This book is dedicated to my father
Harry Frederick Elsmore Macdermott
Motor Mechanic
LST 410
17 January 1943 to 12 November 1944

'Courage is not freedom from fear;
it is being afraid and going on.'

◀ An LCT and a partly loaded Rhino ferry alongside LST 427, with fully loaded Rhino passing. (G. Melford collection)

▼ Crew members of LST 416. (G. Raitt)

▲ LSTs 365 and 368 deliver urgently needed equipment to the Normandy beaches. (C. Powell collection)

▶ Ambulances draw up to LST 416 to evacuate wounded. Notice the army serial number 1480 on her bow. (J. McFadden collection)

Ships Without Names

The Story of the Royal Navy's Tank Landing Ships
of World War Two

BRIAN MACDERMOTT

ARMS AND
ARMOUR

Contents

Arms and Armour Press
A Cassell Imprint
Villiers House, 41–47 Strand, London WC2N 5JE.

Distributed in the USA by Sterling Publishing Co. Inc., 387 Park Avenue South, New York, NY 10016-8810.

Distributed in Australia by Capricorn Link (Australia) Pty. Ltd, P.O. Box 665, Lane Cove, New South Wales 2066.

British Library Cataloguing-in-Publication Data: a catalogue record for this book is available from the British Library

ISBN 1-85409-126-3

Designed and edited by DAG Publications Ltd. Designed by David Gibbons; edited by Michael Boxall; layout by Anthony A. Evans; typeset by Ronset Typesetters, Darwen, Lancashire; camerawork by M&E Reproductions, North Fambridge, Essex; printed and bound in Great Britain by The Bath Press, Avon.

▲An unloaded LST 324 sails proudly up the Solent returning from 'the far shore', probably sometime in June 1944. The dustbin aerial of her Type 271P radar unit can be seen just below the flags on her mast. (Portsmouth Publishing & Printing Company, ref. 2867)

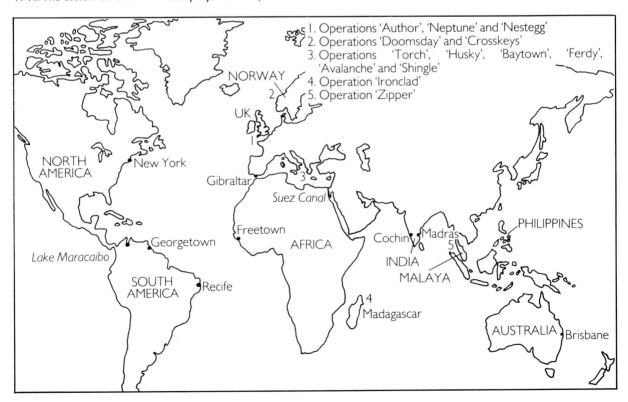

1. Operations 'Author', 'Neptune' and 'Nestegg'
2. Operations 'Doomsday' and 'Crosskeys'
3. Operations 'Torch', 'Husky', 'Baytown', 'Ferdy', 'Avalanche' and 'Shingle'
4. Operation 'Ironclad'
5. Operation 'Zipper'

Introduction

LST ... Landing Ship, Tanks. Conceived in the mind of Prime Minister Winston Churchill; designed and built in the USA; pushed from pillar to post in the Mediterranean; hammered into the ground on the Normandy landings; assisted the liberations of Norway, Denmark and the Channel Islands; and sent to the Far East. Attacked by aircraft, mined, bombed, torpedoed, shelled and sabotaged. The history of the LST in 56 words.

As far as I can tell, Churchill never once set foot aboard an LST. However, he avidly followed their progress around the world. In his book *The Second World War*, he wrote: '... [the LST] became the foundation of all our future amphibious operations, and was often their limiting factor'. (By 'limiting factor', he meant their availability.)

My father served in LST 410 as a Motor Mechanic. He never spoke much of his wartime days, but if a D-Day documentary film ever appeared on television, he would perch up on the edge of his armchair and exclaim 'Watch out for the Four-Ten!'. We never did see her.

It wasn't until May 1989, seven years after my father had died, that I found myself compelled to find out what LSTs actually looked like. I was amazed to discover that virtually nothing had been written about them, so I embarked on my own personal research project. These 'ugly ducklings' captivated me. I needed to know more.

Within a few weeks I had made contact with scores of ex-LST men through the LST & Landing Craft Association and, later, the LST Club. I had found a 'family' of ships and sailors. Letters, diaries, photographs, artefacts and memoirs arrived in the post at a rate of knots. The telephone seemed to be forever ringing.

I had no choice. So much information about the life and times of the Royal Navy's LSTs had come to light, this book simply had to be written.

However, it can only provide a 'general view'. For every ship and crew man mentioned in these pages others were just as active, but went unobserved. The tapestry of each landing was so vast that no one person could have had sight of every LST, enshrouded as they often were in the smoke and din of action.

What is an LST?

Four types of LST saw service during the Second World War.

1. The *Maracaibo LST*. These were conversions of three oil tankers: *Bachaquero, Misoa* and *Tasajera*. While they cannot be thought of as being prototypes in the strict sense of the word, they were used as a 'test bed'.

2. The LST(1) *Boxer* class. These were the first true LSTs to be built. There were just three of them: HMSS *Boxer, Bruiser* and *Thruster*.

3. The LST(2). Powered by diesel engines and built entirely in shipyards in the USA.

4. The LST(3). Powered by steam engines and built in Britain and Canada. Deliveries started just as the war was coming to a conclusion.

However, it is primarily about the LST(2) that this book has been written. The reason for this is that they were transferred to the Royal Navy in large numbers and saw service throughout the critical periods of 1943 and 1944.

The LST(2) was designed and built as an all-welded hull – a complete departure from the standard British shipbuilding technique. Their primary function was the transportation by sea of tanks, vehicles and troops to be disembarked directly on to beaches. A port or harbour with cranes was simply not required.

To perform this task, the LST(2) was built to a length of almost 328 feet with a beam (width) of just over 50 feet. The problem of making them shallow enough to run up on to beaches but also seaworthy enough to cross the sea was overcome by providing a system of ballast tanks.

A large anchor and winch were provided in the stern. This was known as the kedge anchor. At a carefully predetermined spot on the run up to a beach, the kedge anchor was let go. This was then used to haul the vessel off the beach when it was ready to depart.

The ships were powered by 1,800bhp twin shaft diesel engines, built by General Motors, giving a maximum speed of just over 10 knots.

The bow doors opened to reveal a watertight ramp which could be lowered to give access to the tank deck.

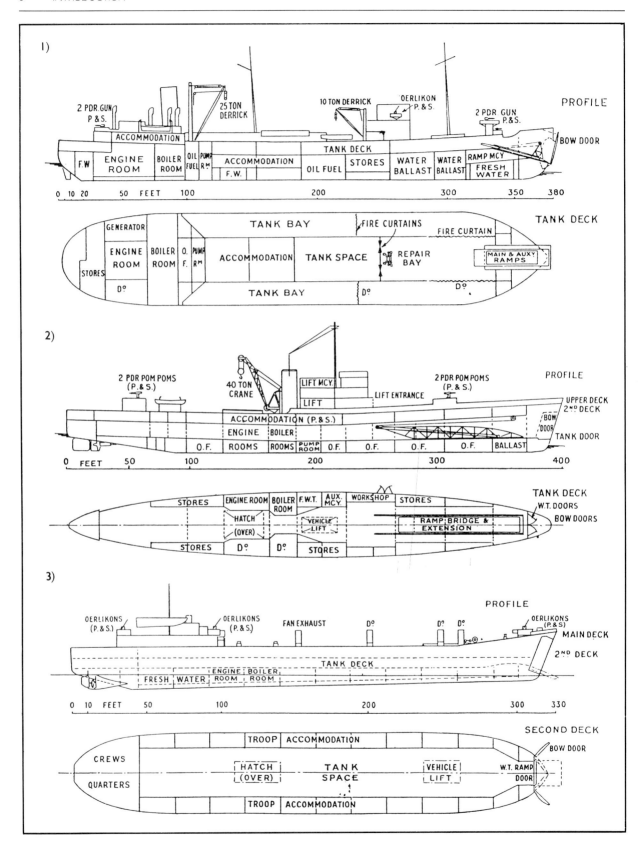

1)

PROFILE

2 PDR. GUN P. & S.

25 TON DERRICK

10 TON DERRICK

OERLIKON P. & S.

2 PDR. GUN P. & S.

BOW DOOR

ACCOMMODATION

TANK DECK

| F.W | ENGINE ROOM | BOILER ROOM | OIL FUEL | PUMP R'M | ACCOMMODATION F.W. | OIL FUEL | STORES | WATER BALLAST | WATER BALLAST | RAMP MCY FRESH WATER |

0 10 20   50   FEET   100   200   300   350   380

TANK DECK

GENERATOR

TANK BAY

FIRE CURTAINS

FIRE CURTAIN

STORES

| ENGINE ROOM | BOILER ROOM | O.F. | PUMP R'M | ACCOMMODATION | TANK SPACE | REPAIR BAY | MAIN & AUXY RAMPS |

D°

TANK BAY

D°

D°

2)

PROFILE

2 PDR POM POMS (P. & S.)

40 TON CRANE

LIFT MCY.

LIFT

LIFT ENTRANCE

2 PDR POM POMS (P. & S.)

UPPER DECK
2ND DECK

BOW DOOR

ACCOMMODATION (P.& S.)

ENGINE   BOILER

TANK DOOR

| | O.F. | ROOMS | ROOMS | PUMP ROOM | O.F. | O.F. | O.F. | O.F. | BALLAST |

0   FEET   50   100   200   300   400

TANK DECK

W.T. DOORS

BOW DOORS

| STORES | ENGINE ROOM | BOILER ROOM | F.W.T. | AUX. MCY. | WORKSHOP | STORES |

HATCH (OVER)

VEHICLE LIFT

RAMP BRIDGE & EXTENSION

| STORES | D° | D° | STORES |

3)

PROFILE

OERLIKONS (P. & S.)

OERLIKONS (P. & S.)

FAN EXHAUST

D°

D°   D°

OERLIKONS (P. & S)

MAIN DECK

2ND DECK

TANK DECK

| FRESH WATER | ENGINE ROOM | BOILER ROOM |

0 10 FEET 50   100   200   300   330

SECOND DECK

BOW DOOR

TROOP ACCOMMODATION

CREWS

QUARTERS

| HATCH (OVER) | TANK SPACE | VEHICLE LIFT | W.T. RAMP DOOR |

TROOP ACCOMMODATION

Outline sketch plans: 1, The *Maracaibo* class; 2, The *Boxer* class; 3, The LST(2); 4, The LST(3). Drawings reproduced courtesy of Royal Institute of Naval Architects, from the book *British Warship Design in World War II*.

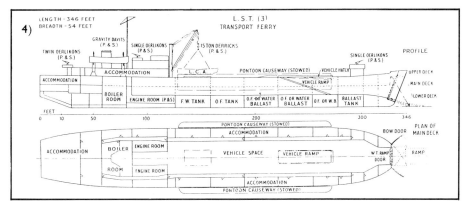

This was approximately 230 feet long by 30 feet wide with a maximum limiting height of just over 11 feet. An elevator with a 10-ton maximum loading was provided to raise vehicles up to the open upper deck.

Official documents give recommended maximum loadings of 18 Churchill or 20 Sherman tanks on the tank deck, with 27 3-ton lorries and 8 jeeps on the upper deck. The exigencies of operational needs meant that these figures would be greatly exceeded on many occasions! LSTs of the 9th Flotilla were noted as carrying 30 Shermans each on one short ferrying trip in the Mediterranean.

A ship's complement would be in the region of 60. They were General Service staff – not Combined Operations. The officers would include a Lieutenant-Commander as CO; two Lieutenants; a Sub-Lieutenant; and an Engineering Officer. Most would be RNR or RNVR, although Flotilla Leaders generally had an RN officer as CO. On 'the lower deck' were the petty officers; motor mechanics; signalmen; telegraphists; electricians; stokers; seamen; cooks; stewards; sick berth attendant; and supplies assistant. The crew's quarters were mainly aft.

Accommodation for the troops in transit was on both sides of the ship below the main deck and comprised seating, messing, lavatory and shower facilities, and bunks. Twelve officers and 165 troops were allowed for, but often this number was easily doubled during shorter runs.

Armament comprised one 12-pounder situated aft and six 20mm Oerlikon guns. Four were mounted around the wheelhouse area, the remaining two being fitted on the upper deck in a forward position. Some vessels were fitted with twin Oerlikons.

A wide variety of roles

When Churchill first had the idea for the LST, he could little have imagined what a wide variety of roles these vessels would eventually play apart from carrying tanks.

Ammunition sometimes totally filled the tank space as did mobile artillery and motor transport; food and rations were carried; railway trucks were taken to Cherbourg, France, and to the Far East; refugees were evacuated; POWs were transported; tank spaces were converted to form a floating ambulance – even surgical operations were performed aboard; fresh water and diesel fuel were carried in the appropriate tanks; mules were transported; rice was carried for the relief of Singapore; radar units were taken to operations; Tank Landing Craft were piggybacked on the upper deck; and on one occasion a German midget submarine was brought back to Britain from Rotterdam.

An immense range of soldiers and airmen of all nationalities were destined to see the inside of an LST – the Desert Rats; the 7th Armoured Division; the 51st Highland Division; the Free French, and many many more.

Churchill could hardly have known that even while beaching trials were taking place in 1943, far-sighted businessmen were already seeing the commercial potential of the LST. By 1948, an ex-LST(3) was sailing on a commercial ferry service between Preston and Larne. What we now know as 'roll-on/roll-off' ferries are direct descendants of the wartime LST.

The United States LST Association has already published the story of the LST from the American viewpoint in the book *Large Slow Target*. I hope that this British viewpoint will provide a balance to that publication. I also hope that it will place the LST in its rightful context within British naval history.

Records do not indicate how many men actually served in Royal Navy LSTs during the Second World War, but at least 145 of those men gave their lives. Their story is recorded within these pages.

I heartily thank the men of the LSTs for playing their part in securing the freedom which I enjoy to write this account. I hope their families, like mine, will treasure this book as a lasting tribute to their sacrifice – a sacrifice which we will never fully comprehend.

Why has so little been written about the LSTs? Perhaps it's because they were mostly *Ships without Names*.

▲ One of the *Maracaibo* class
conversions, possibly HMS
Misoa, showing the
drawbridge-like construction

of the bow doors. (Royal
Marines Amphibious Trials
and Training Unit)

▼John C. Niedermair's first
sketch of the LST(2). (From
US Naval Institute
Proceedings, November 1982)

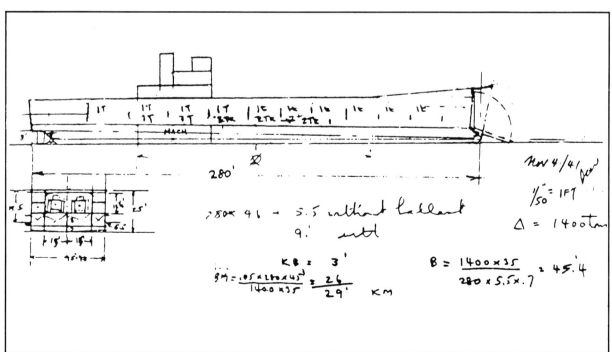

1. The Origins of the LST

The story of the LST began during the First World War when Winston Churchill was planning an amphibious assault for the capture of two Frisian islands – Borkum and Sylt. The basis of this plan, written in 1917, had lain dormant in his mind for many years. In his book, *The Second World War*, Churchill wrote, 'The underlying conceptions of this old paper were deeply imprinted in my mind, and in the new emergency formed the foundation of action which, after a long interval, found memorable expression in the vast fleet of tank-landing craft [*sic*] of 1943 and in the "Mulberry" harbours of 1944.'

In the sullen days following the evacuation of Dunkirk, Churchill's thoughts were firmly fixed on tank warfare – not merely defensive but offensive. 'This required the construction of large numbers of tank-landing vessels, which henceforward became one of my constant cares,' he wrote. With the benefit of hindsight, we can see what a difference there would have been at Dunkirk had the LST been in existence.

Churchill wrote, 'On this same not unfertile 6th of June, 1940, flushed with a sense of deliverance and the power to plan ahead, I began a long series of minutes in which the design and construction of tank-landing craft was ordered and steadily pressed.'

Churchill's first minute of June 1940 referred to 'Proposals for transporting and landing tanks on the beach, observing that we are supposed to have the command of the sea, while the enemy have not.'

Dakar *post mortem*

Operation 'Menace' took place in September 1940. This was an assault on Dakar which failed, but highlighted the need for ocean-going ships which could transport tanks directly to beaches.

In his book, *The Watery Maze*, Bernard Fergusson stated that the Dakar expedition had shown that 'it was impossible to land tanks without the use of a port; and it was apparently impossible to win the use of a port without landing tanks'.

Churchill summoned his Directors of Plans to an after-dinner *post mortem* of the Dakar failure in his underground Blitz quarters on 27 October 1940. He was angry about the apparent peacetime lack of planning for such eventualities. However, the ISTDC (Inter Service Training and Development Centre) had foreseen the requirements of amphibious assault two years previously. Much groundwork had been done on preparing lists of equipment, but the financial constraints of the inter-war years had been prohibitive.

By October 1940, the prototype Tank Landing Craft was undergoing trials. They were originally called Large MLCs and subsequently TLCs – Tank Landing Craft Mk 1. Their design restricted them to use on cross-Channel or short sea operations.

Discussion with the Prime Minister showed that the Dakar problem would constantly recur and that no offensive would be possible until it was solved. Churchill insisted upon the need of a ship which would carry at least 60 tanks and land them on an enemy shore. He told the Admiralty Director of Plans that such ships must be produced and that the Admiralty were to solve the production difficulties involved.

The problem was referred to the Director of Naval Construction who gave an immediate view that such ships, containing a number of entirely novel features, could not be built in less than eighteen months and that he would need time to prepare designs. Furthermore, a ship to carry 60 tanks would be too big. It would be better to build ships to carry 20 to 25 tanks. The specification became what is now known as the LST(1) *Boxer* class.

Keyes meets Sheffer

At that time, the DCO (Director of Combined Operations) was Admiral Sir Roger Keyes. Also at that time, a Lloyds Surveyor, Mr. A. T. Sheffer, was temporarily attached to the DNC's staff. Both men met at the Admiralty. Sir Roger Keyes mentioned the Prime Minister's idea to Sheffer, who replied that he had recently been working on some shallow draught tankers that had been specifically built to cross a notorious sand bar in the

River Maracaibo in South America. The vessels had been designed to carry oil from Venezuela's Lake Maracaibo along a 16-mile channel (which was both shallow and narrow) to the open sea and on to Aruba Island where transshipment took place for transport to the world's oil markets.

Sheffer believed that the Prime Minister's requirements could be met, except for that of speed, by the conversion of some of these tankers. Furthermore, the work could be done in two to three months as opposed to the eighteen months needed for the new construction vessels.

Things moved very quickly and Sheffer was given approval to fly to Harland & Wolff, Belfast, where a set of plans was available. After discussion with the Director of Naval Construction, the decision was taken within 48 hours to convert three of these vessels: the *Bachaquero*, *Misoa* and *Tasajera*. All three had been built by Furness Shipbuilding and North Eastern Marine Engineering Company at Haverton Hill Yard, Stockton-on-Tees. *Bachaquero* and *Misoa* were sister ships, launched on 7 May 1937 and 22 June 1937 respectively. The slightly smaller *Tasajera* was launched on 3 March 1938.

Maracaibos **sail for England**
Bachaquero left Aruba alone in late January 1941 and sailed via Bermuda. She crossed the Atlantic in convoy HX107 as a merchant ship with a full load of fuel oil and arrived at Loch Ewe on 19 February. Sunderland was reached later that month. Here, she was taken in hand for conversion by T. W. Greenwell and Co.

Misoa followed shortly after, in convoy HX108, arriving at Loch Ewe on 26 February. She then sailed for Newcastle where she was to be converted at the High Walker yard of Vickers Armstrong.

Just as *Bachaquero* finished her conversion in July 1941. *Tasajera* arrived to take her place at Greenwell's yard, having crossed the Atlantic in convoy SC36.

To facilitate bow loading, the conversion called for part of the bow to be cut away above the waterline. A rectangular box section was built up on this cutaway, and a large door, hinged at the bottom, was placed at the front of the new assembly. The structure caused a few problems with leakages and, being blunt, prevented the ship from passing through the water with the ease of one with a conventional shape.

A double-ramp device, totalling 68 feet in length when fully extended, enabled tanks and vehicles to drive on and off the ships. Twenty 25-ton tanks or 33 trucks could be accommodated on the tank deck. An access was cut into the tank deck on both sides about midships. A kedge anchor and steam winch were fitted in the stern. Exhaust trunks were fitted to tanks and vehicles while on board.

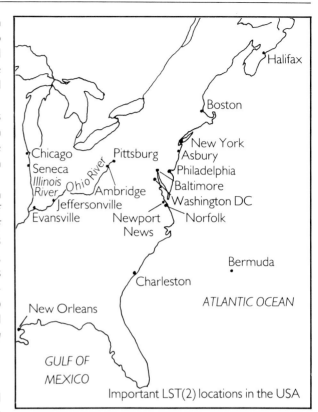

Important LST(2) locations in the USA

When their motors were started up, the exhaust fumes were routed away through the flexible hoses and when the vehicles drove off, the hoses automatically disconnected.

The *Winettes* and the *Boxer* class
Meanwhile, the Director of Naval Construction (DNC) had been considering the following alternatives:

1. A single ship capable of landing sixty 25-ton tanks.
2. Three ships each capable of landing twenty 25-ton tanks each.
3. Fifteen LCTs (Landing Craft, Tanks) each capable of landing four 40-ton or six 25-ton tanks.

At a conference in December 1940, the second option was chosen as being the best. They were originally named *Winettes* but were soon renamed *Boxer* LST(1). Although their construction would interfere with the shipbuilding programme then in hand, with consequent curtailment of the production of nine corvettes, the ships were given sufficient priority to enable them to be finished by April 1942. In January 1941 the order for building the vessels was awarded to Harland & Wolff in Belfast.

Further meetings were held to discuss requirements for 1942, and it was decided that more *Winettes* would be needed. As there were no production facilities available in the UK, the Americans agreed to build the required seven vessels. These were later cancelled, and seven LSDs (Landing Ship, Dock) were built in their place. At about the same time, an English firm, Alexander Brown & Company, had prepared a sketch design for a tank ferry capable of carrying thirty-two 25-ton tanks. This was to have been known as the *Brunette*, but problems were encountered and they were never built. Records indicate that they would have been unseaworthy. In their place came the LCT(3).

It was felt that the *Maracaibos* wouldn't have the necessary speed for assaults, hence the production of the LST(1) *Boxer* class even before the *Maracaibos* had completed conversion. Their steam turbine machinery gave them a much more respectable speed of 17 knots.

To enable them to maintain their speed in a seaway the ramp door was shielded by ship-shaped bow doors, hinged vertically. The ramp door was nearly but not quite watertight. Inside was a watertight door and inside this again was a bridge-type ramp with an extending causeway. The total length of the ramp and causeway so obtained was about 140 feet, but the final structure weighed 90 tons and needed complicated machinery to operate it.

Tanks were carried fairly low in the ship, the tank deck being below the waterline aft. Vehicles could be trans-ferred to the upper deck by a lift. Additionally, a 40-ton crane was fitted so that tanks could either be hoisted aboard through a hatch or hoisted out into an LCT lying alongside.

In August 1941, when it was realized that any invasion of Europe would have to take place on very flat beaches, it was apparent that great difficulties would be encountered with the *Boxer* class as they were designed for a beach of 1-in-35. In fact, their effective working range was between 1-in-35 and 1-in-60. It was pointed out that the only way in which the situation could be improved was by a reduction in the ship's draught, and that on the flat French beaches the *Boxer* class would ground aft. This would leave about 10 feet of water at the bow and it would be impossible to get anything ashore from them unless they were 'dried out' – settled on the beach with no water around them.

Partly because of the novelty of some of the arrangements and partly because of enemy action, the first of the class did not complete until January 1943 – nine months later than planned. This was HMS *Thruster* and she commissioned on 28 January. She was followed by HMS *Bruiser* on 12 March and by HMS *Boxer* on 10 April. These were the first tank landing ships in the world to be specifically designed for the purpose, even though the LST(2)s beat them to the sea by just a few weeks.

▶ LST 410 under construction at the Bethlehem Fairfield Company yard, Baltimore, Maryland, USA, in late 1942. (United States National Archives, ref 19-LCM-LST-410-Y)

UK building capacity fully stretched

By October 1941 plans for the invasion of Europe had begun to receive very serious attention. It was realized that more than 2,000 LCTs of the then existing types would be needed. All possible building capacity in the United Kingdom was already fully occupied and help was sought from the USA by means of the new Lend-Lease Act. The bottleneck in this case was the difficulty of transport and assembly. The existing British types of LCT could not cross the Atlantic under their own power and to ship them in sections would have involved an enormous organization for re-assembly in the United Kingdom. Facilities and labour were simply not available.

British Admiralty representatives in Washington discussed with the American authorities the possibility of building an 'Atlantic TLC', capable of crossing the Atlantic under its own power.

Early in November 1941 the Admiralty sent the following outline requirements to the Bureau of Ships (BuShips) in Washington:

1. Load twenty 25-ton tanks or equivalent with a beaching draft of 3 feet 6 inches on a 1-in-50 beach.
2. Accommodation for full complement and vehicle crews.
3. Speed 10 knots and endurance 10,000 nautical miles.
4. Power-operated bow doors and a simple type of bow ramp.
5. To be capable of carrying an LCT(5) in one piece on the deck.

(Note: The 1-in-50 beach referred to above is from British records. The US records indicate 1-in-100.)

On 4 November 1941 the then Assistant Head of the Design Division at BuShips, Captain Edward L. Cochrane, took the despatch into John C. Niedermair who was Civilian Technical Director at the branch.

In 1975, Niedermair was interviewed for an article entitled 'As I recall . . . Designing the LST', which appeared in the November 1982 issue of the US Naval Institute Proceedings. In that article Niedermair said '. . . the British specified a design to go on a beach whose slope was 1-in-100. I listened to that, and then I started thinking. I got busy and made a few sketches.'

It was apparent that the ships would have to be designed for satisfactory operation under two conditions:

1. A deep-draught condition to give sufficient seaworthiness for long ocean voyages.
2. A shallow-draught condition, with proper trim, for landing on relatively flat beaches with a full load of vehicles.

Niedermair met these needs by providing liquid-ballast tanks which could be filled at sea and pumped out for beaching — a simple principle, but one which had never before been applied to a vessel of this type. Niedermair had previously worked with submarine ballast systems, so the idea was not new to him — just the application.

He went on to say, 'Instead of taking the 1-in-100 slope, I decided that to make this design successful, you have to design it to 1-in-50 . . . I drew the original sketch that afternoon in a matter of a couple of hours.' He went home that night and made a larger drawing, copies of which were sent to England the next day.

The British authorities found the general features acceptable. Their next step was to prepare a set of 'Staff Requirements' — a little over one typewritten page of general specifications for the ship. These were taken to the USA by a small group of British naval officers whose mission was to consult with Buships on the development of the design.

By the time this mission arrived — less than three weeks after the first sketch had been prepared — the preliminary design had been well carried through its early stages. A ship of about 280 feet in length had been investigated but discarded in favour of a larger ship.

There still remained a great number of important problems to be solved, and the British delegation were helpful in passing on their experience of many of those problems. Some of the major features still to be resolved at that stage were the means of operating the bow doors and ramp, the provision of adequate ventilation of the tank space while tank engines were running, and the means for lowering vehicles from the upper deck to the tank deck to permit them to go ashore over the ramp.

Design kept simple

As many of these ships were to be built, one of the cardinal principles of the design was that it must be simple and well suited for available production facilities. It was decided that the hull structure should be all-welded and that it should be made of the smallest practicable number of pieces. To simplify procurement, uniformity of size of steel plates and shapes was also specified. The main diesel engine was a General Motors V12-567 which had been used on railway locomotives but was adapted for marine use.

By early December 1941 the preliminary design of the LST(2) was well under way and was practically complete by the end of that month. From the original 280 feet, the ship was stretched to a length of 328 feet with a beam of 50 feet. This enabled the ship's weight to be distributed over a greater area. A lines drawing depicting the hull form was sent to the David Taylor Model Basin, Washington DC, where a model was built and tested in record time during January 1942. Another set of lines with minor modifications was also tried, but the first model was found to be best.

In January 1942 the New York firm of Gibbs & Cox Inc. was designated to prepare working drawings for these ships.

The cornfield shipyards

On 23 January 1942 the first contract for building LST(2)s was placed. It was becoming apparent that the LST would be required in great numbers, but the shipbuilding industry was being taxed to the limit. New building facilities were needed. As well as the east coast Navy Yards and private firms, other yards were built, organized and operated by bridge-building and steel-working companies with no previous experience in shipbuilding. Here the relative simplicity of the design began to pay big dividends in rapid construction, despite adverse conditions.

Known collectively as the 'cornfield shipyards', five yards were created or adapted on the inland waterways of the Rivers Ohio and Illinois. These were: Seneca (Illinois); Ambridge (Pennsylvania); Jeffersonville (Indiana); Evansville (Indiana); and the Dravo yard at Neville Island (Pennsylvania). This latter yard was chosen as the prime yard. LST 1 was launched there on 7 September 1942.

US Maritime Commission records show that of the total 1,152 LST(2)s actually contracted, all but 101 were constructed. Of these 1,051, 670 were built in the inland yards.

Construction of an LST at Seneca

The Chicago Bridge & Iron Company site at Seneca, situated on the high banks of the River Illinois, extended for some 200 acres. Although work on building the yard didn't start until 1 May 1942, Seneca launched its first vessel, LST 197, on 13 December 1942.

Once the normal teething troubles of the new venture had been overcome, the yard was turning out LSTs at the rate of one every four and a half days.

Over a period of time, the yard developed 'the task system' of building the ships. A total of 378 tasks comprising 1,146 operations was required for each ship. Ship construction time was divided into 20 equal periods. The ship was on land during periods 1 to 18, the last two periods being used to complete the work when the ship was waterborne.

Each ship required in the region of 30,000 parts, 6½ miles of piping system, 13½ miles of electric cable and approximately 130 motors. The cellular construction of the hull consisted of three tiers of box sections 10 feet wide and about 24 feet long on each side of the ship. There were 48 of these box sections to a ship, those for the Seneca ships being prefabricated in Chicago, Greenville (Pennsylvania) and Birmingham (Alabama). They were shipped to Seneca on railway flat trucks.

▲ On 7 March 1943 LST 199 slides gracefully from the slipway of the Chicago Bridge & Iron Company, Seneca, into the Illinois River. (E. Webber collection)

Launchings were carried out sideways – (the River Illinois being narrow) and were quite spectacular. The length of slide was more than 300 feet and the ship hit the water at between 22 and 28mph.

In May 1944 the yard produced nine ships – one in every three and a half days! This meant a 70-hour working week for all employees.

Shipyards involved in building of LST(2)s transferred to the Royal Navy

Shipyard	LST(2) numbers
Dravo Corporation, Pittsburg:	2–5, 8, 9, 11–13
Jeffersonville Boat & Machine Co:	62–65, 76, 77, 79, 80–82
Missouri Valley Bridge & Iron Co:	157, 159–165, 173, 178, 180, 538
Chicago Bridge & Iron Co, Seneca:	198–200, 214–217, 237–239
American Bridge Co, Ambridge:	280, 289
Boston Navy Yard:	301–305
New York Navy Yard	311, 315
Philadelphia Navy Yard:	319–324, 326, 331
Norfolk Navy Yard:	336, 337, 346, 347, 351, 352
Charleston Navy Yard:	358, 360
Bethlehem (Quincy):	361–369, 371, 373, 380–382, 1021
Bethlehem (Baltimore):	401–430
Newport News:	383, 385, 386, 394

▲ 'Black-out Charlie' gives a friendly salute to Leading Seaman Rick Fisher as he paddles past HMS *Bachaquero* at Freetown. (R. J. Fisher)

▼ Lieutenant-Commander McMullan's boat aboard HMS *Bachaquero*, damaged in rough seas. (R. J. Fisher)

▼ A view of Madagascar from HMS *Bachaquero* during Operation 'Ironclad'. (R. J. Fisher)

2. Operations 'Ironclad' and 'Torch'

In 1941 Lieutenant-Commander A. W. McMullan, RNR, was appointed to join HMS *Bachaquero* with what he called the magic words 'In command on commissioning'.

Arthur McMullan had served his apprenticeship with the Lamport & Holt Line. He obtained his Master's certificate in 1929 and joined the RNR. Called up just three days before the outbreak of war, he spent nine months on contraband patrol and at Dunkirk commanded a small vessel which was lost during that operation. By kind permission of Mrs. R. McMullan, some of her late husband's memoirs are reproduced below.

'As may be imagined, the secrecy surrounding the conversion of the *Maracaibo*s was very strict. When I presented myself at Naval HQ and said that I wished to see HMS *Bachaquero* there was silence. Even when I produced my identity card and official appointment from the Admiralty nothing was said about the ship. Eventually, I was ushered into the presence of the Naval Officer in Charge (NOIC) who also seemed loath to tell me about her — even after the most intense scrutiny of my documents.

'It must be remembered that this was my first "big ship" command and I was excited as to what my ship might be. In the end, however, my face must have satisfied and NOIC said to me "She's a Tank Landing Ship." I must have looked blank, as indeed I was justified in so doing. Nowadays, everyone knows what an LST is, but my interview was taking place about eighteen months before the first LST made its appearance.

'NOIC said, "Yes, you are to have the unique job of running a ship ashore on purpose." It sounded like fiction. It was not until later when I first saw this huge ship that I realized fully what might lie ahead.

'A day was fixed for our first big trial of the ship's main function — that of beaching. This took place in the River Wear. On the bridge were Admirals, Captains, Brigadiers and Group Captains — a big event for Combined Operations. At last we touched bottom. The ship was grounded. I breathed again. It was like a nightmare. But there she was, high and dry, bow door open and a Valentine tank crawling into the ship. Despite all attempts at secrecy, the banks of the Wear were lined with spectators.

'The most difficult moment for a new venture was over. It could be done. After that, the trials continued. I never ceased to thrill when the ship's head was pointed for the shore; the engines kept going ahead until she finally came to rest quivering for a second. Always there were senior officers from all three services to witness the beachings and reports went to the Admiralty.

'Sister ship HMS *Misoa* joined our force, commanded by Lieutenant-Commander Grace, DSC, RNR. Grace was senior to me and, therefore, when the two ships were at trials together *Bachaquero* always formed astern of *Misoa*.

'Most of the original trials were carried out in Loch Fyne but then the open beach at Macrahanish Bay, near the Mull of Kintyre, was used. This area was exposed to the Atlantic swell and trials became more difficult. Other trials took place in Scapa Flow.'

McMullan takes *Bachaquero* into Operation 'Ironclad'

In October 1941 HMS *Bachaquero* left the UK on a 17-day voyage to join an assault force in Freetown, West Africa. This force included *Misoa*, and was held ready, possibly to seize the Azores and Canaries. Trials continued here and beachings were made under war-like conditions with RAF bombers and fighter-bombers 'attacking' with flour bags.

The late Arthur McMullan: 'Our unusual appearance always attracted attention. On one occasion as we returned to Freetown after a trial on a nearby beach, a cruiser made a signal to us saying "And what on earth do you do for a living?"'

The force was eventually broken up. *Misoa* sailed for home but *Bachaquero* was ordered to sail for the Middle East via the Cape, calling at Cape Town en route before proceeding to Durban for a refit.

McMullan continues: 'After two or three weeks in Durban we received orders from the Admiralty. We were to proceed to East London (some 200 miles from

Durban) and await a force which was even then on its way from England for that first of our invasions – Madagascar (Operation 'Ironclad'). The people of East London looked after us extremely well and there were many sad hearts when it was time to leave. Orders sent us back to Durban, from where the assault force departed towards the end of April.

'On Sunday 3 May, two days before the invasion, a church service was held on deck. The weather was glorious. Everything was so peaceful that it seemed more like a pleasure cruise than an instrument of war.

'I had to brief the ship's company on the operation. The general objective was the capture of the Naval air base at Diego Suarez, on the northern tip of Madagascar. The Naval objective was to effect a surprise landing and to supply the Army during their advance.

'On 4 May the rendezvous was made and as far as the eye could see, the ocean was full of ships. They formed into their groups and set course for the final approach to Courrier Bay. Darkness fell. The minesweepers commenced sweeping a channel.

'*Bachaquero* anchored in the initial anchorage at 0230. One and a half hours later, the anchor was weighed and at 0415 *Bachaquero* proceeded slowly up the swept channel, picking her way through other ships at anchor and the small landing craft. We had not gone far when a signal was received ordering us to stop. Mines had been discovered ahead. About 0600, a signal was received saying "Proceed towards Blue Beach, keeping in swept channel." We had proceeded two or three miles when another signal was received. It read, "Stop. There are mines in the anchor-

age." I immediately ordered the engines to be put full astern and decided to anchor.

'It was not until noon that we were able to negotiate the channel and reach our mooring position off Blue Beach. During the morning, however, it was found that rocks and the gradient of the beach would cause us to ground if beaching was attempted. The Senior Officer ordered *Bachaquero* to proceed close inshore and anchor near Blue Beach where we were to discharge by derrick into small landing crafts which would come alongside. This was indeed disappointing as not only would it take about two days to discharge in this manner, but all our trials leading up to the invasion seemed to be wasted. All on board were looking forward to beaching in earnest.'

Bachaquero switched to Red Beach

'It was with mixed feelings when the anchor was being weighed that a fast motorboat came alongside to say that a suitable spot had been discovered in the vicinity of Red Beach, some two or three miles away. A signal was made immediately asking for permission to attempt the beaching. This was granted, the only delay being that a minesweeper had to be detailed to sweep us into the beach. Whilst waiting, I gave orders for *Bachaquero* to be trimmed to an even draught and made as light as possible in order to ride over any mines missed by the sweeper.

'The minesweeper, HMS *Cromarty*, arrived and *Bachaquero* was turned to follow close astern of her sweep. Two moored mines were cut adrift and our helm was put over to avoid them.

◄ HMS *Misoa* in a floating dock at Tail of the Bank, Scotland, July/August 1942. (M. Whewell)

'Now in shallow water, *Cromarty* detached and *Bachaquero*'s head was swung round to point for the beach, our beaching point marked by a huge boulder, about 12 feet in diameter, just near the water's edge. I couldn't help wondering if there were any others beneath the surface which might not be discovered until we struck them, possibly with disastrous results.

'It was only a matter of moments after this that we grounded, and I breathed freely when I found that we were on a beach composed of shingle and small boulders. The bow was opened and the steel brow ejected over which our motor vehicles were to drive ashore.

'Then came our greatest disappointment – we discovered that the ship had beached on a bank, or false beach, close inshore and that there was a greater depth of water at the end of the brow than there was at the bow of the ship itself.

'An attempt was made to disembark the vehicles by lashing a portable wooden structure to the end of the brow. An additional 12 feet nearer the beach was attained where the water was shallow enough for the landing to be attempted.

'Whilst shells from *Laforey* screamed over us, three Bren gun carriers successfully negotiated the passage and reached dry land by their own power. The next three vehicles became waterlogged and had to be drawn ashore by 50 or 60 soldiers pulling as in a tug-of-war.

'By now the time was around 1715 and the tide had risen so that no more vehicles could be landed. I decided to withdraw and, with permission, attempt another beaching. Just before 1730, we were afloat again. When about one mile from the shore, the ship's head was pointed for the beach. "Full speed ahead" was rung on the engines.

'I shall never forget my feelings as we rushed towards the beach. The engines were kept at full speed until about 200 yards from the shore. The Engineer Officer had given her everything we had got. I visualized the bottom being torn out. Force our way through the bank? It looked as though we would force our way through the island! And so thought the 50 or 60 soldiers. They let out a cheer as they saw us coming – then, as we came closer and they saw the speed, turned and fled! However, we did stop and the vehicles were able to land in about 6 inches of water.

'The First Lieutenant, H. E. James, RNR, had done such excellent organizing with the commanding officer of the troops that the ship was emptied of vehicles in the almost unbelievable time of thirteen minutes. It was just on high water when we were ready to attempt the unbeaching. By use of the powerful stern winch and by wriggling the ship in coming astern on alternate engines, *Bachaquero* was safely unbeached by 1900.'

Lessons learned

Operation 'Ironclad' was unique in that this was the first operational use of a Tank Landing Ship anywhere in the world.

Bachaquero came back to the UK in the late summer or early autumn of 1942 and was taken in hand for refit at Falmouth. As was usual, there was great official interest in her and Lieutenant-Commander McMullan was sent for by the new Chief of Combined Operations, Admiral Lord Louis Mountbatten. McMullan was shown a scale model of the LST(2)s which were then being built in the USA, designed partly as a result of trials with his ship. McMullan said in his memoirs, 'As I saw some of these results, I felt that the hard work of the previous fifteen months had been well worthwhile.'

Operation 'Ironclad' showed up the need for a method of bridging the gap between the ship and the shoreline. This need was met by the pontoon causeway which had been developed by the Americans. *Bachaquero*, *Misoa* and *Tasajera* were all adapted to carry six 60-foot sections of this causeway in time for the Operation 'Torch' landings in North Africa in November 1942.

Operation 'Torch'

Exactly according to plan, *Bachaquero* parted company with her sister vessels at 1800 on Saturday 7 November 1942, and set a course of 220° for position 'CW'. Four trawlers acting as minesweepers accompanied her.

A submarine marked the position, McMullan noting the time of passing as 2044.5 – half a minute ahead of schedule.

By 2250, an eastbound convoy of merchant ships was seen crossing ahead of the minesweepers. At 2310 McMullan observed one of these vessels, the *Paul Whitman*, on a converging course on the starboard beam. He immediately ordered 'full speed ahead' and helm 'hard-a-port'. The two ships collided, but *Bachaquero* sustained only very minor damage to her stern.

Long blasts were sounded on her siren as she made for her beach, where she grounded at 0400 approximately 150 yards from the shore. Her six sections of pontoon bridging were erected and landing of vehicles started at 0650.

Whilst preparing the pontoons, *Bachaquero* was attacked from the west by a twin-engined bomber. She and other vessels nearby opened fire causing the bomber quickly to alter course for safety over the hills. By 0745, she had unloaded 79 vehicles and had refloated.

Over the next few days *Bachaquero* assisted the unloading of *Mark Twain* and *Mary Slesser*, finally proceeding to Arzew. The three *Maracaibo*s then provided a ferrying service along the north coast of Africa.

▲Some motor mechanics took part of their diesel engine training at the rear of Andrew's Garage, Bournemouth. In this 1942 photograph, LST 410's three motor mechanics are seen. Back row, top right (capless): Harry Macdermott. Front row, seated, second from left (with cap): Jimmy Millbank; extreme right (capless): Alan Tate. (B. Macdermott collection)

▶Captain LST – Fischer Burges Watson, DSO, RN. This photograph was taken at Harwich, sometime after his LST command had terminated. (IWM ref A29651)

▼ The two New Jersey hotels – HMS Asbury. (T. Hill collection)

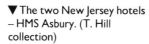

3. Men and Ships Come Together

Records indicate that the manning situation of LSTs in 1942 was somewhat unclear, and that the shortage of motor mechanics in particular was acute.

From October 1942 to February 1943 many hundreds of men left the UK bound for the USA and the LSTs. The great majority of these men were billeted in HMS Asbury – two New Jersey hotels taken over by the Navy as an accommodation base. They were the New Monterey and the Berkeley Carteret in the Asbury Park area.

First impressions

After a short stay at Asbury Park, some men found themselves making a train journey of several hundred miles down to New Orleans. Sonny Griggs (LST 199): 'We stood on a quayside in New Orleans and looked out across the Mississippi at four strange-looking ships tied up on the other side. They looked like small tankers, but what created the most interest was what we thought were funnels spaced out along the deck. I said to my mate, "There you are, Lofty, I told you we were picking up a convoy escort ship. Struth! Jerry will have to have his finger out to catch us in one of those – look, six funnels!" What we thought were funnels were, of course, the tank deck ventilators!'

Jack Haslett was with Lieutenant-Commander Bell, RNR, just after seeing LST 324 for the first time in Philadelphia Navy Yard. Bell said disdainfully, 'After being at sea for 25 years, I never thought I would have to sail in a ship with front doors and traffic lights.' (The traffic lights were used to control traffic leaving the tank deck.)

According to Lambton Burn in his book *Down Ramps*, when Lieutenant-Commander R. J. W. Crowdy, RNVR, arrived to collect LST 417, he found the hustle so great that he had no chance of checking on the acceptance conditions and asked for time before signing the documents. His request met with a drawled: 'Sorry, Cap'n, but dat'd mean holdin' up produkshun.' He signed!

Jack French joined LST 363 in Boston Navy Yard early in 1943 as a Leading Signalman. 'The galley was really up-to-date with cafeteria messing. We each had an individual compartmented tray. At meal times, we would queue at the long grill and have our meals served to us in a civilized fashion. Everything was labour saving. No more spud peeling – it was all done in an automatic peeler.

'Iced water fountains were another innovation unheard of in the RN. All the light switches were of the spring-loaded twist on and off type. There were fans in the messdecks, wardrooms and cabins.'

Sub-Lieutenant Les Roberts, RNVR, joined LST 366 at Boston in December 1942. 'When we originally took the LSTs over from the shipyard, they were simply floating tin cans. There was not a porthole or scuttle anywhere, other than for steering purposes in the wheelhouse. We were supposed to live in artificial light. By very devious means, 366 left New York with scuttles in all living spaces and lino on hitherto bare steel decks. We were experts in scrounging!

'The CO's accommodation was roomy and divided into day and night cabins. The cabins for the Number One and senior engineer were almost identical, with a very adequate desk, but no settee. Other officers' cabins were very cramped. There were double-bunks along one side, a settee and a folding bunk above it on the other side. On the bulkhead between them was a huge metal shelf about six or seven feet up, from which hung fixed metal coat hangers. This left about three square feet of deck. In time, the spare bunks were removed and the infamous shelf lowered to make a writing desk. With some wood I scrounged from Chippy, I made myself a bit of a wardrobe in an alcove.

'On the credit side, bunks were provided with box spring matresses and ample bed linen. The wardroom had a metal table and about a dozen steel chairs. Cutlery and table linen were of the best.

'Messdecks were sparse and furnished with folding bunks – again, these took up a lot of space, particularly when let down. At some time after leaving the States, the crew of LST 366 ripped theirs out (with permission) and slung hammocks. There was far more room.

'The galley was large and well-equipped – all stainless steel. A neat little sick bay earned a couple of house points as did the ship's office. It had adequate filing cabinets and two typewriters . One was a "standard" machine and the other for signals – it printed capital letters only.

'The chartroom was spacious and contained a large settee, but the bridge was just a box without a lid. We found that it needed to be much higher – there was a large "blind spot" at the bows. During operations, a Forecastle Officer had to guide the bridge on beaching (or coming up to a "hard") by counting down "40 feet to go . . . 30 feet to go . . ." etc, etc.

'Armament was not given to creating confidence – an ancient 12-pounder aft and six 20mm Oerlikons. It was galling to see the US LSTs bristling with 40mm Bofors guns to spare.

'Too much electrically-operated gear was boxed up beyond reach. The motor for opening and closing the bow doors was an example. The one in LST 366 went on the blink and just could not be reached for inspection or repair. From that day on, we opened and closed one door by a system of wires on the for'ard winch. In fact, we used to frighten the life out of people on the shore – we just used to let this door *fall* open – wham!'

Burges Watson appointed as Captain LST

Lieutenant (S) Arthur Bailey, RNVR, was serving in HMS *Nigeria* when she was torpedoed during Operation 'Pedestal' in August 1942. He went with her to the Charleston Navy Yard, USA, but left her in January 1943. 'My destination was New York and my appointment was to LST 361. The officer intended for LST 320 hadn't turned up and I found myself reporting to Rear-Admiral Fischer Burges Watson, DSO, then serving in the rank of Captain. He looked at my wavy stripes and mumbled something about having asked for a straight striper. However, after some probing questions, he said that as I was the first to arrive I could have the job as his secretary. As his name is rather unusual, one of his first instructions to me was, "Don't forget, Bailey, one 's' and no hyphen."

Admiral Sir John Cunningham, KCB, MVO, personally chose Burges Watson for the post of Captain LST. He came from a long line of seafarers – there had been a Watson in the Royal Navy since Nelson's time.

Born in September 1884, the son of a Rear-Admiral, he was educated at Ashdown House, Forest Row, and HMS *Britannia*. He was a keen rugby player, playing for the Royal Navy from 1907 to 1911 and England in 1908–9. During the First World War he commanded destroyers and served in *Loyal*. Later in the war he commanded *Tempest* and *Shakespeare*. He was awarded the DSO in 1917. Promoted to Captain in 1921, he subsequently commanded the cruiser *Caledon* and became Captain of the Dockyard, Gibraltar. In 1928, he was President at the first of the *Royal Oak* courts martial. By 1928 he was Naval Assistant to the Second Sea Lord (Admiral Sir Michael Hodges) and in 1930–31 was Flag Captain in HMS *Nelson* to that officer when C-in-C Atlantic Fleet. As a Rear-Admiral he commanded the New Zealand Station from 1932 to 1935 and retired in September 1935. He was recalled when war broke out and initially served as a Commodore of convoys before being appointed Captain LST.

◀ LST 319 undergoing beaching trials in icy waters near Philadelphia, late 1942/early 1943. (J. Peplow collection)

4. The LSTs Set Sail

LST 301 – the first British LST(2) in commission

In October 1942 the liner *Queen Mary* left Greenock for Boston, USA. On board was 18-year-old Norman Barrass (LST 301): 'The *Queen Mary* had rammed and sunk her escort, the cruiser HMS *Curacao*, and had had some repair work done on her bows. She took us across the Atlantic, and we arrived in Boston where we were marched off to the US Navy barracks known as Wells Fargo. We joined LST 301 and she was commissioned on 6 November 1942. I was an officer's cook but soon joined in with the PO cook and his mate to make it easy going on everyone in the galley. The galley itself was very well laid out and I soon settled down to learn about messdeck catering and how to make bread.'

Peter Lacey (Telegraphist LST 301) remembers that they left Boston on 17 November 1942 with Lieutenant-Commander Hoyle as Commanding Officer and sailed alone to Halifax, Nova Scotia, arriving there on 19 November.

Another Telegraphist in LST 301 was Norman Aspinall: 'At Halifax, we were loaded with Canadian tanks and vehicles and did some practice landings outside the harbour on a nearby beach. When the trials were completed, the tank space was loaded with timber and the bow doors welded up for safety.'

Lewis Markham (Signalman LST 301): 'When we left Halifax for the UK on 6 December 1942 in convoy SC112, the weather was awful – gale force winds. About one day out, the main steering broke down and the ship had to be hand steered from the tiller flat. Able Seaman Terry was steering when, suddenly, a cable on the equipment parted. The backlash hit him and somehow he ended up with a fractured skull.' At 2216 on 7 December LST 301 sent the following message to Halifax: 'Am returning base. Steering gear defective. One man for hospital. Fracture of skull. ETA 0600/8.'

Lewis Markham (LST 301): 'After repairs, we left Halifax in convoy SC113 on 16 December. Everything iced up on the journey which took us past Greenland and Iceland. We arrived in the Clyde on New Year's Day, 1943 – the first LST(2) to reach England.'

From January to May 1943 LST 301 became a focus of attention for the 'top brass'. Dates are uncertain, but during those first five months of 1943 she was tested with Vehicle Landing Ramps (VLR) around the Portland and Weymouth areas. The Admiralty was on hand to film the trials. It also seems likely that mobile radar units were tested in her at this time, and several weeks were spent on the sands at Appledore, Devon, where the Army performed trials with her.

LSTs suffer manning problems

The Americans wanted LSTs desperately for their campaign in the Pacific. This led to heated debate between Washington and London as the British authorities had requested the first 200 LSTs to be made available to the Royal Navy. However, the Admiralty War Diary for 29

▲LST 301 undergoing trials with vehicle landing ramps (VLR) on the port and starboard sides, early in 1943, probably at Instow, Devon. (Royal Marines Amphibious Trials and Training Unit)

◀ A truck makes its cautious way along the VLR from LST 301 during trials. (Royal Marines Amphibious Trials and Training Unit)

◀ LSTs 412 and 324 unloading logs at Freetown. LST 324's radar unit is visible under her mast. (IWM ref A17842)

December 1942 noted that only 49 LSTs had been allocated and crews had been arranged. The British Admiralty Delegation in Washington were striving for a further 26 and requested crews be sent out from Britain as soon as possible. The diary went on to say, 'Prospects of obtaining 30 other LSTs to complete to 105 are dependent on future grand strategy. Crews should be earmarked.'

During the last two months of 1942 and the first four months of 1943, 68 RN LST(2)s had been commissioned in the USA. In July and August another twelve were received, making a total of eighty. LSTs 13, 81, 82, 216 and 217 included above were not used as pure LSTs – their story is told later. This brings the total figure back down to 75 – the figure mentioned in the December 1942 War Diary entry. The others that had been hoped for weren't transferred to the RN until late 1944, when a total of 35 were received between October and December.

Commissioning dates for British LSTs

Year	Month	Name or Number	Total
1941	July	*Bachaquero* and *Misoa*	2
	December	*Tasajera* (uncertain)	1
1942	November	301, 302, 303, 304, 361, 362, 363, 365	8

Year	Month	Name or Number	Total
1942	December	305, 319, 320, 321, 364, 366, 367, 401, 402, 403, 404, 405, 406, 407, 408	15
1943	January	322, 323, 324, 368, 409, 410, 411, 412, 413, 414, 415, 421, HMS *Thruster*	13
	February	416, 417, 418, 419, 420, 422, 423, 424, 425, 426, 427, 428, 429, 430	14
	March	8, 9, 11, 12, 62, 63, 65, 159, 160, 161, 162, 198, 199, 200, HMS *Bruiser*	15
	April	13, 64, 163, 164, 165, HMS *Boxer*	6
	July	79, 80, 81, 180, 214, 215, 237, 238, 239	9
	August	82, 216, 217	3
1944	October	280, 538	2
	November	2, 5, 157, 289, 311, 315, 326, 331, 336, 337, 346, 351, 360, 369, 371, 373, 380, 382, 383, 385, 386	21
	December	3, 4, 76, 77, 173, 178, 347, 352, 358, 381, 394, 1021	12

LSTs 324, 412 and 421 sail for West Africa

Unknown to crew members at the time, the LSTs were destined for operations in the Mediterranean – the lucky ones via Bermuda, others via the UK. However, LSTs 324, 412 and 421 were given a task to perform en route.

In January 1943, the British Admiralty Delegation in Washington suggested that two or three LSTs should be utilized as a special measure to carry timber from Georgetown (British Guiana) to Freetown (Sierra Leone). The timber, greenheart logs, were required for a jetty to be built at Freetown.

Jack Haslett (LST 324): 'I joined the ship as Navigating Officer. Lieutenant-Commander Bell, RNR, was the commanding officer. At the end of February 1943, we received orders to sail to New York as one of three ships to be detached for special duties. The other two were LST 412 (Lieutenant-Commander Richard 'Yogi' Brown, RNR) and LST 421 (Lieutenant-Commander Machin, RNR). In view of the considerable cargo-carrying capabilities of these ships, the powers that be decided to use us to carry stores to the Shell oil refinery at Curaçao in the West Indies.'

Gwyn Evans was Quartermaster in LST 412: 'We left New York in convoy on 13 March 1943. Our course for the next few days was about 180° South. We arrived at the Dutch island of Curaçao around 24 March and unloaded our oil well equipment. This was our first taste of the tropics – but the type of ship we had sailed there in constantly reminded us that this was no pleasure cruise. On 30 March, the swing bridge in the capital, Willemstadt, opened and our voyage continued.

'We were in Port of Spain, Trinidad, by 2 April and had to wait two days for a convoy onwards. The three LSTs left this convoy off Stampa Island, British Guiana, on 7 April and we all arrived at Georgetown.'

Jack Haslett (LST 324): 'We were ordered to embark a local pilot and sailed along the coast for a while, and then 20 miles or more up the Essequibo River until we reached a clearing in the jungle. The greenheart logs were all ready for loading. The Admiralty had arranged for a tractor to be supplied to each ship at Georgetown, the theory being that each log could be towed up the ship's ramp and into the tank space in less than ten minutes. The towing by tractor method proved impracticable. Instead, we stationed the tractor ashore and winched the logs on board by means of wires, snatchblocks and rollers – but it was slow!

'Meanwhile, the ship's loading steadily progressed, only enlivened by an occurrence in LST 421. Early one morning, the bosun's mate sent a seaman to fetch a handy billy from the bosun's store. The youth came back at high speed with a white face – "There's an alligator in there!" –

and so there was! The alligator was shot and the skin eventually decorated a wardroom bulkhead. History doesn't relate what happened to the ramp sentry.

'We finally sailed back down the river, through the overhanging trees of the jungle, to arrive at Georgetown where we had to load more logs from a jetty. I felt comfortable in the knowledge that we would have plenty of wood to hang on to if we were ever torpedoed. My illusion was soon shattered – during loading, a log was accidentally dropped. It sank like a stone. The logs were over 60 feet in length and very heavy.'

Gwyn Evans (LST 412): 'During our stay in Georgetown the local population made us feel very welcome and ensured that we were well stocked with Demerara sugar. We left Georgetown on 16 April and still headed south, crossing the Equator and passing the mouth of the River Amazon before arriving at Recife, Brazil, on the morning of 28 April.

'Leaving Recife on 4 May 1943, we were escorted across the Atlantic by six BYMSs and arrived at Freetown, Sierra Leone, on 13 May. In temperatures over 100° we unloaded the logs from Brazil together with the cans of beans and spinach we had brought from the USA. Sometime between our arrival on 13 May and our departure on 23 May in company with LST 324, we acquired a monkey, which we called Jacko. He became a firm favourite with all the crew. One of his tricks was to jump on the back of our dog, bite his hind leg and jump out of his reach all in one swift movement. As food was plentiful at this time, feeding him was no problem. Later in 1943 in the Med, food became scarce and he was reduced to eating onions. He died in Taranto and was sadly missed.'

LSTs 324 and 412 left Freetown on 23 May 1943 and sailed via Gibraltar into the Mediterannean Sea to arrive at Algiers on 8 June. For reasons unknown, LST 421 left sometime later.

Burges Watson sails with the 1st LST Flotilla

In New York early in 1943, Captain Burges Watson gathered together what was to become the 1st LST Flotilla. This was made up of LSTs 302, 303, 304, 320, 361, 362, 363, 401, 402 and 403. All ten had been commissioned during November and December 1942, and had made their way to New York via Norfolk, Virginia. Records do not indicate why, but Burges Watson chose LST 320 as his ship.

On the morning of 27 January 1943 the 1st Flotilla sailed from New York. They hadn't gone far before mechanical problems befell all of them to differing degrees. Burges Watson's LST 320 with LSTs 302, 361, 401 and 403 had to turn back to New York. The other five had made it safely

to Bermuda by 31 January, although they had experienced a moderate ENE gale en route. LST 362 reported heavy rolls of 25°–30° and a recommendation was made that cargoes be held in place by welded battens as opposed to wire and chain lashings.

One of the major problems which most LSTs suffered in those early days was within the steering gear. The gear was motor-operated and had a solenoid brake for quick stopping of the motor to prevent over-riding. Solenoid coils burnt out regularly.

With repairs completed, Burges Watson left New York in LST 320 on 23 February 1943. LSTs 302, 361, 401 and 403 were definitely with him. It is likely that five other LSTs sailed for Bermuda at the same time, but records are unclear.

They arrived in Bermuda on 27 February. In his report to the Senior British Naval Officer Western Atlantic (1 March 1943), Burges Watson said that the ships had encountered two periods of bad weather and both on the starboard beam. In the first, ships rolled 15°–20° with a period of roll of 7 to 8 seconds. In the second, the roll increased to 20°–25° with a period of roll of 9 seconds.

Burges Watson went on to say, 'Having watched the ships carefully, it is considered that it would be as well to fit all future construction with bilge keels, for it seems that the rolling of LST when sea is abeam is out of all proportion to the amount of sea which makes the roll.'

He also reported that vehicles would need far more securing chains in operational use and that ... 'Apart from leeway, which is considerable, heavy rolling reduces the speed through the water by 40% or more. The passage was made with engines turning at 220 revolutions which should give 9 knots, yet speed through the water dropped to 5½ or slightly less during the second period when rolling was heaviest.'

The Convoy

To the LST skippers t'was 'Burgo' who spoke,
  'If you split up the convoy my heart will be broke.
So let each noble vessel proceed out of port,
  Assemble and take up the station she ought.
Come speed up the revs and keep into line,
  Just keep well closed up and all will be fine.
Draw wide the Boom Gate and let's out to sea'.
  T'was thus cried the Captain of All LST.

Ten ships left the wharf and set out on their way,
  But 'ere long there were two that returned to stay
Alongside the pier with defects in the clutch.
  'God damn!' cried old 'Burgo', 'This is just too much!
Come slap on the oil and sweat up the nuts,
  Take down the injectors and purge out their guts,
But keep the props turning and we'll out to sea'.
  T'was thus cried the Captain of All LST.

Some little time later t'was patent to see
  Disaster had caught up with still other three,
As they pulled out of line with their cargo a mess
  And headed right back for re-stowage, I guess.
'Come haul on the lashings and tighten the screws,
  Use each man you've got and your LCT crews,
But get it secure and ready for sea'.
  T'was thus spake the Captain of All LST.

Soon the darkness had swallowed the other five craft,
  Not one of them showing a guiding light aft
To the ship next astern, so when morning light shone
  Each found itself in a world of its own.
'Come shoot at the sun, take a snap at a star,
  Plot your position and find where you are,
Lay truly the course and come in from the sea'.
  Cried the Spirit of Captain of All LST.

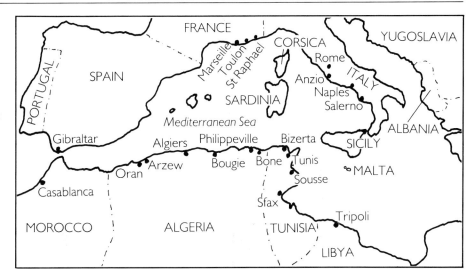

◄◄ Lieutenant-Commander Richard ('Yogi') Brown, RNR, aboard LST 412. (J. H. E. Haslett collection)

◄ Crew members of LST 401 have just emerged from below during the voyage from Bermuda to the Mediterranean. (F. Hooper collection)

The 1st LST Flotilla sails from Bermuda

The 1st Flotilla was brought together again and sailed for Gibraltar on 3 March 1943. Gibraltar was reached on 23 March, the flotilla having sailed 3,593 nautical miles at an average speed of 7¼ knots. The passage was without incident apart from engine and steering motor failure.

In his report dated 8 April 1943 to C-in-C Mediterranean, Burges Watson wrote, 'Although [the breakdowns] were principally of a minor nature, and all but two were successfully repaired at sea, the large number is disconcerting. In addition ... there were frequent temporary steering motor failures caused by sticking contactors and many ships found it necessary to keep a permanent watchkeeper in the tiller flat to clear the contactors.'

The ships and cargoes were desperately needed in North Africa. Nine of the ten vessels in the flotilla sailed for Oran and Arzew on 26 March 1943, leaving LST 362 to follow on 1 April. The vessels off-loaded their cargoes in either Oran or Arzew and quickly settled in to ferrying runs along the North African coastline to such places as Algiers, Bougie, Philippeville and Bône.

Tasajera torpedoed

On 17 January 1943 *Tasajera* was sailing at a speed of 9 knots on course 093° having left Algiers. It was just before 1900. The sky was partly cloudy, but visibility was good. She couldn't have been far from the coast.

The splash of two aerial torpedoes dropping into the water was heard – the first struck *Tasajera* on the starboard side amidships, blasting a hole of 30 feet by 20 feet. Her commanding officer, Lieutenant-Commander Jelling, RNR, immediately ordered the wheel to be put hard-a-starboard. The second torpedo passed harmlessly but very close ahead.

Tasajera began to list heavily and Jelling made full speed for the beach. Water had entered the fuel line and all bunkers, and by 1920 she had lost steam pressure. The main engine and ballast pumps were shut down.

HMS *Polruan* was standing by, so Army personnel were transferred to her. It was now about 2000 and *Polruan* had taken *Tasajera* in tow. By 2040, however, it was apparent that the ship was going to stay afloat so the order was given for the tow to be slipped. The engineers had worked hard to clear the fuel line and by 2050, 180lb pressure was showing on the boilers. A speed of 6½ knots was soon attained and *Polruan* escorted her to Algiers where they arrived in the early hours of 18 January.

A survey of action damage was carried out in No. 1 Dock, Oran, on 13 March. The damage was found to be greater than anticipated. An estimate of 2½ to 3 months was given as being required for repair locally, so it was decided to make temporary repairs to enable *Tasajera* to sail for the UK at about the end of April.

Misoa attacked by aircraft

On 4 February 1943 *Misoa* was in convoy between Oran and Algiers, steering 074°. She was Commodore of the convoy. At 0235, two torpedo tracks were observed crossing from her starboard to port bow and just astern of *Bachaquero*. Commanding officer Grace ordered an emergency 45° turn to port. Five minutes later an escort reported attacking a submarine. By 0250 the convoy had resumed its intended course.

Between 0330 and 0440 aircraft could be heard passing over the convoy at about 1,500 feet. During this time, they made five passes before dropping flares about four miles off *Misoa*'s starboard quarter. Grace made an emergency alteration of course of 45° to port to bring the flares astern. Ten minutes later more flares were dropped, and

▲ Lieutenant P. G. Farwell, RNVR, takes a sighting from the bridge of LST 365. This LST, together with LST 305, sailed across the Atlantic in the ill-fated convoy SC122/HX229 in March 1943. (The late J. Bayley collection, courtesy Mrs J. Bayley)

▲ The cramped conditions in the cabin of Lieutenant J. Bayley, RNVR, in LST 365. (The late J. Bayley collection, courtesy Mrs. J Bayley)

another 45° turn was made. At 0458 an aircraft attacked low on the starboard bow but no bombs or torpedoes were observed. More flares were dropped and emergency 45° turns were made. Shortly after 0500 another aircraft attacked, dropping two torpedoes. By 0535 all was quiet and the convoy resumed course.

Thirteen LSTs sail for England

From late March to mid-May 1943, thirteen LSTs left the USA bound for Liverpool. They were LSTs 63, 64, 164, 198, 200, 305, 319, 321, 365, 366, 406, 418 and 424. Most crew members recall carrying a mixed load of tanks in the tank deck, tons of tinned milk in the troop spaces and lengths of steel rail on the upper deck. LST 366 carried drums of aviation fuel. The bow doors were welded up for the Atlantic crossing.

Lieutenant-Commander C. C. Reynolds, RNR, was in command of LST 418. She sailed in convoy SC127 from Halifax, Nova Scotia, just after midday on 16 April 1943. LST 424 is believed to have been with her. The weather was reasonable on the first day, but the wind soon backed to SE Force 5 causing the ship to roll heavily.

LST 418 suffered the same steering gear problems as her sister ships. By late in the day on 18 April her helm indicator was showing 20° to starboard when the rudder was actually 25° to port. Hand steering from the tiller flat was employed until a temporary repair could be effected.

However, the steering continued to fail at least once a day for the rest of the voyage.

It must have been most unpleasant for the crew as Reynolds reported heavy snow squalls, Force 7 to 8 winds and a rough sea with a high following swell. The ship rolled and pitched heavily. The 350 tons of steel rail stowed on the deck had the effect of reducing the roll, but Reynolds noted that the ship showed signs of stress in a head sea.

John Holden (AB) was in LST 418: 'Those of us who had previously served in ships with submarine detection equipment and depth-charges didn't fancy being a sitting duck on the Atlantic in an LST, particularly as U-boats were at high strength in this area at that time. However, after a few scares and zigzagging all over the place for seventeen days, we finally arrived in Liverpool.

'The cargo was unloaded and modifications were made to the ship, the main one being the fitting of twin Oerlikon 20mm guns in place of the original single mounts. After this we were off to the Clyde to commence exercises. The weather was pretty grim. We were constantly wet through with rain and sea spray, doing endless landings on the beach from early morning to late evening. The worst part was if we lost our kedge anchor wire by dropping the stern anchor too soon. Apart from the Skipper losing face in front of the other LSTs, it was a cold, wet job for a boat crew to fish for the cable with grappling hooks. The practice paid off, however, as we never once lost our kedge anchor during operations in the face of the enemy.'

5. Operation 'Husky' – the Invasion of Sicily

Disposition of operational LSTs as at mid-June 1943

Clyde area: 14 LST(2)s plus HMSS *Boxer*, *Bruiser* and *Thruster*.

Mediterranean: 51 LST(2)s plus HMS *Misoa*.

Others: HMS *Bachaquero* was in the Clyde undergoing refit. HMS *Tasajera* was in the London area for repairs. LST 13 arrived in Liverpool 13 June 1943 but was for conversion to Fighter Direction Tender. Twelve more LSTs were in the USA, of which LST 81 and 82 were converting to LSEs; LSTs 216 and 217 were for conversion to Fighter Direction Tenders with LST 13; the remaining eight LSTs did not leave the USA until August 1943. (Four other LSTs were to be handed over later in the year to the Greek Navy, but operated under the control of Captain LST.)

By mid-June 1943, those involved in operational planning must have been somewhat happier with the LST situation. The accompanying Table shows the disposition of the Royal Navy's LSTs at that time. Crew members knew that something was building up, but they could only guess as to what. In the Clyde area, practice landings were proceeding apace, and in the Mediterranean LSTs were shuttling along the North Coast of Africa in support of the advancing troops. Ferrying trips were also being made to Malta.

It is easy to think of the Mediterranean as 'small'. However, the scale of the operation facing the LSTs and the armed forces becomes apparent when one considers that the top speed of an LST was about 10 knots and that the distance between Gibraltar and the Suez Canal is nearly 2,000 miles. Malta and Sicily are approximately midway.

At the beginning of May, Captain LST, Fischer Burges Watson, had arrived in LST 320 at Bougie and established his shore base there in a requisitioned villa which overlooked the harbour. His staff comprised a Staff Officer (Operations), Lieutenant-Commander R. H. D. Olivier; a gunnery specialist; two engineer officers; and his secretary, Lieutenant Arthur Bailey, RNVR. The Army

▲Officers of LST 366. From left to right: Sub-Lieutenant L. Roberts, RNVR; Lieutenant R. W. Norris, RNVR; Lieutenant-Commander N. Hall, RNR; Lieutenant W. D. Smith, RNR; Lieutenant (E) C. G. Lewis, RNR. (L. Roberts collection)

'lent' Captain LST a Humber staff car, complete with two drivers who enjoyed being away from their unit and drawing their daily tot.

In late June 1943 he and his staff re-embarked in LST 320 and proceeded to Sfax at the beginning of July. There, they would load with many others for Operation 'Husky' – the invasion of the island of Sicily.

The 2nd LST Flotilla arrives in Alexandria

On 4 June 1943 the 2nd Flotilla (less LST 413 which followed later) arrived in convoy GTX1 at Alexandria, Egypt. The Flotilla comprised LSTs 323, 364, 367, 368, 404, 405, 407, 409, 411, 413, 414, 415 and 416. Almost immediately they entered the Suez Canal bound for Port Tewfik (Port Said) where their cargo of stores was unloaded. Difficulty was experienced as no Bills of Lading were carried.

◀ A vehicle being raised to the upper deck in LST 427 at Sousse. The elevator guides were removable, giving greater space on the tank deck. (G. Melford collection)

On 6 June construction of American Naval Pontoon Causeway for use with LST(2)s was started at Alexandria. It seems that these were constructed in two parts, nicknamed *Mary* and *Lily*.

As a portent of things to come, an official report for the period stated that the ships arrived extremely short of spares. It was also noted that some of the ships' companies were in a rather unsettled state, suffering some hardship in matters of pay, leave and ordinary amenities. The condition of some of the ships left much to be desired.

Exercises were carried out with available vessels from 10 to 24 June, but some ships did not have the benefit of even one trial beaching. LSTs 417 and 425 were detached from their own flotilla and sailed from Bizerta on 12 June, arriving in Alexandria on 19 June. On 22 June the commanding officer of LST 425, Lieutenant-Commander C. M. V. Dalrymple-Hay, RN, took command of the 2nd Flotilla from Lieutenant-Commander Clitherow (LST 415).

50th Division troops were loaded at Alexandria, and the Flotilla sailed from there on 24 June in convoy MKS16, bound for Tripoli. One of the pontoons broke up en route, but the salvaged pieces were successfully towed into Tripoli.

During trials off Tripoli on 5 July, LST 409 struck a mine under her stern. Fortunately no one was injured and the damage was repaired in time for her to take part in Operation 'Husky'.

LST 429 – first RN LST to be lost

On 3 July 1943 LST 429 became the first British LST to be lost. She had loaded at Sousse with motor transport, stores and about 200 tons of ammunition. She sailed in convoy en route to Sfax towing a causeway. It is believed that men of the 51st Highland Division were also on

board. At about 2055 that night, the electrics mechanic making his rounds in the fore part of the tank space noticed a small fire under the engine of a truck. He raised the alarm immediately.

Because of the highly dangerous nature of his cargo, 429's commanding officer, Lieutenant-Commander Jenkins, RNR, took the preliminary precaution of lowering both her boats into the water together with the Carley floats.

Before long, thick smoke appeared and the fire got out of control even though hoses, on full pressure, had been placed down all the tank deck ventilators.

A quarter of an hour passed and the fire seemed to have subsided, but then suddenly increased rapidly. Jenkins put all his confidential books into the strong box from the chartroom and locked it – a standard procedure for a commanding officer about to 'abandon ship'.

It was now about 2130 and LST 303 had sent her boats across to help survivors, the risk of explosion being too great to allow 303 to come alongside. Just a few minutes later, small-arms ammunition started to explode. The order 'prepare to abandon ship' was piped. Jenkins ensured that all hands were on the deck before he reluctantly gave the order 'abandon ship'. The officers made a search before abandoning ship themselves.

By 2200, with all hands clear, 429 was well alight with explosions increasing all the time. Some twenty minutes later, a massive explosion occured and the vessel was engulfed in flames from bow to stern. When last seen, only her bows were above the water. On a happier note, it was found that not a single man, Army or Navy, had been lost.

According to Lieutenant-Commander Parker, RNR, there would certainly have been loss of life if it hadn't been

▶ Once at the top of the elevator, the vehicle is reversed off, parked and lashed down among the tank deck ventilators for its passage to Sicily. Lying alongside LST 427 is LST 401. Note 401's strange bridge extension. (G. Melford collection)

for the determined action of Petty Officer Sidney Ellis. In his recommendation for Ellis to be 'mentioned in despatches', Parker wrote: 'In about one hour Petty Officer Ellis rescued over 80 survivors in the whaler ... He later went back and rescued one soldier suffering from shock who had been observed on the poop of LST 429 silhouetted against the flames. LST 429 blew up whilst the whaler was returning.'

The report was forwarded through the usual channels; Commander Alison of LST 302 noting '... this Petty Officer ... displayed much initiative and good seamanship under difficult circumstances'. Captain LST concurred as did the Awards Committee and Admiral Cunningham. This was probably the first award to a member of an LST crew.

Lieutenant-Commander Jenkins concluded his report by saying 'No cause for the fire has been ascertained ... no suggestion, other than spontaneous combustion can be offered'.

It was subsequently ordered that fire sentries be stationed so that any small fire could be dealt with immediately.

The invasion convoys sail

John Holden and LST 418 were in the Clyde: 'We knew the time had come to put all our practice into action. Admiral Lord Louis Mountbatten, Chief of Combined Operations, visited the LSTs in the Clyde on 14 June and addressed some of the ships' companies.'

Over the next few days, the Clyde LSTs were loaded with Canadian tanks and troops. Les Roberts (LST 366): 'We loaded the 12th Canadian (Fore River) Tank Regiment. As they were a new regiment, they had no real emblem. Lieutenant-Commander Hall was a fine oil painter, so he painted them a pennant on canvas, which included the "12" and a leaping salmon.'

The LSTs left the Clyde in three convoys over a period of about eight days in late June 1943. KMS18A comprised

▶ LST 427 and part of the invasion convoy approach 'Bark South' Beach on 10 July 1943. (G. Melford collection)

LSTs 301, 305, 319, 321, 365, 366, 406 and 424. Departure date was 20 June. KMS19 followed on 25 June comprising LSTs 63, 64, 164, 198, 200 and 418. Last away were *Boxer*, *Bruiser* and *Thruster* in KMF18 on 28 June. En route the convoys called at Gibraltar and Algiers. It was from the latter that they sailed as part of the invasion force on 5 July.

Other convoys were formed by the LSTs already out in the Mediterranean and sailed from Tripoli and Malta. These included MWS36, SBS1 and SBM1. Records have not survived to show accurately which LSTs were in which convoy. MWS36X from Tripoli on 8 July included those which had gone out to Alexandria and Port Tewfik. SBS1 was an LCT/LCR/LCG convoy from Sfax on 7 July, for which Captain LST had appointed Commander J. H. Alison, RN, to lead with LST 361. Burges Watson was in LST 320 with convoy SBM1 comprising 26 LSTs, also believed to be from Sfax.

Saturday 10 July 1943

In the early hours of 10 July 1943 the invasion convoys approached the southern tip of the island of Sicily, in the vicinity of Cape Passero. Almost complete surprise had been achieved, even though the convoys were made up of hundreds of vessels.

Dalrymple-Hay (SO LST 425) sailed with convoy MWS36X from Tripoli on the morning of 8 July. By the afternoon of the 9th the weather had begun to deter-

iorate, sea and wind increasing considerably. The pontoons in tow of LSTs 415 and 416 both started to break up, but with the help of a tug one and a half pontoons were saved.

Reports indicate that there was considerable confusion over beaching arrangements. Beaches which had been thought suitable for the LSTs turned out to be unsuitable and much delay followed. Commanding officers had to take the initiative themselves and seek suitable landing spots. However, this was the first time that LSTs had been used operationally and many lessons had to be learnt. A source of some confusion must have come from the fact that LSTs had Army identification serial numbers painted on their bows very close to their own number.

Commander Alison in LST 361 experienced difficulty in beaching at Amber Beach and stuck fast at about 1240 with 4 feet 6 inches of water at the ramp end. Only the tanks could be driven off as other wheeled vehicles would have 'drowned'. The loads of LST 402 (Lieutenant-Commander Sprigge, RNR) and LST 304 (Lieutenant-Commander Fotheringham, RNR) were particularly required on the same beach so they had to beach their vessels hard aground near 361. Both ships cleared their cargo in under four hours even though vehicles were disembarking into 3 feet of water. Soon afterwards, LST 302 (Lieutenant-Commander Stanley, RNR) brought in one of the pontoons and positioned this close to LST 402. The pontoon was used continually thereafter.

Four LSTs were allocated to the HOW Sector of Amber Beach. LST 413 was the first of these to go in and landed successfully at full speed at about 1430, with a water gap of just twenty yards. Her pontoons could not be used because of this short gap but there was still 3 feet of water at the bow door. Royal Engineers promptly used girders to make a temporary bridge. LST 409 came in at 1830 and had been unloaded by dark.

Although there had been sporadic air attacks and enemy gun fire during the day, no reports of casualties to LST crew or ships was reported except to LST 407. LST 323 shot down a Junkers Ju 88. By nightfall on the first day, twenty LSTs had sailed empty for Malta. LST 413 was attacked by aircraft in one of the Malta convoys just off Sicily and successfully shot her attacker down in flames.

The next day, just before noon, Burges Watson brought LST 320 alongside LST 361 which was still stuck on Amber Beach. A girder ramp bridge was assembled between the upper decks of the two ships and vehicles were able to drive from 361 onto 320. LST 320 then sailed down to the rocky area at the eastern end of the beach to unload. Captain LST had chosen this area from reconnaissance photographs in preference to the sandy area originally allotted to him.

▶ Five LSTs head for the beach on 10 July 1943. One commanding officer likened it to a cavalry charge. (D. Barnard, photograph taken from LCI(L) 318)

In his report, Burges Watson said: '... the strata of the rock was flat and not on edge. Ships were beached at 2–4 knots and ran up perfectly to put their ramps down dry. In some cases, ships had difficulty in getting off, having run up so far on the hard rock surface. The old trick of jumping the ship's company right aft in unison always shook a ship free.' LST 363 (Lieutenant-Commander McReynolds) was the first to beach on 'Rocky Beach' as it became known.

On 11 July at first light, LST 367 beached on HOW Sector followed shortly after by LSTs 368 and 407. LST 407 had gone in on GEORGE Sector the previous day but had suffered near-miss bomb damage before being able to discharge her load and had to withdraw. Her commanding officer had been wounded and the ship had lost her kedge anchor. When she came in to HOW Beach, she rode up the beach much higher than the other vessels, due to not having a kedge anchor, and stuck fast. All attempts to haul her off failed. She remained as W/T guard ship, fighter direction ship and HQ ship for the Senior Naval Officer of the landing until 6 August when she was able to sail for Bizerta.

By 13 July the ferry service was well under way. LST 320 and three others arrived from Malta at 0830 that morning and unloaded on 'Rocky Beach'. The loads of four freighters were desperately needed, and the LSTs were assigned to place themselves alongside to offload the freighters' cargo. LST 320 took off 47 assorted vehicles and four guns in ten hours, beached at 2350 that night and discharged in 1 hour and 20 minutes. Burges Watson praised Lieutenant Richards, RNVR, 320's First Lieutenant, for his fine work of organization.

Operation 'Husky' had been a success and the Allied forces gradually pushed the enemy farther north. The LSTs maintained reinforcements and supplies to the island from Malta and North Africa during the following weeks. In due course, landings were possible at Avola, Syracuse, Augusta, Catania, Taormina and St. Teresa on the west coast, and Palermo, Termini and Milazzo on the north coast.

Approximately 76 US LSTs had invaded the southern ports of Licata, Gela and Scoglitti in what were known as the 'Joss', 'Dime' and 'Cent' forces. The British beaches were referred to as 'Acid' and 'Bark'.

70 per cent losses among LSTs had been expected

Les Roberts (LST 366): 'Our second commanding officer, Grandage, was no bearer of hearsay, but later told us after conversations with Captain LST that up to 70% losses among LSTs had been reckoned for at Sicily. Could this be why we were so desperate for spares the whole time we were in the Med? And why any badly damaged LST was cannibalized?

'LST First Lieutenants were usually RNR officers. Not only did they bring a wealth of professional skills to the job but also the know-how of dealing with shortages of all kinds. For example, I was crossing Tripoli harbour in a motor boat with 'Smithie' (First Lieutenant, LST 366) when we passed a sunken Italian cruiser. His eyes lit up. We rapidly returned to LST 366 for tools and were soon aboard the cruiser, disconnecting the steering wheel in the wheelhouse. This was subsequently re-sited in 366's tiller flat and connected up to the emergency steering.'

LST 424 mined off Sousse, 30 July 1943

The weather off the Tunisian coast on the night of Friday, 30 July 1943 was fine and clear. The Mediterranean was calm.

Calm ... until 2146 when LST 424 struck a mine under her port bow. A column of water shot 50 feet into the air and the ship shook violently from stem to stern. Able Seaman Tappin was manning one of the forward Oerlikon guns. The blast blew him into the air and overboard.

424 was returning from the 'Acid North' Beaches of Sicily in convoy at a speed of 8 knots. She was lead ship of the starboard column, four cables off the starboard beam of the SO 7th Flotilla in LST 319. LSTs 365 and 416 were the other ships in the convoy.

They were steering 290° and were just over five miles from the Sousse Pier Head Light when the explosion occurred. 424's commanding officer, Lieutenant-Commander Grandage, RD, RNR, immediately ordered maximum speed. Course was altered towards a beach some four miles distant. The engine room replied with 330 revolutions.

As the First Lieutenant, Engineer Officer and Shipwright started their examination of the damage, 'prepare to abandon ship' was ordered. The ship appeared to be going down by the head. The full extent of the damage could not be ascertained because of the darkness and the need to keep watertight doors closed.

Grandage stuck to his decision to run for the beach. He no doubt breathed a sigh of relief at 2213 as 424 ran onto the sand just under a mile from the Sousse Pier Head Light. Soundings were taken. She was aground from stem to the bridge in 6 feet of water with 16 feet under her stern.

Able Seaman Tappin was recovered unharmed apart from a strained neck. He was a good swimmer and was already wearing a life-belt. Tappin shouted to LST 416, which was following 424, and a Carley float was lowered for him. An LCI astern of 416 eventually picked him up.

In daylight on Saturday, 31 July, a full examination of the damage was undertaken. On the deck, it was found that the welding along the seam from the forward end of the after hatch on the starboard side was open out to the side and for 18 inches down the ship's side. Below, the full extent of the damage was seen when the manhole door to compartment A404W was taken off. A hole about 20 feet across was found in the ship's bottom at the junction of compartments A404W, A406W and A403V. Three bulkheads had gone. The three compartments and the bilge control room were wide open to the sea. The tank deck in the vicinity was bulging upwards by about 12 inches. In the bosun's store (A308A) the deck had been forced upwards to within a foot of the deck above and had torn away from the ship's side.

At 1515 that day, she was floated off the beach and made Sousse Harbour under her own power. Adjustments were made to the ballast to overcome the loss of buoyancy. Floating with a slight list to starboard, she was secured to the Phosphate Quay with a draught of 3 feet 3 inches forward and 9 feet aft.

Sometime in early August Grandage took her to Bizerta. Even in moderate sea, she pounded heavily and further buckling of damaged plates took place.

Grandage went to see Burges Watson at Ferryville to ask for a new command. Captain LST discussed this with him but said that he could not give any guarantee that it would be possible. At that moment the Captain happened

◄ Three LSTs unload on 'Rocky Beach' on 11 July 1943. Notice the hand-painted army serial numbers. Serial number 325 is believed to be LST 427. (G. Melford collection)

to look out of the window and saw one LST ramming the stern of another. He quickly commented, 'Well, if those two copulating in the fairway have an offspring, perhaps I could manage it.' Grandage soon took over command of LST 366.

LST 414 hit by torpedo-bomber, 15 August 1943

In the early hours of the morning of Sunday, 15 August 1943, Lieutenant-Commander Dalrymple-Hay, RN, was at the head of a small convoy bound for Bizerta from Malta in LST 425. He was Senior Officer of the 2nd Flotilla. The convoy was just over four miles from the Cani Island Light, with HMS *Albacore* as escort.

At about 0130 his attention was drawn to LST 414, some three miles astern (LST 414 had been towing 416 since 0745 the previous day). She appeared to be on fire. As neither sound nor shock had been heard or felt, it was assumed that the fire had been caused by an electrical fault.

In fact she had been attacked from the north by a torpedo-bomber aircraft. The OOW, Lieutenant Robertson, RNVR, had only spotted the aircraft just as it dropped the torpedo at almost pointblank range – the torpedo hit the water just 200 yards or so off her starboard bow. The aircraft passed ahead of the ship as it turned to make its getaway. Moments later (evasive action had been almost impossible due to having 416 in tow) the torpedo ripped into 414's midships.

Fires started in the passenger equipment store (A315A) and oil fuel on the tank deck caught fire. Fumes from the oil fuel were uncomfortably dense. 414's damage control parties performed excellent work in getting the fires under control.

At about 0135 Dalrymple-Hay gave the order 'hard-a-port, flank ahead' and made his way up to 414. Although by this time the fire appeared to be out, minor electrical explosions could still be seen in the darkness.

In the meantime, 414 had slipped her tow rope from 416 and had made an attempt to proceed under her own power, but because of the damage to the hull and flooding of the auxiliary engine room, this had to be abandoned. 414 requested 425 to take her in tow. By 0300 414 was in hand-steering behind 425, progress towards Bizerta being made comfortably at 4 knots with bulkheads holding and making no water.

Flag Officer, Tunisia, had advised the escort that no tugs were available at Bizerta. Dalrymple-Hay intended to tow 414 up to Ferryville, using LST 413 as a 'stern tug'. However, a message sent by 414 at 0605, the contents of which are unknown, caused him to come to the decision to beach her at the earliest possible moment. So it was that just before 0700 LST 414 beached on a sandy strip north of Bizerta.

Only one man, Leading Seaman Edward Jasper, had been killed in the attack.

When the damage to the ship was inspected, it was found that a hole 50 feet long by 15 feet deep had been blown 10 feet into her. The upper deck had cracked right across, and a further crack extended a distance of 30 feet before the after hatch. Flooding in the auxiliary engine room had been uncontrollable and the generators had

▶ During the build-up of reinforcements, LST 427 has only one more load for the elevator. (G. Melford collection)

◀ LST 367 is showing two black balls on her mast. According to the manual of seamanship, this signified 'out of control'. One can speculate whether she went out of control approaching the pontoon causeway (partly obscured by the tank) and rode up on the beach. (IWM ref NA4265)

become immersed which put the pumps out of action.

In his memo of 15 August 1943, addressed to Captain LST, Dalrymple-Hay said, 'I have to submit, regretfully, that 414 must be regarded as a total loss. Her back is in all probability broken and she is badly hogged.' Ferryville Dockyard noted, 'To effect repairs, work would entail renewing complete midship portion for a length of 70 feet to 80 feet, with vessel in dry-dock for about two months. Extensive girdering would be necessary before an attempt could be made to move the vessel, and this could not be guaranteed. LST 414 has been cannibalized to a considerable extent.'

9th LST Flotilla leaves the USA

On 16 August 1943 Commander Garth H. F. Owles, RN, led the eight LSTs of the 9th Flotilla away from Norfolk, Virginia, USA, in a large convoy bound for North Africa. The LSTs were destined for an operation in India, but the authorities were to take great advantage of their capabilities while they were passing through the Mediterranean. Each ship carried either US Army or Navy personnel, together with a number of hospital ship officers and men. All vessels carried an LCT on the upper deck, between 312 and 560 tons of cargo fuel in the forward ballast tanks and all (except LSTs 214 and 237) carried steel rails weighing between 193 and 250 tons on the tank deck.

In his report on the passage, Commander Owles graphically described his experience of the LST in bad weather. 'The weather began to deteriorate during the first watch on 16 August. On 17 August and 18 August the wind blew from SW Force 6 to 7. During this period, ships rolled and pitched very violently. The roll was so quick that "sea legs" availed nothing and it was always necessary to hold on to something. All bunks are fitted fore and aft and it was very difficult to stay in them. At times the effect of the pitching was somewhat alarming until one became used to it. Ships would rear up and then crash down on to the next approaching wave. The whole of the forward part of the ship could be seen to move in a vertical direction in a gradually diminishing "waving" motion.

◀ This aerial view of LST 214 is believed to have been taken while she was on passage from the USA to North Africa in August 1943, as part of the 9th LST Flotilla. The men sunbathing appear to have implicit faith in the lashings which secure the LCT to the upper deck. (US Naval Institute)

"Ripples" travelled fore and aft along the upper deck, and vehicles on the upper deck in LST 215 had the appearance of travelling along a very uneven road.'

The weather improved for the remainder of the voyage, but the action of the sea from 27 August to 1 September '... caused a continuous quick roll and occasional "shudders" which were tiring and uncomfortable'.

LSTs 215 and 180 performed well with no breakdowns whatsoever on the voyage. The other vessels suffered the usual steering problems. On 27 August LST 237 collided with SS *Jubal A. Early*. On 3 September LST 238 collided with an unknown corvette causing serious damage to bow doors and operating gear.

From the moment of arriving in the Mediterranean, the flotilla never again worked as a complete unit which caused Owles great difficulty in his administration. LST 239 stopped off at Gibraltar on 1 September to attend to major steering defects, while the remainder of the flotilla completed the 4,000 nautical mile journey to arrive at Oran on 3 September. Owles reported that the port authorities at Oran were extremely unco-operative and it was difficult to persuade them of the necessity to disembark quickly so that the flotilla could continue. In some ships, US troops remained on board for five more days after arrival. Libertymen were frequently insulted or attacked and the atmosphere was noticeably 'anti-British'.

The story of the 9th Flotilla continues in the following chapters so as to maintain events in chronological sequence.

Composition of Flotillas in September 1943

Flot.	Senior Officer	LSTs
1st	Alison	302, 303, 304, 320, 361*, 362, 363, 401, 402, 403.
2nd	Clitherow	323, 364, 368, 404, 405, 407, 409, 411, 413, 414, 415*, 416, 422.
3rd	Hore-Lacy	322*, 324, 367, 408, 410, 412, 417, 419, 420, 423, 426, 427, 428, 430.
4th	Dalrymple-Hay	8, 9, 11, 12, 62, 65, 159, 160, 161, 162, 199, 425*.
7th	Sutton	301, 305, 319*, 321, 365, 366, 424 (out of action).
8th	Rudyerd-Helpman	63, 64, 164, 198*, 200, 406, 418.
9th	Owles	79, 80, 180, 214, 215*, 237, 238, 239.

Notes: LSTs 163, 165 and 421 were Unallocated. * denotes Senior Officer's vessel. There were no 5th or 6th Flotillas at this time.

▲The date of this photograph is unknown, but depicts a flotilla of LSTs loading at Bizerta. (G. Melford collection)

▼LST 199 on the beach at Reggio during Operation 'Baytown'. (IWM ref NA6216)

▲Lieutenant-Commander L. J. Smith, RNR, on the beach at Vibo Valentia following Operation 'Ferdy'. LST 65 is in the background. (IWM ref NA6417)

6. Operations 'Baytown' and 'Ferdy'

One of the most significant, and often overlooked, landings of 1943 was that of 3 September – Operation 'Baytown', the crossing of the Messina Straits from Sicily to 'the toe of Italy'. Twenty-two LSTs took part in this operation: LSTs 8, 9, 12, 62, 65, 160, 161, 162, 199, 301, 323, 366, 403, 404, 405, 409, 413, 415, 416, 417, 422 and 425.

Surviving records have enabled the following report on how the operation was conducted to be compiled on a daily basis. The vessels were supposed to be from the 2nd and 4th Flotillas, but six vessels were missing for unknown reasons. Captain LST added four ships to the group because of this (see 23 August entry).

Sunday 22 August: From Ferryville, LSTs 8, 9, 404, 413 and 415 to Karouba to load.

Monday 23 August: 2nd and 4th Flotillas completed loading at Karouba and proceeded to anchorage in Bizerta Bay at 1730. Great difficulty was experienced in getting permission from the US authorities to allow ships to leave the loading berths when ready and this resulted in serious congestion in the channel. Dalrymple-Hay noted 'a bad time was had by all'. LST 199 grounded when getting away from the oiling berth but got away in time to join the group. Just outside the breakwater, US LST 209 rammed LST 425 port side amidships. No serious damage was done, and she was able to continue in the operation. Captain LST sent a message (timed at 1847) adding LSTs 301, 366, 403 and 417 to the group.

Tuesday 24 August: Group sailed 0800 to Port Augusta with HMS *Gavotte* and one ML as escort.

Wednesday 25 August: At approximately 0200, both HMS *Gavotte* and LST 417 broke down and were left behind to make for Malta. At dawn LST 415 and others opened fire on a 4-engined aircraft which flew down one of the columns at 2,000 feet. It dropped recognition signals and turned away to starboard. Arrival time at Port Augusta was between 1830 and 2000.

Thursday 26 August: Unloading commenced at the submarine basin and ships returned to anchor berths in Augusta Harbour where such overhauls as time permitted were carried out.

Friday 27 August: All at anchor in Harbour.

Saturday 28 August: Small air raid at 0800 when LST 62 was near-missed. SO 4th Flotilla inspected and addressed ship's company of LST 62 as five men had been reported to have refused duty the previous day. The men were sentenced to cells by NOIC Augusta.

Sunday 29 August: A day of heavy showers. SO 415 walked round LSTs 160 and 162. Fair sized raid was made at 2045 with many flares being dropped. Smoke cover was drawn up from the tank deck and this proved effective. Ron Kelly (LST 162): 'The flares lit us up like daylight and during the 1¼-hour raid we had near-misses on both sides.'

Monday 30 August: At 0545 LSTs 9, 162, 301, 366, 403, 409 and 425 sailed for Catania. They were out of the way prior to two small raids at 0705 and 0840. They sailed to Catania to load, returning to Augusta on completion at about 2130. SO 425 noted that the Army loading authorities were most helpful and concurred that wherever possible flotillas should work as a unit.

Tuesday 31 August: LSTs 8, 12, 62, 65, 160, 161, 199, 323, 404, 405, 413, 415, 416, 417 and 422 proceeded to Catania to load, where they arrived at 0815. SO 4th Flotilla visited Flag Officer Sicily (FOSY). Vessels loaded by 1545 but held up by personnel ships entering harbour. Arrived Augusta 2100.

Wednesday 1 September: All at anchor, Augusta. Dalrymple-Hay, his Navigator and the commanding officer of LST 404 were taken up the Sicilian coast to look at the objective. Dalrymple-Hay reported that … 'This trip proved of inestimable value on D-Day'.

Thursday 2 September: FOSY briefed all commanding officers at a meeting at 0930. They were to be split up into three groups. The 2nd Flotilla was to land the 1st Canadian Division on FOX Beach. The 4th Flotilla and attached ships were to land the 5th Division on GEORGE and HOW Sectors further up the coast. The whole party sailed in two convoys. The 2nd Flotilla cleared Augusta shortly before midnight.

Friday 3 September: 4th Flotilla left Augusta shortly after midnight. Dalrymple-Hay and others reported that the turning lights on the Sicilian coast were confusing and not marked as they were supposed to be. This resulted in his group turning too soon. However, his preview of the coast prevented him landing in the wrong place. The GEORGE group also turned too soon and had to be chased out of the FOX area.

Les Roberts was in LST 366. 'The bombardment from both the Army on the North Sicilian coast and from cruisers in the Messina Straits had turned the area into a thick fog. There seemed to be ships everywhere. The cordite fumes had us in tears. Just ahead of us was an American minesweeper. With one of the loudest bangs I have ever heard, she simply disappeared. She must have found a mine.'

It is thought that the first LST to touch mainland Italy that day was LST 301 on HOW Sector. As the ship hit the beach, a member of an onboard tank crew lost his footing and slipped into his vehicle. In grabbing for support he fired off two rounds from a gun. Two soldiers were hit and wounded.

As soon as 301 was on the beach, her commanding officer was summoned by the Principal Beachmaster (Commander RN) who reprimanded him for beaching without orders from him. LST 301 was ordered to withdraw as there were no exits for vehicles from the beach. 301's commanding officer pointed out that he couldn't withdraw as he had no ballast to release, and was hard and fast aground. The Beachmaster didn't seem to comprehend the relevance and still ordered 301 off the beach as he walked away.

Bearing in mind his primary duty was to get troops and equipment ashore, 301's CO consulted the Army commanding officer on board. He fully concurred and by 0720, eight Sherman tanks, a bulldozer and a tank fitted with bridging gear were off the ship and heading for an exit 300 yards up the beach to the north.

As the sand was very soft and no beach roadway had been provided, he decided to pull off the beach and await an opportunity to beach nearer the newly found exit in order to give his cargo of wheeled vehicles a chance. The berth was occupied by LST 366, so he waited until she had finished, re-beaching at about 0900. Once unloaded, she sailed for St. Teresa, arriving at about 1300, where loading up began immediately.

LST 415 arrived at Gallico Beach (HOW Sector) at 0900 while our own shore batteries were still firing from the Sicilian side. She beached with LST 162 subsequently beaching on her starboard side and LST 161 200 yards to port.

LST 425 beached at 0840. A bomb dropped between her and 417 but without causing casualties or damage apart from a large splinter through the seamen's heads (lavatories).

The first LSTs to beach on FOX Sector came under fire from a shore battery but none was hit and the battery was soon silenced.

LST 425 pulled off and proceeded to St. Teresa. LST 405 seemed to be uncomfortably high up the beach as 425 left, so 413 and 422 were instructed to render assistance if required.

On her first return trip, LST 425 rammed LST 162 in the stern while trying to beach in the dark. Ron Kelly of LST 162 said, 'It's a good job she did hit us and retired, otherwise she would have wrecked an LCT lying alongside us.'

Once the initial assault was over and LST 366 was clear of the Straits, Les Roberts was able to snatch a couple of hours on his bunk. He must have been tired. Not even the sound of an 8,000-ton freighter carving a 'V' shape into 366's starboard side woke him. The gash stopped less than a foot from his cabin.

Saturday 4 September: LST 162 left the beach at 0500 and went to Catania to load with tanks and steam-rollers, arriving at 1030. She left at 1230 together with LSTs 323 and 417. LST 425 on ferrying. In accordance with orders, LSTs 301, 366 and 403 were sailed for Tripoli and LSTs 162, 323 and 417 were sent to Milazzo. LST 415 received FOSY's 041115B (See Operation 'Ferdy').

Sunday 5 September: Charts found by LST 425 in order to get to Termini. At 2230 LSTs 160, 199, 404, 405, 409, 413, 416, 422 and 425 sailed for Termini together with six LCI(L)s, 2 MLs and SS *Astra*. They passed through the Straits of Messina and reached Termini at 1535 on 6 September. LST 62 was not considered operationally sound and was left behind to continue the shuttle service between St. Teresa and the Italian mainland.

According to Dalrymple-Hay in his report on the operation, many more loads could have been taken but the Army authorities did not co-operate. Some ships were so overloaded that much time was taken unbeaching. Ships were held waiting off the beaches for some time and it was difficult to raise the Signal Station.

Both commanding officers of LSTs 301 and 415 complained about the lack of beach roadway. That of 301 said that this '. . . might have had serious consequences had there been much enemy opposition'. Apparently, the supply for HOW Sector had been delivered further up the coast. The commanding officer of LST 415 suggested that '. . . turnround of ships could be quickened by carrying this on board'.

Disposition of vessels after the Operation:

To Termini LSTs 160, 199, 404, 405, 409, 413, 416, 422, 425

► Wrecks of vehicles and debris are strewn across the upper deck of LST 65. Her LCV(P) hangs precariously from the starboard davit. (IWM ref NA6423)

To Tripoli   LSTs 301, 366, 403
To Milazzo   LSTs 162, 323, 417
              (They returned to 'Baytown' area, then proceeded to Termini.)
To Riposto   LSTs 8, 9, 12, 65, 161, 415
              (LSTs 8, 12, 161 and 415 went to Messina to unload and then went to Termini. LSTs 9 and 65 took part in Operation 'Ferdy'.)
Shuttle   LST 62

Operation 'Ferdy'

Operation 'Ferdy' was originally scheduled to take place on 6 September 1943. The object was to land 231 Brigade at Gioja, some miles behind enemy lines. This would help speed up the advance of XIII Corps; interfere with the enemy's programme of withdrawal and road demolition; and, in the words of Flag Officer Sicily, 'put some Germans in the bag'.

The Naval and Military Commanders were Captain Ian Black, RN (SNOL(L)), and Brigadier Roy Urquhart of 231 Brigade. Their HQ ship was to be LCI(L) 263. (Captain Ian Black was SNOL(F) during Operation 'Baytown'.)

Following Operation 'Baytown', Flag Officer Sicily sent a secret hand message (timed at 1115 on 4 September) to Ferry Control CLC and Senior Officer LST 425. It called for them to assemble the following in the vicinity of Mortelle, to the NW of the Straits of Messina, by 1700 on Sunday 5 September: six LST; eight LCT; six LCI(L); and 32 LCM. The initial destination was Riposto, presumably for loading.

The message was received at 1330 by the SO of 4th Flotilla in LST 415. LSTs 8, 9, 12, 65, 161 and 415 were allocated to the operation.

LST 415 stopped loading at St Teresa at 1400 and rounded up the flotilla to arrive at Gallico by 1700. They were unbeached again by 1830 and proceeded with all dispatch to Riposto.

Beaching did not take place until noon the next day, Sunday 5 September. The flotilla was unbeached by 2000 and formed up to proceed to Gioja, weighing anchor at 2130. The weather wasn't good – rain and squalls. By 2300, LST 415 had received orders that the operation was postponed and that he was to anchor off Messina along with the other LSTs.

The next morning, Monday 6 September, LSTs 8, 12, 161 and 415 were called into Messina to unload. Flag Officer Sicily then ordered the empty vessels to sail for Termini, which they did at 1630. Although they didn't know it, they were on their way to load to take part in Operation 'Avalanche', the invasion of Salerno. LSTs 9 and 65 were left behind – still loaded.

Operation 'Ferdy' was put into action for real on Tuesday 7 September, when the assembled force proceeded at 1830. The commanders had had less than 24 hours to re-assemble the craft and hold the necessary briefings. There was no time for rehearsal, but as the plan was comparatively simple and the personnel experienced, that was accepted.

The force comprised three groups:

Group One: HDML 1128 with five LCI(L) towing ten empty LCAs.

Group Two: HDML 1277 with nine LCI(L).

Group Three: LCI(L) 263 (the HQ ship) with eighteen LCTs.

LSTs 9 and 65 were scheduled to sail so as to arrive off the beaches at 0530 on D-Day, 8 September. Support was to be provided by 2 LCGs, 2 LCFs and HMSS *Aphis*, *Erebus* and *Scarab*. They faced a 50-mile sea crossing. This passed without incident and the lowering position was reached at 0150. The first LCT went in at 0535 followed by others. Over the next 90 minutes, the landings were under continuous attack. It seems that the enemy, instead of being some miles south, were actually passing at the time of the landing. Captain Ian Black reported '... large numbers of guns and machine-guns were brought to bear'.

Because of the shelling, LSTs 9 and 65, together with LCTs 702 and 306, were ordered not to enter harbour without further orders. The LCTs were carrying petrol, ammunition and stores.

By 0730, LST 65 was being shelled. Flag Officer Sicily decided that it was essential to get at least one of the LSTs on to the beach as the guns and vehicles were of great importance to the Army. He realized that some of the shellfire would cause damage. However, it was the lesser of two evils, as things would certainly get worse if the Army didn't get their much-needed equipment.

At 0800, LSTs 9 and 65 were ordered towards the beach, led by HDML 1128, an LCG and two LCFs. They were greeted by continuous shellfire and Captain Black ordered LST 9 to withdraw. It seems that one of her engines had become defective.

LST 65 carried on. Her commanding officer, Lieutenant-Commander L. J. Smith, RNR, wrote in his report, 'During the run in, I was engaged by the shore batteries and in spite of evasive action taken by me (zigzagging), hits were being registered on the ship as I approached. I ordered flank speed and ran hard up the beach.'

On board LST 65 at the time was Telegraphist Stanley Batty. 'We steamed at full speed for the beach. I remember it was a beautiful, sunny day. The enemy must have thought we were mad, as we made a smashing target. We were hit many times mainly by 88mm shells.

'Our leading hand dashed into the wireless cabin, where I was on duty, and put all our codebooks and confidential papers into the weighted bag provided for the purpose and ditched them over the side, as per Admiralty instructions. I was ordered to make a "Mayday" signal in plain language saying that we had been hit many times; had casualties amongst the crew and troops; had a fire on the upper deck; and that one of our bow doors was jammed shut. I remember thinking that apart from all that, we were OK. Suddenly, a shell cut through the corner of the wireless cabin, throwing bits of asbestos and debris all over me. Luckily for me, it must have exploded further inboard.

'We beached at full speed and a brave soul on a bulldozer pulled the remaining bow door open. This enabled the troops, equipment and wounded to be put ashore swiftly, but still under very heavy gunfire. The beach party did a marvellous job under great stress.

'I remember that Sick Berth Attendant Burton did a fine job tending to the wounded with what must have been just a small first-aid kit. I also remember Able Seaman Maynard who stayed on the upper deck operating the lift to get the vehicles from the upper deck to the lower deck. He also helped put out the fire.'

Lieutenant-Commander Smith was ordered by the Beachmaster to move the ship's company ashore. Stanley Batty remembers grabbing a jug of rum as he ran for the beach and the shelter of a tunnel. 'One of our gunners asked the Skipper for permission to go back aboard to his Oerlikon gun. He was sure he had spotted one of the enemy gun emplacements on the hillside. The Skipper denied the permission, saying that we were now under the orders of the military. However, the gunner somehow got permission from the Army and dashed back to the ship. He made it to the gun, but was instantly riddled from head to foot with gunfire. Later, when they carried him back into the tunnel, one of our officers lifted a bloody scrap of the gunner's clothing . . . and sadly shook his head.'

In the early afternoon, LCT 306 was sent into harbour, followed shortly after by LCT 702 and LST 9 which beached alongside LST 65. After unloading, the crew of LST 9 also spent the night in the tunnel with the men of LST 65.

Captain Ian Black recommended Lieutenant-Commander Smith for a decoration, saying, 'This officer . . . displayed great courage and determination in entering harbour while under heavy shell and mortar fire . . . By his determination, he materially helped the military situation which at that time gave rise to some anxiety.'

Flag Officer Sicily wrote, 'I cannot speak too highly of the conduct of this LST, which has been praised by XIII Corps Commander and all who saw it. The guns she carried were in action a few minutes after she beached and helped to relieve a difficult situation.'

However, Captain LST was not so impressed. In a report he wrote, 'LST 65 gives a perfect example of a case where the ship should have backed off as soon as the tank deck was cleared. Here was a steep-to beach with nothing to prevent a quick backing off, and return when the upper deck load had been transferred to the tank deck.' (See Chapter 7 – Lessons Learned.)

Lieutenant-Commander Smith sailed with LST 9 back to Messina where he made a preliminary report to Flag Officer Sicily. LST 65 stayed on the beach for some days before being patched up and sailed to Naples for more permanent repairs.

Smith recommended the following crew members for an award, believed to be a mention in despatches: Able Seaman Maynard; Lieutenant Murray, RNR; Sick Berth Attendant Burton; Ordinary Seaman Wood; Warrant Engineer Baker, RNR; Acting Petty Officer Freestone, RN; Petty Officer Hill, RN; Engine Room Artificer Stevenson, RN; Ordinary Seaman Uren, RN; Stoker 1st Class Fullager, RFR; Stoker 1st Class Andrews, RN.

7. Operation 'Avalanche' – the Salerno Invasion

LST convoys for Operation 'Avalanche'

TSS2	Tripoli	0500	6 Sept 1943	20 LSTs
TSS3	Tripoli	0600	7 Sept 1943	17 LSTs
FSS2	Bizerta	0530	7 Sept 1943	20 LSTs
FSS2X	Bizerta	0630	7 Sept 1943	18 LSTs
FSS2Y	Termini	0500	8 Sept 1943	16 LSTs (14 known to be British)
FSS3	Bizerta	1315	7 Sept 1943	18 LSTs
NSF1	Oran	1500	5 Sept 1943	*Boxer, Bruiser, Thruster*

The early days of September 1943 saw the LSTs involved in feverish activity. The 9th Flotilla had arrived in North Africa and was undergoing severe difficulties in unloading ready for its voyage to India. The 2nd and 4th Flotillas were regrouping after Operation 'Baytown' and LSTs 9 and 65 had just taken part in Operation 'Ferdy'.

There was no rest. Operation 'Avalanche' was planned for 9 September. The objective was to land the Allies at Salerno so that they could move round the coast and capture the vital port of Naples.

Approximately 57 British LSTs were mixed with approximately 52 US LSTs in Operation 'Avalanche'. Sadly, even the official historians reporting on the operation shortly afterwards were unable to state which vessels had sailed in which convoy.

SO 2nd Flotilla, Lieutenant-Commander Dalrymple-Hay, RN, was in charge of convoy FSS2Y due to leave Termini at 0500 on 8 September. He left the 'Baytown' beaches on 5 September in LST 425 with LSTs 160, 199, 404, 405, 409, 413, 416 and 422 in company. En route, both LST 409 and 416 had to attend to 'flapping bow doors' in a heavy sea and poor visibility while passing through the Straits of Messina.

At 1500 on 6 September the vessels arrived in Termini where Dalrymple-Hay was instructed to await orders. He noticed many wrecks masking the way to the loading berths. He also knew that an operation was in the offing, but what, where and when was still unknown.

By nightfall, he was told that it was imperative that he take his vessel and two others into the inner harbour to load. Having observed the numerous wrecks in daylight, Dalrymple-Hay appointed his Flotilla Navigator, Lieutenant Peter Wilcockson, DSC, RNR, to mark out a makeshift channel by placing the ship's emergency lights on certain buoys in the vicinity of the wrecks. This was done and the three vessels were safely berthed by 2300.

Despite this hazardous venture, no loads arrived for the vessels until about 1030 the next day. The other ships were berthed just outside the harbour during the morning. There was a slight swell, so they had to keep their engines

▶ LSTs 304 and 409 at Bizerta. (J. F. G. Fotheringham)

◄ From left to right, LSTs 320, 401, 304 and two other unidentified LSTs. (C. Hooper collection)

► HMS *Thruster* at speed in the Mediterranean. (H. Reid collection)

running at half speed to enable them to stay on the beach.

Confusion reigned. Dalrymple-Hay could find no one who actually knew what was being planned. During the morning, Lieutenant-Commander Clitherow arrived in LST 415 with 8, 12 and 161. LSTs 162, 323 and 417 also arrived. LSTs 415 and 199 loaded US personnel and equipment of the 189th Artillery. Despite protests by Clitherow, about 200 tons of loose stores in the form of petrol and ammunition were loaded. For reasons un-known, LST 8 did not load.

LST 417 torpedo-bombed

During the evening of 7 September LST 417 was anchored about one mile off Termini, fully loaded with troops and vehicles. Although the crew didn't know it, she was awaiting sailing orders to take part in Operation 'Avalanche'.

John Bell was aboard LST 413: 'A torpedo-bomber attacked across our bows. No-one fired at it because it was showing a light.'

At about 2120, a torpedo from the bomber struck 417's port rudder. The violent explosion sent many soldiers and ratings into the air and overboard. About 25 feet of the ship's stern was blown away and cracks appeared in the deck plating in front of the bridge. Watertight doors and hatches were immediately secured.

Boats from numerous surrounding vessels were sent to help. LST 162 came alongside to port, while three LCIs manoeuvred on to the starboard side. Troops and wounded were taken off by these craft, but before long, LST 162 received her sailing orders and had to cast off. LCI 288 took off casualties and LCIs 115 and 306 were lashed to LST 417 to tow her to the beach where head ropes secured her to the shore. All the ship's crew could

be accounted for, but sadly five had died at the moment of impact and another died later from wounds received.

The next day, she was refloated and taken to a more suitable part of the harbour where unloading of vehicles could take place. Temporary repairs were put in hand to keep her afloat. However, it was reported that she was in danger of breaking her back.

The Salerno convoys set sail

Starting at 0500 on Monday 6 September, the LST invasion convoys left from their ports in Sicily and North Africa. Captain LST sailed from Tripoli with LST 320 in convoy TSS2, which suffered little or no enemy inter-ference en route. However, LSTs 12, 199 and 415 were not so lucky on their passage from Termini. At 1400 on 8 September they were attacked by four Messerschmitt Me 109s. Bombs dropped around 199, but fortunately caused no damage. About four hours later they were attacked again, this time by rocket bombs. In the clear atmosphere, the bombs could be seen plainly all the way down, but again no damage was done.

John Holden (LST 418): 'During our voyage, the soldiers received lectures from their officers with maps spread out on the upper deck under the sunny Mediterranean blue sky. On the afternoon of 8 September, our commanding officer spoke to us on the SRE, telling us that we were heading for the Bay of Salerno. This time it would be a much sterner task than the Sicily job.

'At 1830 that evening, we received the news that Italy had surrendered. We chatted excitedly with the troops hoping that this news would make things easier for us.'

Les Roberts (LST 366): 'Each LST had an SRE – sound reproduction equipment as termed by the Americans. The British would know it as a Tannoy. It was used to play

radio or music throughout the ship when things were peaceful. It could also be used to pipe orders. One could hear a little "click" as a Quartermaster changed over. At sea en route to Salerno, the SRE was on to broadcast the news. The momentous announcement was heard that Italy had capitulated. The news reader followed with a wonderful piece of oratory ... "Mussolini's dreams lay in ashes ... proud pretender brought to his knees ... a dynasty had passed into oblivion ..." Then a "click" – "'ands to Supper! 'ands to Supper!" Empires might crumble and history might be in the process of being re-written, but at half past six in the Royal Navy, 'ands still go to supper! Perhaps it's that adherence to tradition that makes the Royal Navy great.'

John Holden (LST 418): 'Night fell. It was a beautiful night. The sea was calm and the moon was full. Visibility was so good that I wondered why the enemy hadn't discovered us. Just before dawn, we could tell that we had arrived by the different sound of the ship's engines. It now seemed that we were creeping along like thieves in the night. Then, suddenly, the bombardment of the beach began. It was absolutely deafening. The flashes were blinding and continuous, lighting up the bay. We could do nothing but wait. If we ever thought our task here was to have been made easier by the capitulation of the Italians, we could now see how wrong we were.'

Burges Watson goes ashore

Many of the British LSTs were conveying DUKWs and towing causeways. At 0615 on Thursday 9 September, Burges Watson received a signal from the Senior Naval Officer of the landing (SNOL/Q) ordering him to send in the LSTs with DUKWs followed by the ships with causeways.

At 0815 he left LST 320 in HDML 1207 for the beaches and was happy to find that five LSTs had already beached with ramps dry and the causeways not required. It is thought that he landed on 'Roger' or 'Sugar' Beaches.

Commander Alison took LST 361 into 'Roger Amber' Beach, being shelled by an 88mm gun on the approach. Four or five shells fell close, but no damage was done. He went in with a causeway, but found that the beaches were so good that it wasn't really needed.

Lieutenant-Commander McReynolds, RNR, was ordered to take LST 363 down the swept channel for 'Sugar Green' Beach in company with other LSTs carrying DUKWs. His nine DUKWs were launched at 0835 at which time the ship was being straddled by intermittent fire from shore batteries.

A few minutes later, an 88mm shell sliced through a truck on the upper deck, pierced the main deck, and went through the troop showers and general store on the starboard side. LST 363 eventually beached on 'Sugar Amber' at 300 revolutions just before 1030 with the ramp high and dry, followed soon after on her port side by Commander Sutton, RN, SO of the 7th Flotilla in LST 319. While unloading, LST 365 came in on the starboard side of 363 and collided with her, causing holes in the troop deck approximately 14 feet and 6 feet long respectively, by 8 inches wide.

Commander Sutton reported that there was much smoke in the area and he himself had had great difficulty in finding a suitable spot on which to beach. LST 366 was only feet off the beach when frantic Aldis lamp signals from a Beachmaster warned them that the beach was heavily mined at that point.

Lieutenant-Commander Bell, RNR, in LST 324, also found it impossible to see the beach or beach marks at times when running in. He beached nearby and was ordered to make smoke as shells were pitching close to his starboard side. 365's starboard door collided with 430's port side. However, he found that smoke was sucked into the tank space by the fans. This he said delayed unloading and hindered other LSTs during beaching.

Three LSTs under attack

Matters became most unpleasant for the three LSTs. They were beached at the end of a road leading to an airfield, and all vehicles disembarking from them had to pass up this road. By 1100 the enemy battery had found the range and Commander Sutton reported that shells were falling 50 feet from 319's ramp. Numerous vehicles were hit and set on fire causing many casualties and delaying the unloading. The deep and rough sand was also causing problems. Tractors from 25-pounder batteries had to go up the beach then haul the guns off the ship's ramp by wire, even though some wire netting roadway had been laid. To add to Sutton's problems, the bow waves from other LSTs beaching lifted 319's bow and moved it on two occasions and the roadway had to be relaid.

LST 363 unbeached just after 1130, her unloading being noted as having taken 1 hour and 22 minutes. The movement of the water caused the stern of 365 to shift round and hit 319. As 363 turned away from the beach, one gun shelled her continuously and scored two hits on the starboard side – one above and one below the waterline. Four crew members were wounded by shrapnel and AB Sheppard was later transferred to the hospital ship *St. David*.

Soon afterwards, Sutton observed a dive-bombing attack on some US LSTs to his port side. One of the aircraft flew parallel to the shore and across the stern of 319 and 365.

At the same moment, LST 430 was coming in on 365's starboard side. 365's starboard door collided with 430's port after davit causing much damage. By this time, 430 had come to rest on a 'false' beach and was nearly beam on to the main beach. (False beaches were shelves of sand in the shallows.) A shell entered the ship's side, starboard aft, immediately above the main exhaust. This was followed almost at once by another which scored a direct hit on the bridge, seriously wounding Lieutenant-Commander Laws, RD, RNR, in the back, legs and arms.

Lieutenant Davey, RNVR, the First Lieutenant, assumed command of LST 430 and unbeached her. As he turned her for the run to the beach, a third hit was scored. This went through the port side and into the tank space causing further damage and casualties. He eventually beached her some 100 yards to the south of the beach limits, where the sand wasn't firm enough for wheeled vehicles. However, four tanks were discharged.

As he started to pull off the beach, another shell struck her – this time entering the tank space from the starboard

side. A truck containing ammunition was set alight. Warrant Engineer Miller, RNR, was principally involved in getting the fire under control in a very short time. Although he was aware of the contents of the truck, Miller initially tackled the fire alone, the truck crew and other military personnel having run for the beach.

LST 430 was still not out of trouble. A fifth shell struck, holing an oil fuel tank 6 inches above the waterline. A few minutes later, another shell passed through the upper-works of two trucks on the upper deck, but failed to explode until it hit the sea.

Lieutenant Davey reported that seven serious casualties had been sustained on board, six being military personnel.

LST 430 finally beached alongside 319, hitting her with her starboard quarter on the approach causing a split and bending two frames.

Also having trouble with false beaches was Lieutenant Commander Fotheringham, RNR, in LST 304. On 30 August he had loaded vehicles of 65th Field Regiment of the Royal Artillery together with 171st Anti-Tank Battery at Tripoli. Personnel were embarked on 2 September. On 4 September he sailed for Sousse, towing a 75-foot section of damaged pontoon in company with LSTs 302, 324, 361, 362 and 402. From Sousse he sailed in convoy.

Fotheringham made a run for 'Sugar Amber' Beach at 1230 but brought-to on a false beach. A shell smashed through the ship's siren. He managed to get off and attempted a landing further south. On this second run in two more shells struck LST 304. Only superficial damage was done, but three men had been injured. Although the landing was eventually a good one, the sand was too soft for wheeled vehicles and he was ordered to unbeach and make another attempt closer to LST 365. At 300 revolutions she again brought-to on a false beach. Fotheringham ordered the forward ballast compartments to be filled in order to lift the stern, but the ballast pumps soon became choked with sand. The port engine over-

◄ LST 419 lowers her ramp on the beach at Salerno. She has a confusing three digit army serial number below her LST number. Two more LSTs are further along the beach. One of these appears to have been damaged and set on fire. (G. Melford collection)

▶ HMS *Boxer* has her brow up to a pontoon causeway. (A. B. Stakemire collection)

heated, so assistance was called for. LCT 164 attempted to help, but it was the tug *Hengist* which finally refloated LST 304 at about 1830.

Another attempt was made to beach on 'Sugar Green'. The run in was made with the starboard engine on 300 revolutions, but with the port engine at slow ahead. The port engine started to function normally during the run in and a good landing was made. The ramp was lowered at 1930 and discharge had been completed by 2140 at which time LST 304 took aboard two officers and 30 other ranks of German PoWs.

During the day, approximately 60 casualties had been brought aboard LST 319. As she was a Flotilla Leader, she carried a doctor – Surgeon Lieutenant Thomas, RNVR.

Jim Brend was a leading supply assistant in LST 319 on that day. 'The ship's company went ashore picking up all the wounded they could find. The ship was filled up – stretchers all over the tank space and the wardroom was used as an operating theatre.' The doctor had to perform a number of amputations on board while Sick Berth Attendant McCulloch attended to the less serious cases. The wounded commanding officer of LST 430 was embarked, and Sutton commenced to unbeach LST 319 at 1410. Some difficulty was experienced as he was wedged between 430 and 365, but once clear he turned and left the beach at full speed. Fortunately for the wounded, the hospital ship *St. David* was nearby and 319 was able to go alongside. As the sea was calm and the decks of the ships were at a similar level, the transfer of wounded was comparatively easy. Sutton then formed up with sixteen other LSTs and made for Tripoli as Commodore of the convoy. Of those sixteen, LSTs 322, 367, 419, 420, 427 and 428 were detached for Milazzo and LST 408 was detached for Ferryville with a broken propeller.

In Tripoli the next day, the damage caused to LST 363 was inspected. It was discovered that Lieutenant-

Commander McReynolds had completed the operation and sailed back to Tripoli, blissfully unaware that the first shell that hit his ship the previous day had lodged, unexploded, in a fuel tank.

Confusion in the Gulf of Salerno

When Lieutenant-Commander Dalrymple-Hay arrived with his convoy in the early hours of 9 September, it was apparent to him that the situation was in a state of much confusion. US LST 16 had been sent in to the beaches at Paestum and was reported as being under heavy fire. Beaching orders were cancelled and Dalrymple-Hay was ordered to close Admiral Hewitt's flagship, USS *Ancon*. He went aboard and was taken to the conference room with Lieutenant Commander Pattie, USN, Senior Officer of US LST 358. Pattie was described by Dalrymple-Hay as 'being most helpful and co-operative throughout [their] associations, creating an impression of quiet and thorough resourcefulness, and energetic efficiency'.

An argument was in progress between senior US naval and military officers, indicating that things were not going too well. Both Pattie and Dalrymple-Hay volunteered to take their LSTs in to unload vehicles and personnel, but suggested that bulk stores be left on board. The army were insistent that each ship be fully unloaded and much argument ensued. It was arranged that US LST 358 and her group would go in to beach at first light on 10 September, followed by some of the British LSTs. However, the beaching signal did not arrive until 0800. In the meantime, according to Dalrymple-Hay, contradictory signals were arriving by the minute and there was little or no co-ordination.

The British LSTs then received instructions that they were to take part priority over the US LSTs. More contradictory signals were received and it subsequently transpired that LST 415's group should not have been unloaded. Lieutenant-Commander Clitherow reported that '... staff work broke down completely. Hundreds of contradictory orders were given by various officials; all without reference to each other. One order was actually given at one stage to reload an LST as they were not ready for her to unload. She was 90% empty at the time.'

There were some heavy air raids during the morning and either LST 160 or 161 was damaged by aircraft gunfire, the First Lieutenant and three crew members being wounded.

Unloading of the British LSTs continued during 11 September and finally DUKWs were sent out to complete offloading of bulk stores. Lieutenant-Commander Clitherow in LST 415 was ordered to pull off a pontoon which had been blown ashore during the night.

LST 425 claims to have shot down an Me109 during one of the many daytime attacks. An aircraft landing strip had been established inshore of 'Red' Beach and Spitfires and Lightnings of the Allied air forces began to arrive. As they circled to land, all the beach defences opened fire. LST 415 was the nearest ship, so Lieutenant-Commander Clitherow immediately broadcast a message to cease fire. When the aircraft came round again at about 500 feet, the leader was shot down. The pilot survived and walked up the ramp of LST 420 – unharmed but rather irate.

At 1520 on 12 September Dalrymple-Hay received sailing orders and formed up in a convoy of seven US LSTs and twelve British. The destination was unknown, but was subsequently discovered to be Termini. At 1030 the next day, the following were detached for Palermo: LSTs 12, 160, 161, 199, 404, 405, 409, 413, 415, 416, 422 and 425. On arrival, LSTs 12, 160 and 415 were ordered back to Termini.

Dalrymple-Hay was scornful of the fact that the flotilla could not work together again – a situation which was to recur many times over the next year or so, and scorned by more flotilla leaders. He went on to report: 'Lack of appreciation of LST or interest in them regarding such essentials as water, stores, spares, machinery maintenance and loading, together with complete lack of co-operation between Military and Ferry Control Naval authorities regarding time makes an LST commanding officer's life anything but a bed of roses.'

Lessons learned

On 18 December 1943 Captain LST sent his report on lessons learned in the four operations of that summer and subsequent ferry service to C in C Mediterranean. He was emphatic that it was the responsibility of commanding officers to see that loading authorities were prevented from overloading their ships. Among other matters, it was recommended that bow doors should remain shut when

▲ A view from the forecastle of HMS *Boxer* as mobile artillery crosses the pontoon causeway. (A. B. Stakemire collection)

beaching in close proximity to ships already beached and that they should be shut before backing off.

Beaching may have seemed to be somewhat haphazard, and indeed much of it must have been dependant upon the skill and knowledge of the ship's commanding officer. However, in true naval style, it seems that a procedure called 'the positioning ship' method of beaching had been discussed in August 1943. It was proposed that one ship approach the beach, release the causeway it had had in tow and moor to it. The vessel would then unload and remain holding the pontoon steady while other LSTs came in to unload in succession. However, it was found that if, as at Salerno, the beach was under fire, a positioning ship would soon be wrecked if it had to remain in the same position for hour upon hour.

Commander Alison proposed that the initial ship attach the pontoon to its ramp after beaching with an extra foot to her draught than operational trim, and then unload.

▶ Trucks position themselves to reverse into HMS *Thruster*'s lift, situated immediately below her bridge. *Thruster*'s commanding officer, Lieutenant-Commander A. W. McMullan, RNR, noted that he made five follow-up trips to Salerno. During these trips, *Thruster* unloaded 388 vehicles at an average of 1.14 minutes per vehicle. (H. Reid collection)

Twenty minutes before completion, she would call the next ship to come in alongside, which would flood down, and then take the pontoon under its own ramp. The 'positioning ship', now being empty, could back off. The process would be repeated until all ships were unloaded.

Another method discussed was for LSTs to beach initially only long enough to unload the tank deck – about five to ten minutes. The ship would then back off and another take her place. Thus by the time the fourth ship of a series had unbeached, the first should have been able to transfer all her upper deck vehicles via the elevator down to the tank deck and be ready to beach again.

An entry in the C in C Mediterranean's War Diary on 22 September 1943 read: 'Captain LST was warned that no reduction in LST effort could be expected until Tripoli is cleared of stores. The movement of personnel and vehicles from North Africa to Italy will then centralize on Bizerta where British LST . . . together with US LST . . . will form a regular ferry service operating for a period of approximately two months'.

Burges Watson pays tribute to the LSTs

As part of his report on lessons learned, Burges Watson made the following statement: 'I should like to pay tribute to the excellent work put in by all Commanding Officers of LST. For the most part they are from the RNR, many with little actual RN experience or training. They are used to handling their ships in the Merchant Navy manner of extreme caution and slow speed. They have had to forget all their "safety first" methods, and have been urged by me to move at what is to them high speed, in bomb blasted harbours full of wrecks and with very little sea room. Finally, to push their ships ashore in an apparently reckless manner. They have risen to the occasion magnificently. Likewise, the Engineer Officers have been forced against

their judgement, founded on Merchant Navy high standards of safety, to keep their machinery going long past the total hours of running which should bring a periodic overhaul. Officers and men have worked very long hours without complaint. It is most urgently represented that this high pressure must be relaxed soon in the interest of morale, and wear and tear on material.'

C in C Mediterranean, Admiral Cunningham, in his covering letter to The Admiralty said, 'There is no doubt that the performance of the LSTs was of the highest order and in the best traditions of the service, contributing very largely to the success of both operations.'

Salerno postscript

Les Roberts (LST 366): 'There was little amusement in the tiny harbours often used by the LSTs. Mail was nobody's business and was often weeks, even months, in arrears. Mail was something never to be denied fighting men, anxious for news of those back home. LSTs were not "on the books" of regular bases in the Med, and, therefore, few shore staff bothered about them. It was only the ingenuity of all ranks aboard that saw them through.

'Crews laboured with little respite while ferrying reinforcements and supplies to one beach-head after another. Each trip meant securing tanks and vehicles for the sea passage, initiating army personnel into the "do's and don'ts" of life aboard ship and keeping normal watches once clear of the harbour.

'On one of our trips, we carried Goumier tribesmen with their wives, goats, mules and chickens. No sooner were the Goumiers aboard than they started lighting camp fires! It took hours to establish some semblance of order.

'But there was one thing no-one could sort out. The tribesmen did not look for a loo when they needed to answer calls of nature. By the time we got to Naples, the stench, if the wind had been in the right direction, could have been used against the Jerries! We hosed the whole ship down when they left with every drop of carbolic we had. We even took a chance and kept the bow doors open for the first hour on sailing away from the beach. It was a long time before we could breathe comfortably.

'It was a rare trip when we were not called to "action stations" and that could mean goodbye to a meal – unless the cooks could be spared to make some corned beef sandwiches. We had to "live with" the corned beef sandwich. However, 366 did have a wonderful change of diet for a while when we acquired a consignment of tinned salmon. After weeks of the stuff, though, we all felt we were sprouting gills. It got so bad that one evening sitting in the wardroom in harbour, Smithie suddenly piped up, "Anyone fancy a corned beef sandwich?" . . . and we all did!

'At some stage, we brought out some US Rangers – every man was nearly asleep on his feet after having held some strategic point for days against overwhelming odds. Compared with these blokes, the film-famous "Dirty Dozen" look like bank clerks. The unit included a tall, lean, Texan Padre. He had crew cut hair and toted a gun low on each hip. He saw me look up at the dog-collar and then down at the armoury. He grinned and said, "I figured this out a long time ago, son. Just when I might be yelling for the Big Guy to get my butt out of some mess, there would probably be 50,000 other guys on at him already." He patted the guns – "Just in case he's busy!"'

The 9th LST Flotilla in the Med.

At 0500 on 11 September Commander Garth Owles sailed eastward from Algiers with seven LSTs of the 9th Flotilla and ten US LSTs of the 25th US LST Group. LST 80 had been sent to Algiers to unload ammunition and joined the convoy at about noon the next day. By 1430 on that day, Owles received orders to take his ships and the US 25th Group back to Algiers, where arrival was made at 1900. He was ordered to unload LCTs and all cargoes, and to proceed with all despatch to Bizerta for further orders.

LST 238 had damaged bow doors, so it was decided not to unload her. LST 180 had a large quantity of cargo which was, apparently, difficult to unload, so she also was not worked upon.

The remaining six ships unloaded as much as possible before 1830 on 15 September and sailed in company at 1900. They were LSTs 79, 80, 214, 215, 237 and 239.

Arrival in Bizerta was made on the morning of 17 September and ships proceeded to the embarkation berths at Karouba. One LST was required urgently to proceed with a group leaving the harbour at dusk that

evening, and Owles detailed LST 214. She sailed to Taranto and did not again rejoin the flotilla.

On 19 September LST 79 was ordered not to load but to sail for Algiers to have her LCT launchways removed. This vessel also would not rejoin the flotilla – her story follows later in this chapter.

A mixed force of British Army, US Army and RAF units were loaded on the remainder of Owles' ships and he sailed for Catania in company with five US LSTs and two escorts. From Catania he sailed to Taranto and back to Bizerta, from where LST 238 sailed for Port Said on 27 September followed by LST 180 about a week later, believed to be carrying spare bow doors for LST 238.

Owles and his depleted flotilla made a further trip to Taranto, where he was ordered to embark 78th Armoured Division of Eighth Army for transport to Manfredonia. In view of the urgency of the operation and the fine weather, he agreed to load 30 Sherman tanks in each LST together with a full upper deck load of Bren gun carriers and wheeled vehicles, even though this would take the ships over their normal weight limits and the tracked vehicles would cause damage to the upper deck. Cargo fuel and rails were still on board.

The ships were berthed against a quay wall which had been slightly knocked away towards sea level to enable LSTs to berth. However, when the ships berthed it was found that the ramp was inclined at a sharp angle, the ramp end being about 2 feet above the berth. This was overcome to a certain extent by 'packing', but the weight of the first tank on the outer edge of the ramp pushed the ship away from the quay, straining the berthing lines. One snapped under the pressure and it was realized that there was great danger of either seriously damaging the ship or losing a tank in the harbour. The problem was overcome by placing a tank on the road above the quay, some 40 feet away, and making the ship fast to it. All remaining ships loaded by this method, the only casualty being the town's tram service in that quarter which had to be suspended for the day.

Escort for the four British LSTs and US LST 372 was provided by HMSS *Aire* and *Pollock*. Between them, the LSTs were carrying about 60 officers, 780 men, 150 Sherman tanks and 140 other vehicles. Two destroyers from the Adriatic Patrol joined for a while. En route the ships entered Bari in darkness and sailed again at 0500 on 4 October. Manfredonia was reached by 1100. The western part of the harbour was full of wrecks so the East Mole was chosen for landing. British LSTs were drawing 14 feet 6 inches aft and 8 feet 6 inches forward but successfully berthed on the Mole, even though at least one vessel appeared to ground slightly while turning. Owles wrote: 'No naval staff were available at the port and the handling of berthing lines was carried out by Italian youths and children, several hundreds of whom appeared to watch the proceedings.'

The quay wall was high and made of stone, so the lessons learned at Taranto were put into operation. One tank was disembarked at the expense of some anxiety and a broken 2½ inch wire, but the remainder landed without difficulty. During the afternoon, LST 411 and US LST 73 arrived with the remainder of the Armoured Division.

All vessels sailed the next day, 5 October, for Taranto. LST 411 and US LST 73 were detached to Bari at the request of NOIC, leaving the remainder to arrive in Taranto by the early afternoon of 6 October.

Owles sailed at 0900 on 7 October with the following vessels under his orders: LSTs 80, 215, 237, 239, 363; US LSTs 356, 372, 378; US SC 693 (as escort). An exceptional squall occurred just as the ships were leaving Taranto and LST 363 was blown into the nets of the outer boom. A propeller became fouled and she had to be left behind. In the late afternoon of 7 October LST 319 (Commander Sutton) was sighted with three Italian submarines nearby. Sutton made a signal to Owles expressing the hope that they were on their way to give themselves up.

The US LSTs and escort detached to Bizerta during the night of 9/10 October and Owles' group arrived at Algiers at 1300 on 11 October. The ships berthed immediately and loading of LCTs, launches and miscellaneous cargo and stores for Ceylon started without delay. He was told that only LSTs 80, 215 and 239 would proceed to India to join LSTs 180 and 238 who were already there. (HMSS *Boxer*, *Bruiser* and *Thruster* also went to India.)

On 14 October Owles left Algiers to join an eastbound convoy with the following under his orders: LSTs 80, 215, 237, 239; US LSTs 17, 21, 25, 72, 175, 176, 208, 209, 261; five merchant vessels. En route LST 237 was detached for Bizerta on 16 October, the remainder arriving at Port Said on 23 October ready for their passage through the Suez Canal at daybreak the next day.

Commander Owles was able to report that ships in his company experienced no enemy activity whatsoever while in the Mediterranean and Adriatic. All ships had run well, and up to arrival at Port Said approximately 12,300 nautical miles had been covered. They had been under way or on passage for all or part of 84 days of the 98 days since commissioning.

LST 79 hit by glider bomb

LST 79 sailed from Algiers on 28 September 1943 under orders from the commanding officer of the French escort ship, *Fortune*. The destination was Ajaccio on the western side of the island of Corsica. On board were personnel and vehicles of British, US and French services as well as

▲ LST 79 lost at Ajaccio on 30 September 1943, having been in commission for just 75 days. (R. Robertson Taylor)

the steel rails and diesel oil which LST 79 was supposed to be transporting to India.

In his report to Captain LST, Lieutenant-Commander Robertson Taylor, RNR, noted that LST 79's passage to Ajaccio was uneventful, but in unsettled weather with fresh shifting wind and heavy rain in squalls. About two hours out from Ajaccio, what was thought to be an enemy reconnaissance aircraft was noticed high above.

Upon arrival at Ajaccio, a pilot went aboard LST 79. Wind conditions were difficult for berthing and about 1¼ hours were needed to secure the ship's bows to the Quai Capucines and commence unloading. The French vehicles were urgently needed and were disembarked first.

Just before 1500, a Junkers Ju 88 passed over the harbour. Nearly two hours later, another Ju 88 came over and was attacked by Spitfires. This was followed almost immediately by a formation of nine Dornier Do 217s. They were coming from the south at a height of about 4,000 feet and were first spotted about four or five miles away. Spitfires engaged these, also.

Robertson Taylor ordered 'action stations'. Several glider bombs were dropped, one hitting the mole about 500 feet to port of LST 79. A few moments later, a second bomb slammed into the port side of 79 and entered one of the fuel oil tanks. The ship burst into flames immediately. The tank space was flooded with water, fuel oil burnt fiercely and the ship listed about 5° to port. Sections of the main deck and elevator plating had been blown out, the twisted remains landing up to 100 yards away on the quay. The main deck had been blown upwards and folded back over the forecastle and fore part of the bridge deck. Flames and dense smoke rose more than 200 feet.

The ship was alight from the bows to abaft the bridge. The pumps and electricity supply had been knocked out so nothing could be done to fight the fire. Robertson Taylor knew the main engine room was still intact, so he took the ship away from the quay until the stern anchor pulled her up.

The order to abandon ship was finally given at approximately 1815. Nothing more could be done. The ship continued to burn fiercely until structural damage internally overcame her efforts to survive. As if exhausted, she sank at 2300, only the mast and flag deck being visible above the water.

The enemy action had claimed one man killed; three men missing, presumed killed; and eleven men, including the ship's First Lieutenant, wounded.

The French authorities awarded Robertson Taylor the Croix de Guerre Française avec palme de bronze. The citation read: 'On September 30th, 1943, during a violent air raid on the port of Ajaccio, with magnificent presence of mind, manoeuvred his ship, which had been hit by a bomb and was burning fiercely, in order to remove it from the vicinity of the harbour until the fire and the imminent risk of explosion compelled him to order "abandon ship". His coolness in danger aroused the most intense admiration among his comrades, both Allied and French.'

Lieutenant-Commander Robertson Taylor subsequently went on to command LST 8 through the Anzio build-up and invasion of Normandy. When the ship went to the Mersey for tropicalization he was appointed deputy to Commander Parker, RNR, who was setting up the LST base at Tilbury. Robertson Taylor eventually succeeded Parker, and became Officer-in-Charge of the Tilbury base until demobilization.

LST 418 torpedo-bombed

John Holden was aboard LST 418 on the evening of 21 October 1943 as she was making her way to Bizerta from Oran in convoy MKS28. Twenty-three miles off Cape Tenez, fifteen enemy aircraft came in low to attack the convoy.

John Holden (LST 418): 'As the planes approached, they split up and were difficult to follow as they wheeled their way around the convoy. Suddenly, there was a huge explosion from our starboard bow and a column of water shot 30 feet into the air. We had been hit by a torpedo. The ship stopped dead, as if it had run into a stone wall. The stern jumped up and crashed back down, throwing most of us off our feet. A couple of American Seabees were blown into the sea by the blast, but they clung to some oil drums until they were picked up by an escort vessel and safely returned to 418.'

The ship began to settle by the head with a list to starboard of 8°. Lieutenant-Commander Reynolds wrote in his report that several compartments had been flooded to a depth of 7 feet, so counterflooding was resorted to. This reduced the list and held up some of the inflow of

water. One pump had been damaged in the explosion. Other damage included the truck elevator motor which was blown from its bed and the magnetic compass blown from position. The barrel of one 20mm Oerlikon burst by a premature explosion. The ship's steering gear also became defective, but somehow Reynolds managed to maintain convoy position and arrived at Oran in the early afternoon of 22 October.

Ten crew members had been injured. Four were taken to hospital together with four American troops. Twenty-eight others suffered minor injuries. The ship was repaired in Oran and was back at sea, sailing loaded for Naples, by 26 November.

LST 12 damaged by mine

In the early hours of 13 November 1943 LST 12 was on her way empty to Ferryville, Bizerta, in company with LST 62. They were sailing at 6 knots through a rough, head sea. The wind was strong and it was raining heavily in frequent squalls.

They were passing about three miles off Zembra Island at 0355 when LST 12 struck a mine close to the starboard door, blowing a hole approximately 18 feet by 20 feet in her side. Tom Hill was a signalman aboard: 'I was about to leave the messdeck to take over the morning watch – I got to the bridge in record time!'

LST 12's commanding officer, Lieutenant-Commander A. R. Wheeler, RNR, reduced speed and headed towards Zembra Island. LST 62 followed and stood by. Although badly holed, it was decided that the ship could make Tunis or Bizerta, so they made their way back into the war channel at 0500.

The weather was not in LST 12's favour, so she anchored in the lee of Cape Farina. Conditions improved and she was able to proceed to Bizerta Bay where she arrived during the mid-afternoon of 14 November. Fortunately, no casualties had been sustained. LST 12 was temporarily repaired at Ferryville and sailed via Augusta for Taranto where she was docked in the Tosi Yard in January 1944. She was there until June.

US LSTs leave the Mediterranean for the UK

The authorities wanted the LSTs back in the UK for a planned maintenance and training period prior to the forthcoming invasion of Normandy. Great debate ensued as to when and how many should return to England, as the invasion of Anzio was on the horizon.

The first batch of US LSTs left Gibraltar on 13 November 1943 in convoy MKS30, followed by the second wave on 21 November in MKS31. Two more batches were planned for December, but these didn't leave until early January 1944.

▶ A topical cartoon from a crew member of LST 416.

LST 418 suffers weather damage

On the night of 31 December 1943 many LSTs in port would have been welcoming in the New Year. For LSTs 411 and 418, both in different parts of the Mediterranean, it would be a night to remember for other reasons.

LST 418 left Naples 'in ballast' at noon on 30 December, bound for Bizerta in company with LST 198 (SO 8th Flotilla). By 1400 the next day they were encountering heavy weather off the NW coast of Sicily – wind was westerly Force 6/7, sea and swell 54.

LST 418 started to pitch and pound heavily so most of the ballast compartments were ordered to be filled. Within a few hours, cracks began to appear all over the upper deck varying between 3 inches and 3 feet. However, one on the fore side of the main hatch extended across the deck for some 15 feet. Numerous other fractures of bulkheads began to appear throughout the ship.

John Holden (LST 418): 'It was quite the worst weather we had encountered in the Med – we were tossed around like a cork. The high seas smashed our lifeboat, wrecked the ranges in the galley and put our gyro compass out of action. It was lucky that we weren't carrying troops on this trip, because I don't think we could have coped with 200 seasick soldiers; and they would have been, for at times it seemed that the ship was standing on end. What a way to start 1944!'

The ship also had a damaged starboard propeller and the commanding officer had great difficulty keeping her hove to. The wind had shifted to NW Force 8 with a high confused sea and swell, but the ship eventually managed to make Palermo safely by noon on New Year's Day 1944, where defects were made good.

LST 411 hits mine off Corsica

Douglas Wilkinson, a leading supply assistant, served in LST 411 since her commissioning in Baltimore, USA, in January 1943. 'After the initial Salerno landing, we were ferrying troops and equipment between Milazzo and Salerno until the end of September 1943. From then on, we ran between Bizerta and Taranto, Bari, Barletta and Manfredonia on the Adriatic side of Italy. We had also been to Calvi, Ajaccio and Maddalena Island.'

LST 411 left La Maddalena, off the north-east tip of Sardinia, at 1500 on 30 December 1943, bound for Bastia with just over 100 US troops aboard. In company was SS *Empire Lass*. Escorts were HMSS *Clacton*, *Polruan* and *Hoy*. HMS *Clacton* was ahead of LST 411, *Empire Lass* astern. *Polruan* was to starboard and *Hoy* was off to port.

A speed of 6.2 knots was maintained as the ships sailed through a calm, clear night. A rendezvous had been arranged at a point six miles off Bastia for 0710 the following morning. The ships arrived approximately on time at what they thought was the rendezvous point. However, they were a few miles out. The reasons for this are unclear, but are thought to have been beyond their control. No ML escorts were to be seen. A few minutes later, the wind started to freshen from the north with rain and sleet. LST 411 made a signal to *Clacton* to the effect

▲ Leading Supply Assistant,   happier time aboard LST 411.
Doug Wilkinson, during a   (D. J. Wilkinson)

that she proposed waiting at that position until met. Within a few more minutes the wind speed had risen to Force 8, sea 6. The rain and sleet brought visibility down to practically zero.

LST 411 made a signal to the Senior Officer Inshore Squadron at 0815 advising him that they had arrived and were awaiting instructions. SOIS replied that MLs were on their way out.

Just after 0830, *Clacton* appeared to move to starboard and almost immediately struck a mine. A large column of smoke rose from her port side. LST 411 found that she needed revolutions for 7 knots before she would answer the helm in the rough sea, so her commanding officer, Lieutenant-Commander John Douglas, RNR, signalled SOIS: '*Clacton* hit, standing by to pick up survivors.'

Polruan was able to get to the stricken vessel first while 411 closed to the leeward of the wreck as soon as she could. Engines were stopped and she rolled 35° degrees each way in just four seconds. A couple of vehicles on deck

broke loose. Within five to ten minutes of the explosion, *Clacton* had listed to port and had broken in two.

By 0900 the wind was so strong that revolutions for full speed had to be used by LST 411 before she would steer. At 1000 she passed to the windward of *Clacton*, the wind blowing north Force 9.

Two minutes later, 411 struck a mine almost amidships on the port side. Lieutenant-Commander Douglas immediately ordered the abandon ship bells to be sounded, but they had been put out of action in the explosion. The Engineer Officer, Roger Buckley, RNR, reported that both the main and auxiliary engine rooms had flooded. The ship naturally stopped. The First Lieutenant and Quartermaster were ordered to go below and pipe up the US soldiers and ship's company to abandon ship stations.

Nearly an hour passed by before all men were on deck and the Carley floats sent overboard. The soldiers were put over the side into them and cast off so that they floated away from the ship. Water was by now breaking over the main deck aft where the wounded were being held. The sea was so great that nothing was able to get alongside – the commanding officer called for volunteers to man the motor whaler.

Warrant Engineer Buckley, Chief Petty Officer Wilmott and Petty Officer (Telegraphist) Braddock took up the challenge. On lowering, the sea caught the whaler and there was great difficulty in fully releasing it. After spending about an hour in the ferocious sea, the whaler was smashed against HMS *Polruan* but not before the excellent work of these three courageous men had saved the lives of nineteen hands.

By noon, the sea was washing all over the upper deck, so Douglas finally abandoned ship by simply stepping off the side at 1220. He was picked up by ML 121 and taken with others to Bastia where they were given beds and blankets at the American Sick Quarters.

Two crew members of LST 411 lost their lives that day. It is thought that Stoker 1st Class C. Pearce was killed in the auxiliary engine room at the time of the explosion. EM 4th Class R. J. Plenderleith was rolled under a PT boat which was attempting to rescue him and was killed by the boat's screws. Plenderleith was recovered and buried at sea three days later in the presence of his commanding officer and SOIS. LST 411 eventually broke in two and was found beached some eight miles south of Bastia.

The loss of the two ships was probably unnecessary. It was well-known that the area around Bastia was an extensive minefield and E-boats from Elba were continually laying mines off the entrance. Gales at that time of the year were another factor. The risks had been pointed out to the authorities just five days previously when it was found that a road was open between Ajaccio and Bastia.

8. Operation 'Shingle' – the Anzio Invasion

At the beginning of 1944 weather in the Mediterranean was extremely poor. The Greek LST 37 was driven ashore at 0350 on 6 January under Plane Island Lighthouse. She was on passage between Catania and Bizerta in company with sister Greek LSTs 33, 35 and 36.

Les Roberts of LST 366 remembers the weather: 'I often jammed myself between the gyro compass and the side of the bridge when she was rolling like a barrel. With the Kapok life-jacket over one's duffel coat, it was a bit of a squeeze, but it meant that you were wedged in very snugly once you were in position.

'On one occasion we were making about 3 knots over the ground into a head sea. Standing on an open bridge with winds gusting to 70 or 80 knots and hail and sleet hammering on your face does not make for happy watchkeeping. Lieutenant-Commander Grandage, RNR, was on the bridge with me; neither of us could see a thing, when I suddenly remembered a "dodge" from my coastal forces days. This was to put one's face into the wide end of a megaphone and peer out of the 2″ or so diameter end. Although the field of vision was restricted, it was better than none at all. And it was better to hear the hail rattling on the megaphone than on your face. "Now that's a very good idea, Roberts," said Grandage. Imagine my pleasure in being able to say to a professional seaman of many years' standing. "It's an old RNVR trick, Sir."'

Background to the operation

Much debate had taken place between the Combined Chiefs of Staff, Winston Churchill and President Roosevelt concerning the proposed Operation 'Shingle'. A full account of these high-level talks can be found in Churchill's book, *The Second World War*, but suffice it to say here that the LSTs were, as ever, in desperately short supply.

A schedule for refitting and training had been worked out to enable the LSTs to be ready for Operation 'Neptune' (the naval aspect of the forthcoming invasion of Normandy – Operation 'Overlord'), but this clashed with the demands of 'Shingle'. In November 1943 US LSTs started heading for the UK in convoy MKS30. However, the haggling continued until it was agreed that the Mediterranean LSTs could be held for the operation.

Vessels of the British task force were commanded by Rear-Admiral Thomas Troubridge, RN, in HMS *Bulolo*, and were assigned to the 'Peter' Beaches just north of Anzio.

▼ LST 401 displays some LST humour. Painted above the bow doors are the words 'Is your journey really necessary?'. (W. Collison collection)

▲Ron Kelly and LST 162's
dog, Pepsi. (R. Kelly)

The American task force was commanded by Rear
Admiral Frank J. Lowry, USN, in USS *Biscayne*, and was
assigned to the 'X-Ray' Beaches to the south of Anzio.

A force of US Rangers under Colonel W. O. Darby was
to be put ashore on 'Yellow' Beach, inside Anzio harbour.
LST 410 was the only LST assigned to this group.

Although 'official' histories indicate numbers of LSTs in
each group, it is apparent from actual records that the
operational plans were amended right up to the last
minute.

Anzio was a small town, typical of many seaside bathing
resorts with sandy beaches, and hotels and well-to-do
villas huddled along the waterfront. The tiny harbour could
only accept vessels of less than 10 feet draught. The
beaches were susceptible to the effects of surf. Inland, the
terrain was flat and cultivated up to the Alban Hills, some
miles distant.

▶ Exact details are unknown,
but this photograph is
believed to have been taken
at Naples while LST 366 and a
sister ship were loading up.
The LST alongside is carrying
a radar unit – she could be
either LST 305 or 430. (US
Naval Institute)

Vessels converge on Naples and Salerno

From 14 January 1944 LSTs began to prepare for the
operation. *Boxer*, *Bruiser* and *Thruster* sailed from Port Said
in the late afternoon of 16 January. *Boxer* and *Bruiser* were
ordered to Castellamare; *Thruster* was ordered to Naples.
All three vessels arrived at their respective ports on 20
January. It was a race against time – they were due to sail
for Salerno at 1400 the same day.

However, they had to unload before they could reload
for 'Shingle'. Early in the morning of 20 January, *Bruiser*
disembarked one LCM, two LCS and one LCN with
crews, officers and men belonging to Party Major 30.
Subsequently, she unloaded 50 tons of cased stores,
timber, four workshop trucks and two trailer pumps
before embarking 63 vehicles, ten motor cycles, personnel
and LCS 46. *Boxer* loaded similarly, but because of
problems with her port bow door, did not complete until
0900 the next day.

Invasion convoys sail

At 0030 on Friday 21 January Commander Alison sailed
from Salerno in LST 361 as Senior Officer of 'Peter' Group
B, together with nine other LSTs, including 303, 304, 320,
363 and 402. It seems that each vessel had 22 DUKWs
aboard as well as vehicles, guns and personnel.

Boxer and *Bruiser* left Castellamare at 1005 and had
caught up with *Bulolo* (already in convoy) by 1115. *Thruster*
didn't leave Naples harbour until 1305, having embarked
twelve officers and 363 men of the US Army; seventeen
half-tracks; one trailer; twelve 2½-ton trucks; five jeeps;
three bulldozers; and one mobile crane. Just outside the
harbour, a tug delivered to her two 175-foot pontoons
lashed together. On these were a bulldozer, a jeep and a
2½-ton truck. She joined her convoy by 1800.

'Peter' Group C, under Commander Dalrymple-Hay in LST 425, sailed from Castellamare at 1100 in company with seventeen British LSTs. He was followed at 1250 by LST 319 as Senior Officer of convoy NAM2 made up of 32 British LSTs.

Arrival at Anzio

By the very early hours of 22 January, Commander Alison had arrived in LST 361 with Group B and anchored off Anzio. *Boxer* and *Bruiser* also arrived; LCS(M) 63 and LCS 46 were swum off the ships respectively.

At 0320, Group B commenced swimming off DUKWs. Once these had all gone, they were able to bring their upper deck vehicles down to the tank deck via the elevator. As it was dark, Lieutenant-Commander J. F. G. Fotheringham, RNR, in LST 304, gave permission to switch on the traffic control lights to amber. This together with two red lights at the far end of the tank deck provided enough light to assist the work without shining upwards. Just before 0400 the tug *Weasel* placed a pontoon causeway alongside Commander Alison's LST 361 and the Party Chain got to work. Over the next four hours, Dalrymple-Hay arrived in LST 425 with 'Peter' Group C, as did Commander Sutton in LST 319 with his follow-up group.

By 0700, the Party Chain had set up the pontoon on LST 361 and she was ready for 'Peter Amber' Beach. She went in at 0745 at 9½ knots, slipped the causeway, but beached with a gap of about 100 feet between her ramp and the causeway. Some manoeuvring followed to get the causeway positioned under the ramp by 0830. At 0900, LST 361 signalled *Boxer* to come in on her starboard side. *Boxer* moved in but received another signal to come in on the port side instead. She was only just able to switch course, but came up firmly on a false beach about 275 yards from the shore. LCT 136 assisted the unloading from *Boxer*.

Meanwhile *Thruster* had arrived and promptly transferred her pontoon to US LST 359 before coming under a bombing attack. She opened fire as several bombs fell harmlessly on her port quarter. Shore batteries began to shell the anchorages just as the first vehicle was coming off LST 361 at about 0930. Several ships nearest the beaches were straddled.

By 1010 LST 303 had beached 60 feet to starboard of LST 361 with her ramp 200 feet short of the shoreline. LST 304 took a pontoon from a tug but had to detail members of her crew to prepare the pontoon for beaching as it had been lashed for ocean passage and no Party Chain had been provided.

During the morning, the shelling from shore batteries continued and *Thruster* noted about six Focke-Wulfe

Fw 190s dropping bombs near her beach. At about this time, LST 362 was hit by a shell in her tiller flat which damaged her steering.

Commander Sutton of LST 319 was getting somewhat impatient that his vessels were being kept waiting. He went to the beaches in an LCP to observe the false beach problem for himself and then went across to *Biscayne*, where he obtained permission to send in some of his group to Anzio harbour. The SNOL wanted *Thruster* and LST 410 into the harbour as soon as possible, but had been unable to contact them. Sutton went back to LST 319, contacted the two vessels and sailed nearer to the harbour.

Beaches under shellfire

During the afternoon, beaching continued under continuous shelling. A flight of Focke-Wulfe Fw 190 came out of the sun and dropped bombs which straddled *Thruster*, but did no damage. LST 304 was straddled by a salvo of three 88mm shells as she went into the beach.

LST 320, anchored in Berth No. 7, was not so fortunate however. At 1240 she was attacked by gunfire. The first shell missed; the second was a near-miss; the third exploded under her starboard bow door; and the fourth was a direct hit on the main deck. It passed through a troop space bulkhead and burst inside the paint locker, blowing a hole in the ship's side and causing a serious fire. Lieutenant-Commander Buckley, RNR, sounded 'fire stations', weighed anchor and proceeded towards the beach in case the fire got out of control. By prompt action of the fire party, LST 320 was able to turn full speed back to the anchorage by 1310, but was still under shellfire.

LSTs 303 and 304 had difficulty unloading as the exits from their beach were difficult for vehicles to negotiate. The sand was soft and all heavily laden vehicles had to be hauled over a steep slope by tractor.

During the afternoon, LST 301 was ordered to transfer her consignment – 368 men of the US 36th Combat Engineers – to *Thruster* which would take them to Anzio harbour. *Thruster* began her approach at about 1520 but a launch came alongside soon afterwards ordering her to wait for a signal before entering the harbour.

At 1545, SNOL of 'Peter' Beach ordered LST 425 with LSTs 413, 409, 407, 422, 405, 404, 368, 65 and Greek 33 to proceed to 'X-Ray' Beaches as 'Peter' was proving difficult to unload across.

LSTs 303 and 401 reported being near-missed by fighter-bombers and *Boxer* was near-missed by shellfire.

LST 363 hit and damaged

LST 363 had been ordered to 'Peter' Beach at about 1500. Because of overcrowding she had to wait until about 1620 before she could make for the pontoon alongside LST 304. The beach came under attack by fighter-bombers and 363 was straddled by two bombs very close. The bridge was momentarily enveloped in smoke and spray. Lieutenant-Commander McReynolds reported that the ship appeared to lift bodily aft. The aircraft also swept the decks with gunfire and Signalman William Smart was killed at his action station on one of the starboard Oerlikons. Leading Signalman Jack French took some shrapnel in his chest. Eight soldiers were seriously wounded. Notwithstanding this attack, LST 363 took the pontoon from LST 304 and commenced unloading by 1645.

LST 410 first LST into Anzio Harbour

LST 410, under the command of Lieutenant-Commander James Kirby Jones, RNR, entered Anzio Harbour at about 1630 in company with boom vessel HMS *Barndale*. They were under continuous shellfire but 410 managed to unload safely. She had brought in 45 vehicles and stores belonging to the US Rangers' 83rd Chemical Battalion and unloaded in just seven minutes. From passing the harbour entrance inwards to passing outwards was 38 minutes.

As 410 came out just after 1700, she signalled *Thruster* that the harbour was now ready for her. *Thruster* was in position within half an hour. LST 319 followed her in but was sent out under shellfire as there was not enough room for her to unload at that time. One shell scored a direct hit on a building near *Thruster* and showered her with rubble. At 1730, Petty Officer Blackadder, previously wounded in *Bruiser*, died.

By 1915, it was dark. *Thruster* had finished unloading and started to leave the harbour in a cross wind and very restricted visibility. Her CO noted that the Mediterranean Pilot stated that 'The Port of Anzio should not be entered without local knowledge'. He found it somewhat ironic that *Thruster* had gone in under shellfire and come out stern first in darkness.

Sunday 23 January

On D+1, vessels continued making their way to the pontoons or into Anzio harbour. Commander Sutton's efforts to beach in LST 319 were again thwarted. At 0640, under constant shellfire, he entered Anzio Harbour. The steering gear failed and the helm went hard-a-starboard, so he ordered full-speed astern and backed out. The steering gear was rectified and he tried again. Once more the steering failed and SNOL ordered him out. By 0800 Sutton had secured to a pontoon on 'X-Ray' Beach and unloaded in just over two hours.

Petty Officer Blackadder of *Bruiser* and Signalman William Smart of LST 363 were both buried at sea off Anzio during the morning.

'Anzio Annie'

LSTs were by now sailing back and forth between Anzio and the Naples area, a ferrying service which would continue for 50 days, almost always under shellfire or bombing attack. One of the major problems was 'Anzio Annie' – a 280mm mobile gun, mounted on railway wheels, which was concealed up in the hills beyond the

◀ LSTs under attack in the Anzio anchorage. (G. Melford collection)

► A view of the tiny harbour of Anzio from LST 427. (G. Melford collection)

town. As far as can be ascertained, 'Annie' never actually hit any British LST, but the 'woosh' of her shells was enough to strike fear into LST crews every time they came back to Anzio.

Some memories of Anzio

Les Roberts of LST 366: 'We were ordered into Anzio harbour in darkness. Nosing into this unfamiliar harbour, we thumped something projecting from a pier and listed heavily to starboard. Everyone was thrown by the suddenness of it. The CO was immediately on the 'phone to the forecastle to find out what we had hit. The reply was that the First Lieutenant couldn't speak. The skipper ordered me to leave the stern winch and go for'ard to investigate. This never happened to John Wayne or Robert Mitchum storming the beaches of Iwo Jima – but the No. I had been thrown so heavily that his dentures had taken flight!

'The stern winch of LST 366 vibrated like mad in top gear. On one occasion, I was in charge aft where we were hauling in the stern anchor coming out of Anzio harbour. The winch vibrated so much that an electrical contact disengaged and it "died" on me. The ship lost sternway and thus had not reached the point where a shell wooshed past the stern and exploded on the quayside. It might have missed the stern winch, of course, but, on the other hand, it wasn't all that far off.

'One night off Anzio we were attacked by glider bomb. The pilot was very good but the ship rolled towards the bomb at the last moment. It seemed to scrape down the side of the ship but exploded on the sea bed in the shallow water. So much water blew into the air we thought we were actually sinking. The explosion left 366 with a slight but permanent hump across the foredeck.

'If there were a lot of Army officers on board, we would hand the wardroom over to them lock, stock and barrel. However, with about seven or eight, we would all muck in. At any mention of "the Officer of the Watch", we would break off what we were doing (even eating), stand for about five seconds, then proceed as before. It would always mystify the Army types until it was explained that it was a mark of respect to the OOW who, at that moment, had all our lives in his hands. It provided great light relief to watch them observe the ritual with us!'

LST 422 hits mine

On Tuesday 25 January, LST 422 loaded at Naples with 63 vehicles and 517 US Army personnel. The vehicles were heavily loaded with phosporous shells, rockets, smoke canisters and ammunition of all kinds together with several cans of petrol on each vehicle. She sailed in convoy for Anzio under the command of Lieutenant-Commander C. L. Broadhurst, RNR, and anchored off Anzio at 0015 on Wednesday 26 January.

It was noted that the weather was deteriorating all the time the ships were in convoy. The wind veered from southerly to westerly Force 8. If ships were allowed to fall just one point from the wind, they would not steer. LSTs 11 and 165 were in collision, and several other collisions were narrowly averted.

At 0520, Broadhurst was resting in a sort of bunk which had been built on the magnetic compass platform. There was a flash followed by a terrific shock of explosion, causing the magnetic compass to topple on to the commanding officer. He was able to slide from under it and make his way to the bridge.

From the bridge he could see 20-foot flames coming from all the tank deck ventilators. The vehicles in the tank deck started exploding and this set fire to the ship's fuel oil which had been sprayed out at the moment the ship hit the mine. The impact caused a massive 50-foot hole on the starboard side in the region of the bulkhead between the main and auxiliary engine rooms.

The after hatch collapsed allowing exploding ammunition and rockets to escape then fall on to the vehicles on the upper deck. Their loads of petrol had been fractured by shrapnel and within two minutes the entire upper deck was a sheet of flame. Soon the bridge was on fire and the ship's LCP was ablaze and dropped from its davits.

Broadhurst was unable to get in touch with the engine room – all power having been lost. It was found impossible to reach the mess decks and tiller flat where the smoke helmet and asbestos suit were kept. An attempt was made to start the auxiliary fire foam motor but this was soon damaged by shrapnel from explosions on the deck.

Army personnel were ordered to abandon ship. Only four Carley floats were left unharmed, so all available floatable material such as loose timber and oil drums was thrown overboard to assist them. LST 301 stood nearby to help.

It was not until about an hour later that the ship's company were ordered to abandon ship, leaving just eight men aboard with the CO. It became apparent that the ship was settling and on the advice of the CO of fire tug ATR 1, the ship was abandoned at 0740. LST 422 broke in two and sank at 1430.

Precisely how many US Army personnel died is not known, but they probably numbered some hundreds. At least 29 crew of LST 422 lost their lives. Ironically, one of the survivors picked up by LST 301 later fell between two LSTs and died.

LSTs attacked by aircraft

Just before noon on Wednesday 26 January, LST 421 came under attack from five or six dive-bombers in Anzio Harbour. One bomb fell very close and 20-year-old Able Seaman John Mawdsley, who was manning a starboard Oerlikon gun, was killed. The blast also killed the ship's dog. One officer and thirteen ratings were injured.

A fire started in the ship's LCP. The petrol tank had been holed and burning petrol was cascading on to the deck below. The fire was put out very quickly, but another fire had started on the messdeck which was full of smoke. All available crew tackled this fire.

NOIC Anzio didn't want the harbour blocked or other ships to be set on fire, so he ordered Lieutenant-Commander Machin, RNR, to leave. Machin requested permission to get the fire under control first, and NOIC agreed. By 1300 Machin was able to report to NOIC Anzio that all was well.

The congestion at Anzio meant that many LSTs were milling around the anchorages. Many attacks developed during the afternoon. At about 1900 LST 425 was bodily lifted out of the water by a bomb which fell within 10 feet of her port side, and much minor damage was caused. LST 403 was near-missed by five sticks of heavy bombs in Anzio Harbour. Four ammunition trucks on the hard ahead of her caught fire and started to explode sending stones and flaming material on to 403's upper deck. She had 137 German PoW on board.

At about the same time, LST 301 was at anchor in Anzio Bay. Her crew could hear an aircraft approaching but couldn't see it because of the smoke-screen. It suddenly emerged from the smoke about 400 yards away, crossed the bows and flew down the starboard side at a

◄ HMS *Thruster* has nosed her way into Anzio's tiny harbour to unload and then embark casualties. (H. Reid collection)

height of about 20 feet. The starboard Oerlikons opened up and many shells were seen to explode in the aircraft's fuselage. When abreast the bridge, the aircraft caught fire and crashed into the sea 50 yards away.

On the afternoon of Saturday 29 January, LST 214 was struck by a shell in Anzio, which killed two or three US soldiers. Minor damage was sustained. She had to sail from Anzio with her starboard bow door only ¾-closed because of projecting torn metal.

Pull your socks up, LST 366!

Les Roberts (LST 366): 'Sometime after the invasion of Anzio, LST 366 and others were anticipating an inspection by some brass hat. As it was winter time, we were in "blues" uniform, but clothing was in short supply. I was summoned to the CO's cabin for the night order book. I found him experimenting with patches of ink on his ankles, hoping that they might conceal the fact that his socks were full of holes. I was able to make a suggestion that if he wore two pairs, then where there were holes on the outer pair there might be solid sock showing on the inner pair. That was what I was doing, anyway!'

LST 418 sunk by torpedoes

On the afternoon of 16 February LST 418 left Anzio alone with 53 empty vehicles and approximately 75 Army personnel on board, bound for Naples. Lieutenant-Commander Reynolds, RNR, was on the bridge and the weather was fine with good visibility.

John Holden (LST 418): 'When we were clear of Anzio, the CO gave permission for those not on duty watch to go below. Having flopped on to my top bunk, too exhausted to undress, I fell asleep.'

Unbeknown to him and his commanding officer, LST 418 had been spotted at about 1430 by *U 230* (Kapitänleutnant Paul Siegmann). It took Siegmann just 40 minutes to position *U 230* in line with 418's stern. He ordered a torpedo to be fired. At 1512 it struck LST 418 right aft, the explosion blowing Ordinary Seaman Stirling into the water.

John Holden (LST 418): 'The violent explosion flung me against the deck head (ceiling), but in my sleepy condition I could not take in the fact that we had been hit. All the lights were out except for a tiny emergency one which was battery operated. Our lockers had fallen over and there was the sound of hissing steam escaping. I and some shipmates ran for an escape hatch in one of the bathrooms and scrambled out.'

Reynolds himself signalled two US LCIs which were following about six miles astern – 'SOS. SOS. Please hurry.'

The engines stopped, all power failed and the ship began to settle by the stern. The power boat was

damaged and hanging from its davit, while the whaler on the starboard side aft was also damaged and could not be lowered. The stern structure had been blown upwards and the upper deck was split right across just in front of the main hatch. The ship's sides had also split in the same position. LST 418 had been damaged on previous occasions and had been patch welded.

Warrant Engineer Robert Reid, RNR, was in his cabin on the starboard side when the torpedo struck. Rushing into the passageway, he found his way barred, the doorway into the messdeck having jammed. He went via the upper deck and down into the engine room, where he stopped the engines and shut off the steam at the domestic boiler. He wanted to get power on the board, but couldn't get near because there was four feet of water in the engine room. The water was coming in through the split which ran right down the ship's starboard side.

Returning to the upper deck, he proceeded to the escape hatch above the petty officer's messdeck. He saw four men trapped and immediately went down to their aid. He sent a messenger for assistance because he

▼HMS *Thruster* unloading at Anzio. A few moments after this photograph was taken, the building at the end of the ramp was demolished by shellfire, showering *Thruster* with debris. (H. Reid collection)

◀ The Anzio Party Chain worked under arduous and dangerous conditions to keep the causeways linked up. Here, LST 403 and US LST 326 wait for the causeways to be positioned under their bows.

◀ Motor transport makes its way to LST 416's elevator at one of Anzio's beachheads. (J. McFadden collection)

◀ Once lowered to the tank deck of LST 416, vehicles move along the causeway to the Anzio beach. Compare this view of the sturdy causeway with that of the unstable VLR under trials with LST 301 in Chapter 4. (J. McFadden collection)

couldn't get the injured men out through the hatch by himself. Able Seaman Victor Russ and John Holden managed to rescue several men from the stricken messdeck and pulled Ordinary Seaman Stirling from the water.

While all this was happening, Siegmann was lining up *U 230* for another attack. At 1537 this second torpedo struck LST 418 in about the same position, sending a column of water into the air. Warrant Engineer Reid found that he had somehow been blown out of the ship and into the water.

Lieutenant-Commander Reynolds gave the order to abandon ship just after this second explosion. The split across the upper deck increased, the ship settled more by the stern and the list to starboard increased.

John Holden and a shipmate managed to jump off the ship together. 'The silence was shattered by the most hideous clanking and banging of metal as the lorries on board slowly sheared from their shackles and crashed down the deck. The ship reared to a perpendicular position and slid slowly beneath the surface. The last we saw of her was the large red circle painted on the bows with the number 418 in white. Then she was gone. A loud hissing as air escaped lasted for several minutes. I was in the freezing water for about two hours before a US LCI picked me up with many others.' LST 418 took 21 of her crew with her.

LST 305 sunk by torpedoes

Kapitänleutnant Paul Siegmann prowled around the Anzio area with *U 230* for four more days. Just after 1700 on Sunday 20 February 1944, he recorded in his log that he had seen two destroyers and an LST. He started his attack, but the destroyers moved too far away – the LST remained.

She was LST 305 – a somewhat unusual LST under the command of Lieutenant-Commander R. Naylor, RNR. Although she had done some work as a 'pure' LST, much of her work at Anzio concerned the RAF and Ground Control Interception (GCI) radar duties.

It is thought that sister-ship LST 301 had undertaken trials with radar units, off Portland, in the early days of 1943. LST 407 certainly carried a GCI unit into Sicily, and LST 430 was also equipped for GCI duties at Anzio. Details of LSTs 13, 216 and 217 which were redesignated Fighter Direction Tenders follow in the next chapter.

It was the fifth consecutive night that LST 305 had sailed to 'Point William' off Anzio, unescorted. On arrival, the engines were stopped and the ship was turned to head 050° at the request of the RAF controller on board.

At 1850 the first of *U 230*'s torpedoes hit the starboard side of LST 305 followed by the second just moments later. A large column of smoke rose up and debris fell all over the ship and on the bridge where the Officer of the Watch, John Aslett, the First Lieutenant, was standing. Lieutenant-Commander Naylor was quickly on the bridge and ordered Aslett to examine the ship.

He found the upper deck torn up and bent forward, standing 20–30 feet in the air. The tank deck was also blown upwards and formed the appearance of a bulkhead. Aslett was unable to get past the wreckage, but was able to report back to his CO that the starboard side forward of that position had gone altogether. He found Flying Officer Jeffries who had been in the radar van on the tank deck. The van had been blown to pieces and the RAF personnel found themselves in water in or below the tank deck. They managed to climb to safety up the inside of the port side of the ship.

LST 305's Engineer Officer, Lieutenant (E) Peter Turnbull, RNVR, was in his cabin at the time of the explosion, but went immediately to his action station in the engine room. By this time, the ship had listed about 15° to starboard. Turnbull ordered the men to pump out various tanks to conteract the list.

HM Trawler *Sheppey* (T292) witnessed the explosions on her ASDIC, and shortly after received 305's emergency signal: 'All ships. This is LST 305. Hit by torpedo. Require assistance immediately.' *Sheppey* approached 305 at full speed and was with her by 1925. Naylor had given the order to abandon ship and the majority of her crew crossed over *Sheppey*'s forecastle-head to safety.

Discussion then took place as to whether LST 305 should be taken in tow. Naylor decided that she was likely to break in two if any towing strain were put on her. He remained aboard *Sheppey* who stood by until daylight.

By 0700 it was clear that LST 305 was sinking by the head and turning on her side. She was completely on her side by 0710. Within five minutes she turned end-on and sank bow first.

No crew members lost their lives, but six RAF personnel were killed.

Extract from Log of LST 305
Sunday 20 February 1944

1850	Hit by torpedo.
1850¼	Hit again. Large hole starboard side. Boats lowered. Starboard B tanks emptied.
1915	Ship listing to starboard. Taking water Auxiliary Engine Room.
1935	Ship T.292 alongside.
1945	Abandoning ship. Listing further. Terrific hole midships. Taking water shaft alley. Flares being dropped.
2000	Aboard *Sheppey*. All ship's company and 5

'Forget it, Buster, Anzio Annie is a goddam gun!' The crew of LST 425 appear to be listening-in to this conversation at Anzio. (US National Archive ref 80-G-358108)

officers on board. 2 RAF officers and 20 ORs on board – six missing. Presume they were in troop compartments when ship was hit. RAF gear destroyed by explosion.

2150   Tug *Prospect* arrived. Considered inadvisable to reboard until day. LST 305 still appears to be sinking. Intend to board at daylight to tow to Naples.

Monday 21 February 1944
0610   Ship appears to be settling down.
0715   Ship sank.

Anzio postscript

Many LST commanding officers reported that, as usual, there was considerable lack of knowledge of LST capabilities by loading authorities. One reported that '. . . it was disheartening to officers and men who know the capabilities of LST to see them so poorly exploited. It is earnestly submitted that it is essential for the "main punch" of an assault to have adequate and expert control at the delivery end … Large convoys of laden LST arrived causing further bunching at the beach-head.'

Lieutenant-Commander Sprigge, RNR, of LST 402 suggested '. . . that consideration be given to the use of a powerful sucker or hopper-type dredger. It is believed that such a vessel could quickly have cut out several more berths for LSTs in the Anzio-Nettuno area.'

Sprigge also noted that his Sick Berth Attendant, R. Bareham, had suggested that a dressing station or sick bay be built in the after end of the tank space. Casualties would suffer less in the tank deck than by having to be taken down by narrow turning gangways to the existing sick bay. It is unknown whether the idea had already been thought of, but a number of LSTs were subsequently fitted with such bays for Normandy. (Details in the next chapter.)

The story of an LST

She's not very good from the looks point of view,
    She's not very old, but don't look very new.
She's broad in the beam and blunt in the bow,
    She's as flat as a flounder and a bit of a cow.
But for those in the know and with eyes that can see,
    She's a useful old tub . . . that LST.

One mast and no funnel, one boat that won't go,
    She plods her way onward with diesels below.
She picks up her cargo through wide open jaws,
    Then toddles along to enemy shores
Where she sticks her snub nose right up on the sand,
    And Pongoes and Tanks go back to the land.

She's not very welcome back at the base,
    She's just a darned nuisance – told right to your face.
We haven't got this, we haven't got that,
    We can't do the job – work off your own bat!
Canteen and naval stores? Good God, man,
    We've only enough for ourselves in hand.

The lads that manned them were painfully new,
    With just a few hands to teach a raw crew.
But they learnt very soon to stand on their feet,
    And scrounge as good as the Navy's élite.
When given a chance to fire off their guns,
    They made it darned hot for the pestilent Huns.

Now they've done a Good Job and astonishment's waned
    That they've returned from the sands again and again,
They've been hit with selections of infernal things,
    But mostly bobbed up with varying grins.
So at last I believe they almost agree,
    She's a useful old tub . . . that LST.

Leading Supply Assistant Alan Birmingham, LST 416.

9. Operation 'Neptune' – the Normandy Invasion

Bad weather continued in the Mediterranean during February 1944. On one particularly bad day, LSTs 64 and 407 together with HMS *Boxer* were all blown aground at Naples.

LSTs for Operation 'Neptune' (the naval part of Operation 'Overlord') started to head for England in January 1944.

Les Roberts (LST 366): 'We off-loaded Free French armoured units at Port Talbot and proceeded to Harwich. We were greeted there with an intensive training programme: how to drop anchor, how to open bow doors, etc ... Our Senior Officer, Commander Jack Sutton, RN, nearly blew a gasket and asked if it wasn't good enough training to do it for (very) real for the past 12 months. The Harwich authorities had us down as fresh from the US builder's yard!'

LST 362 sunk in convoy MKS40

LST 362 sailed from Gibraltar in convoy MKS40 on about 20 February 1944. In company were LSTs 324 (Senior Officer), 413 and 427. At 2100 on 1 March HMS *Rockwood* was ordered to detach from the convoy and escort the four LSTs to their destination ports. *Rockwood* was operating on only one screw. They formed two columns: LST 324 followed by LST 362 in the starboard column, LSTs 413 and 427 in the port column. *Rockwood* took station ahead of them, zigzagging across a broad front. As LST 324 carried Type 271 radar, *Rockwood* asked her to keep a look-out for surface craft.

LST 324's radar was operating at only half power due to a valve having been damaged by the ship's pounding. However, at 0345 on 2 March a contact was made 1,600 yards on the starboard beam. *Rockwood* increased to her maximum safe speed and carried out a starshell sweep along the starboard side of the LSTs. Right ahead of her was a U-boat – believed to be *U 744*. She was about 800 yards away and in an ideal position to fire a torpedo at the LSTs.

Rockwood decided to ram the U-boat. As she closed in on her, a torpedo struck LST 362 amidships. Her back broke immediately and she started to sag. Within a minute, the fore part tore away. It is thought that about 60 Army personnel were in that part. The after section listed 10° to starboard and settled by the head. 'Abandon ship' was given at 0355, but as the vessel seemed to be steadying, the order was belayed. Ballast tanks were used to bring her back on an even keel.

Meanwhile, *Rockwood*'s commanding officer had decided that he didn't have quite enough speed to make his ramming lethal. He altered course to pass 50 feet ahead of the swirl of the disappearing conning tower and dropped ten depth-charges in a tight bunch.

The weather by now had deteriorated – visibility was poor with drizzling rain and a freshening wind.

At 0700, what remained of LST 362 started to list further, so LST 324 was requested to come alongside with her bows abreast 362's bridge. As 324 came near, 362 settled sharply and listed even further to starboard. The order to abandon ship was given and 324 sheared off.

LST 362 sank at about 0720. LST 324 rescued 73 survivors either by boat or by scrambling nets and ladders over her side.

▲ Signalman John McFadden and Leading Telegraphist Bungy Williams relieve the pre-invasion tension below decks in LST 416 with a game of cards. (J. McFadden)

Another contact with the U-boat was made and reported to the escort. LST 324 was ordered by *Rockwood* to proceed; *Rockwood* would pick up any remaining survivors. At that moment, many men were still clinging to the nets and were fast succumbing to cold and exposure.

The three remaining LSTs were able to make the south coast safely. Fifteen crew members were 'missing presumed killed'. Able Seaman Stanley died later on board LST 324 and was buried at sea at 1150 on 2 March.

Lieutenant Newton, RNR, commanding officer of LST 362 at the time, noted in his report the efforts of Leading Motor Mechanic Smith and Leading Stoker Delves who stayed below in the engine room at the pumps until instructed to abandon ship. Chief Petty Officer Reagan was commended for his rescuing of survivors.

From LST 324, Petty Officer J. McKenzie repeatedly went into the water to help survivors at great risk to himself. He finally drifted but managed to hang on to a propeller guard.

In his report, LST 324's CO, Lieutenant-Commander A. J. Bell, RNR, commended the CO of LST 362 for not abandoning ship earlier – the water was apparently so cold that those taken aboard 324 were almost entirely unable to help themselves. Bell also recommended his First

Lieutenant, J. H. E. Haslett, RNVR, for an award for 'His prompt and capable organization of rescue work [which] was most praiseworthy and was responsible for the saving of many lives.' Haslett was 'mentioned in despatches' and later took command of LST 320.

Burges Watson leaves the Mediterranean and the LSTs

On 17 March 1944 Captain LST, Burges Watson, sent the following message to all LST commanding officers in the Mediterranean. 'Hope you have a good and safe passage home and receive some very well-earned leave and rest. I very much regret my command is finished with you. I wish to thank you one and all.'

Exercise 'Tiger'

With the LSTs back in the UK, the authorities were able to arrange various exercises with those vessels that had been refitted in the Mediterranean and with those now coming out of British ship repair yards.

One of those exercises was to become notorious. Exercise 'Tiger' employed eight US LSTs in its make-up of more than 100 ships and craft. In Lyme Bay in the early hours of 28 April 1944, these LSTs, fully loaded, came under attack from E-boats out of Cherbourg.

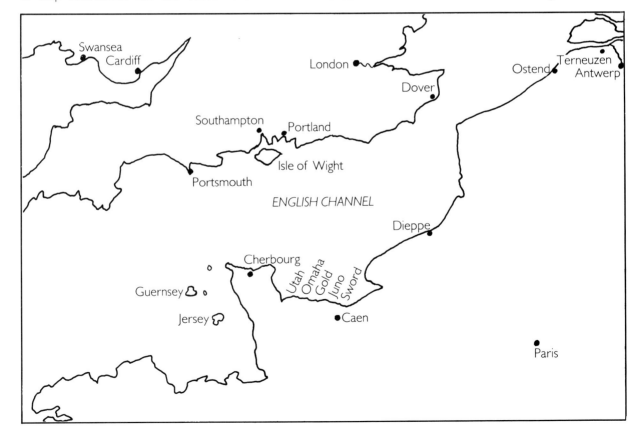

US LST 507 was the first victim of the E-boat force. She was torpedoed with 282 troops on board. US LST 531 was torpedoed and sank with the loss of 424 men. US LST 289 then fell victim to another torpedo. She managed to limp back to Dartmouth with four of her crew dead and eight others missing, presumed dead.

Details of further reading on this exercise can be found in the bibliography.

D-Day, 6 June 1944

By the early days of June 1944, the LSTs were gathering in their allotted forces at Portsmouth, Southampton, Harwich and Southend for the largest amphibious assault the world has ever known – the invasion of Normandy. One newspaper wrote, 'Landing Ships, Tank, Mark 2, are due for as much fame from coming operations as the Spitfire and Hurricane achieved in a similar vital battle four years ago.'

Five beach areas of Normandy were chosen for the landings. In the west were 'Utah' and 'Omaha' Beaches, allocated to US LSTs and US troops. In the east were 'Gold', 'Juno' and 'Sword' Beaches allocated to British and Canadian troops. Official plans indicate that 'Gold' Beach was to be served by US LSTs, whereas 'Juno' and 'Sword' were to be served by British LSTs. However, on the day, it seems that many British LSTs actually went to 'Gold' Beach.

Sadly, the only detailed records concerning the British LSTs which seem to have survived are for 'Juno' Beach. No official reports have come to light concerning the other two beaches or the L1 and L3 assault groups.

Because of the fresh wind and choppy sea, the original D-Day of 5 June was postponed for 24 hours. The weather was noted as having moderated by 2100 on 5 June.

With the 7th LST Flotilla from Harwich

Les Roberts (LST 366): 'One by one, ships of the 7th LST Flotilla cast off from Parkestone Quay, Harwich. It was the afternoon of 5 June. There were many hours to go before 'H-Hour, D-Day, Normandy', but we had some steaming ahead of us before joining our counterparts sailing from ports on the south coast.

'Shore staff and dockyard workers waved and cheered us as the flotilla proceeded downstream in company with a flotilla of US LSTs. The cheering heightened as the little armada broke out battle ensigns. There was no doubt that this was the big one – the long-awaited 'second front'. As far as the LSTs were concerned, the task was in the hands of battle-hardened veterans – some all of 20 years of age!

'Stomach muscles tightened and throats felt dry. But few, if any, would have wished to be anywhere else.

▲Standing room only in LST 320 as she heads for Normandy. (C. Powell collection)

Having come so far – Sicily, Reggio, Salerno, Anzio – everyone felt they had to see it through.

'Navigators checked their charts for the umpteenth time. Gunnery officers checked ammunition readiness. First Lieutenants looked at everything on the tank and upper decks. Engineers looked wisely at their gauges as only engineers can. Commanding officers donned their sphynx masks, designed to hide from everyone's eyes the responsibility that lay heavily on their shoulders.

'As darkness fell, voices softened down to a whisper – a reaction to the cloak of secrecy they felt about them. Hollywood might one day make a film about all this, with bugles blowing and banners waving. But in the meantime, the LSTs knew how to put their trust in silence and in stealth.'

Cacophony of sound

John Holden (LST 322): 'Just before dawn, the familiar cacophony of sound broke out. Heavy gunfire from the cruisers and battleships; the flickering of intense light as shells exploded among the beach defences; the ear-splitting screams of rockets being launched from the supporting craft. As 6 June dawned, we were treated to an amazing sight. There seemed to be thousands of ships of all shapes and sizes as far as the eye could see. Although we were still a few miles from the shore, the noise was absolutely deafening.'

▶ 'Sword' Beach, D-Day, 6 June 1944. Barrage balloons face England as LST 427 moves towards LST 423 on their way in to the beach with their sister vessels. (G. Melford collection)

▼A view from the tank deck of LST 320. Mobile artillery crosses her ramp and on to a Rhino ferry. The stern of LST 412 is just visible. (C. Powell collection)

▲A clear view of the size of a Rhino ferry attached to LST 320. Another LST waits behind with her bow doors open and ramp partially lowered. (C. Powell collection)

◀Now fully loaded, Rhino ferry F94 moves away from LST 320 and heads for the beach along the port side of LST 412. (C. Powell collection)

▶ DUKWs scurry back and forth as LST 408 starts to unload on to a Rhino ferry, as does an unidentified sister ship behind. (G. Melford collection)

Groups 332 and 333 sail from Southampton

The vessels for 'Juno' Beach which loaded at Southampton were split into two groups: Group 332 under Commander Garth Owles, DSO, DSC, RN in LST 215 and Group 333 under Commander C. M. V. Dalrymple-Hay, RN, in LST 425.

They loaded at three of the four hards at Southampton. Group 332 was first during 2 and 3 June, followed directly by Group 333 in the afternoon of 3 June. There was a delay of eleven hours on the carefully worked out loading schedule, due to the Army having lost its convoy somewhere en route. By 4 June, all the vessels of Groups 332 and 333 were at anchor in the Solent.

Many of the LSTs in these two groups had Rhino ferries and/or Rhino tugs in tow. Records are unclear as to exactly why these were provided, but it is thought that allowing LSTs to dry-out on the beaches would make them too easy a target for the enemy. Another possibility is that as the beaches were so flat, the LSTs would ground too far from the shoreline, even for the use of pontoons as at Anzio.

At 1900 on 5 June Group 332 sailed from Area 22 of the Solent, followed by Group 333 at 2145. Passage through the mined area of the Channel was not easy due to a strong cross tide and wind. Ships often had to steer as much as 40° off course in order to stay between the marker buoys. The only known mishap to either group was a serious breakdown of the steering gear in LST 215. Commander Owles reported, 'This entailed a somewhat anxious period from 1030 to 1115 during which time the ship was in unswept water endeavouring to regain the Channel.'

The Rhino tugs and ferries of Group 332 arrived off Normandy intact, but those of Group 333 had not fared so well. Three ships of that group lost their tugs.

Group 332 arrived at the anchorage at about 1300 followed by Group 333 about an hour later. Considerable congestion was noted, not helped by a strong wind, nor by two follow-up groups which also arrived during the afternoon. Group 332 carried DUKWs at their davits, and these were lowered and swum ashore soon after anchoring. Some ships also carried DUKWs in the tank deck. Because of the swell, officers commanding these vehicles were reluctant to swim off the ramp and were subsequently landed by Rhino. This committed most ships to three ferry loads, further delaying matters.

The state of the sea caused considerable movement between the Rhinos and the ramps of LST, over which the Rhinos would load. Most Rhinos were damaged to some extent by the end of the day because of this.

From 1615, about three hours later than schedule, Rhinos were dispatched from the LSTs, the beaches having signalled their readiness to accept loads.

The unloading programme steadily deteriorated. Several Rhinos dried out on the falling tide, others appeared to broach to on the beach and some suffered engine breakdowns. It was almost impossible to get in touch with a Rhino that had cleared its own ship to assist with another. LST 199 had to wait more than five hours for her second Rhino. This left her with just eight vehicles, but she had to wait from 2200 until well into the morning of 7 June for this final load to be taken off.

Enemy activity had been minimal. At about 1730, four small calibre shells fell within 200 yards of LST 215, and a stick of bombs fell on the beach about twenty minutes later. Bombs dropped on the starboard quarter of LST 425 at about midnight.

LST 215 embarked 196 PoWs from a Rhino. They had been sent from the shore without any other guard than the Rhino crew and were immediately put in the tank deck

▶ With about 5,000 vessels in the Channel during Operation 'Neptune', safe navigation wasn't easy. Officers on the bridge of LST 320 keep a careful watch as they return to England for another load. (C. Powell collection)

▼ D-Day dog. (W. H. Owen)

under Seaman guard and searched. At 0745 the next morning, another 184 prisoners arrived by Rhino at LST 215's ramp.

During the hours of darkness, the pilot of one of the Rhino ferries observed a soldier on the beach feverishly waving a red light at him and shouting. The pilot took this to mean that he had to beach his ferry at exactly that spot. However, the soldier was endeavouring to warn the Rhino of the presence of a mine which had been dropped by aircraft on the shoreline. The Rhino hit the mine, damaging several vehicles and injuring military personnel.

By 0900 on D+1, 7 June, LST 215 was able to sail for the UK with LSTs 180, 238, 239, 421, 416 and 11 as the first return convoy. After reporting to the Captain of Northbound Sailings, Owles in 215 was joined by three LSTs from Force 'S' and four US LSTs. Considerable confusion arose over their destinations.

LST 215 was at Southampton's S3 Hard by 2315 that night and prisoners were disembarked – possibly the first to arrive in the UK (at least by LST) during this operation.

LSTs evacuate casualties

The 'medically fitted' LSTs carried three medical officers, including a surgeon, and sixteen sick berth attendants. Many operations were carried out in the small station which was rigged up in the tank deck. The 'fold away' stretcher racks could accommodate 300 stretcher cases, with a further 160 walking cases. Due to the chaos which surrounded the invasion, casualties could expect to be on board their LST for at least 30 hours and one case was noted as being extended to 71 hours.

John McFadden (Signalman LST 416): 'We beached at around 0430 during the morning of 25 June, unloaded and hauled off around 1145. Responding to an urgent signal

►LSTs 365 and 320 on 'Sword' Beach. (J. H. E. Haslett collection)

►LST 320 dried-out on a Normandy beach. (J. H. E. Haslett collection)

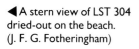

◄A stern view of LST 304 dried-out on the beach. (J. F. G. Fotheringham)

►US LST 505 beached close to LST 304. The kedge anchor cable of 304 can just be seen. (J. F. G. Fotheringham)

◀ LSTs 320 and 415 are ready to return to England carrying wounded. Within six months, 415 would be put out of action by a torpedo (see Chapter 10). LST 320 went on to assist in the relief of Norway and was returned to the USA in 1946. (C. Powell collection)

◀ A wounded soldier shields his eyes from the glare of the summer sunshine as he is carried up the ramp of LST 320. A sentry stands guard – but why? Is she carrying PoWs? (C. Powell collection)

from the Flag Officer British Assault Area, we went alongside the *Cap Tourane* at about 1230 to embark casualties. The transfer of casualties from the immobilized ship was carried out by 1600 under fire from the shore – mostly anti-personnel shells exploding overhead. All hands who could be spared helped carry the stretchers and some minor wounds from shrapnel were suffered. I felt very exposed on the open bridge under what seemed a very small tin hat. On completion, we cast off and proceeded to a safer billet to await a convoy.

'Three of the wounded died and were buried at sea – it was not permitted to land the dead. The casualties were disembarked at Portsmouth during the late evening of 26 June.'

Les Roberts (LST 366): 'One night, we came back to Tilbury with a great many wounded among the survivors of two sinkings. Shore organization was at its best – rows of ambulances drawn up with doctors and nurses at the ready. But the first bloke up the gangway was a Customs Officer – we were still "an arrival from a foreign port"!'

A prize of war

John McFadden (Signalman LST 416): 'On 29 June 1944 on passage empty between Normandy and Portsmouth, we came upon a cargo ship. She was the *Empire Portia* and had been disabled and abandoned about 15 miles south of the Isle of Wight after being struck by a torpedo or mine. A

▶ The tank deck of LST 427 with 456 casualties. (G. Melford collection)

▶ LST 320 approaches a Mulberry Harbour. (C. Powell collection)

▶ LST 427 unloads at what is thought to be the Mulberry 'A' harbour at St. Laurent in mid-June 1944, just before it was destroyed in the great gale. (G. Melford collection)

◀ Trucks head for the Normandy beach from LST 427. (G. Melford collection)

◀ The communications branch of LST 416 – plus rabbit. (J. McFadden)

◀ Petty Officer George Raitt and Chief Petty Officer Harold Warrington of LST 416 share a smile in troubled times. (E. Raitt)

▶ FDT 216 (ex-LST 216) fitted out with radar equipment. (IWM A21922)

boarding party went to examine her. Although taking water slowly she was not in immediate danger of sinking. Our CO, Lieutenant-Commander Braine, RNR, decided to try and salvage her. Towing lines were passed and secured. We eventually beached her near Ryde, Isle of Wight. About two years later I received the sum of £1.7s.1d. (about £1.35) as salvage money. Chief petty officers got £2.0s.0d. (£2.00) and leading hands £1.17s.5d. (£1.87).

Fighter Direction Tenders

As mentioned in previous chapters, a number of LSTs were used to assist RAF radar units, particularly LSTs 305 and 430. LSTs 13, 216 and 217 were converted specifically for fighter direction use, becoming FDT 13, 216 and 217 respectively. Their decks were covered with pig-iron to compensate for the lighter RAF load compared to the heavy vehicles and tanks normally carried.

During Operation 'Neptune', FDT 13 was positioned in the main shipping route, about 40 miles off 'Gold' Beach; FDT 216 was less than ten miles off 'Omaha' Beach; and FDT 217 was less than ten miles off 'Juno' Beach. They maintained these positions for about a week. Various movements were made over the next few weeks, the vessels having done much more work than had been envisaged.

On 27 June FDT 216 relieved FDT 13 off Barfleur. On the morning of 7 July, 216 was being screened by the destroyer, HMS *Burdock* when radar contact was made with an enemy aircraft, subsequently found to be a Junkers Ju 88. Under fire from both ships, the aircraft flew down the port side of 216 at a height of just 20 feet. It turned down her starboard side between her and *Burdock* and then took the same route back to the port side.

The commanding officer of FDT 216, Lieutenant-Commander G. D. Kelly, RNR, said in his report, 'One torpedo was seen to splash about a ½-mile on the port beam and the track was seen approaching the ship. At first, I had hopes it was going to clear us ... At 0059, the ship was struck with a great explosion.'

A large hole was blown in the ship's side and thick, black smoke and reddish orange flame blew out of the elevator hatch up to mast height. The order to abandon ship was given at 0107 and *Burdock* immediately closed to her aid.

FDT 216 began to settle by the head and take on a 15° list to port. By 0145 the pig-iron on her deck could be heard shifting. She turned on her port side, stayed in that position for about 90 seconds, then turned turtle, the full length of her hull remaining visible above water to a height of about ten feet.

A total of 250 men and the ship's dog were picked out of the water in just over 2½ hours, but five RAF personnel could not be accounted for.

Complaints by commanding officers

The LSTs plied back and forth across the Channel to Portsmouth, Southampton and London's West India Docks amid total lack of organization. Given the limited communications facilities of the period and the fact that more than 4,000 vessels were involved in 'Neptune', the chaos is understandable. Much was left to the determination and ingenuity of individual LST commanding officers to get their loads across to 'the far shore' and bring back many hundreds of casualties and PoWs.

Tempers ran high at the disorganization. Commanding officers sent a barrage of memos to RALSCU (Rear-Admiral Landing Ships and Craft Unallocated) complaining

of their inefficient use by the Army authorities. Some ships were being worked intensively without any care for maintenance. On the other hand, in spite of every effort by her commanding officer, one LST remained at Tilbury for eleven days waiting to load.

One commanding officer wrote, 'It cannot be too strongly urged that these ships should either be treated as HM ships and allowed to run as such, or naval officers and crews withdrawn and the ships run under the Red Ensign. The ... control of ships in company for unloading in the hands of the group commander at Anzio resulted in twelve ships unloading in two hours less than eight ships had done under shore control.'

Another commanding officer reported that a round trip to the far shore and back could be done by an LST in 36 hours. Because of convoy arrangements, his average time was 67 hours. He 'respectfully submitted' that with better organization, the same number of loads could have been handled by two-thirds the number of LSTs, allowing greater time for essential maintenance.

His memo continued: 'Sir, during this last 18 months, LSTs have been fighting two battles: one with the enemy and one with our own cloth. The former has proved easier and more exhilarating through accomplishment than anyone anticipated. The latter more exhausting and demoralizing than anyone could imagine.'

▼ 10 June 1944. LST 427 arrives at Gosport Hard with German PoWs. The tudor-beamed pub in the background is still there today, but is now a private house. A small yacht marina now occupies the area to the starboard quarter of the LST. (G. Melford collection)

▲ A fine view of LST 320 in dry-dock, believed to have been taken at Portsmouth during the summer of 1944. (C. Powell collection)

◀ LST 410 fully loaded for another run to Normandy. A PoW takes a break from painting a sister ship to watch her depart. (IWM A24040)

10. The Build-Up —Five LSTs are Lost

The build-up was to continue over many months. LSTs were used to tow out sections of the vast Mulberry Harbour and this was brought into use by mid-June. In due course the ports of Ostend, Antwerp and Rotterdam were opened for use by LSTs.

Les Roberts (LST 366): 'During one beaching, 366's stern anchor was dropped too late. When we dried out, the anchor was about 40 feet astern of us – useless for kedging off the beach. A passing tank recovery vehicle spotted our plight and offered to help. We brought the anchor up and lowered it on to the vehicle, which drove off slowly while we payed out the wire. At the required distance, we put the brake on the winch while the vehicle kept going. With a crunch and a grind, the anchor fell on the sand and was nicely dug in as a bonus. Such is improvisation!'

The 'shuttle service' was soon in place. High in number of runs achieved to Normandy was LST 416. From D-Day until the end of September 1944 she made 28 trips. From the beginning of October 1944 to 6 May 1945, she made 17 trips to Ostend and four to Antwerp.

Operations 'Author I' and 'Author II'
As the American 12th Army Group began to pursue the enemy towards Brest their need for supplies became acute – the beaches of Normandy being some 150 miles in their rear. British LST 421 with US LSTs 344 and 519 were detailed for Operation 'Author I', to land supplies at St-Michel-en-Grève, a small village on the north coast of Brittany.

They left Portland at 2200 on 10 August, escorted by two destroyers, a frigate, the French ship *la Découverte* and the 16th Minesweeping Flotilla (SO in *Shippigan*). The LSTs beached at 1340 on 11 August, being greeted by jubilant villagers and members of the Maquis.

Monsieur Georges Daniel: 'As the tide receded leaving the ships aground, work began in earnest, trucks going to and fro unloading the vital supplies. These large ships made a great impression on us all. We were so pleased to see them as the retreating German army had passed through our village only a few days previously. A panzer had unleashed its firepower on the villagers, killing one and wounding another.' (Monsieur Daniel later became Mayor of the village.)

Because of the success of the mission, Operation 'Author II' was organized. For reasons unknown, LST 421 was replaced by LST 368. However, 421's commanding officer, Lieutenant-Commander J. V. Machin, RNR, was ordered by C in C Portsmouth on 17 August to '... proceed forthwith to 40 Berth Southampton to take passage in LST 368 as Senior Officer of LSTs 368, 344 and 519 taking part in this operation'.

The LSTs sailed at 1700 on Saturday 19 August surrounded by six minesweepers led by *Shippigan*, together with Motor Launches 117 and 124. Fog was encountered en route, seriously delaying the ships. By now

▼ Lieutenant-Commander J. H. E. Haslett, RNVR, was in command of LST 320 from July to November 1944. In August of that year he took an ENSA party across to Normandy in 320. Included in the party were Diana Wynyard, Gertrude Lawrence, Ivor Novello, Margaret Rutherford, Joan Benham and Jessie Matthews. (J. H. E. Haslett collection)

time was so short that the LSTs made for the beach at full speed without waiting for the channel to be swept. They beached at 2130 in the nick of time as far as the Army were concerned. They had only enough petrol to drive their trucks to the beach.

Operation 'Anvil'

The American invasion of southern France on 15 August 1944 was code-named Operation 'Anvil'. It is thought that FDT 13 took part. The only British LST(2) involved was LST 12 which had remained in the Mediterranean following the mine damage sustained on 13 November 1943. From September 1944 she operated off Yugoslavia and Greece.

Bruiser and *Thruster* loaded at Oran. They sailed on 15 August and were approaching the landing beaches at St Raphaël by late afternoon. They were ordered in to Delta Green Beach at Bougnon Bay, but grounded a considerable distance offshore. Three lengths of pontoon were needed to enable *Thruster* to unload, completion not being until 0030 on 16 August.

The two ships made ferrying runs between the beaches and l'Ile-Rousse, Corsica, up to 25 August. *Thruster* is

▲ HMSS *Bruiser* and *Thruster* during the landings in southern France, August 1944. (H. Reid collection)

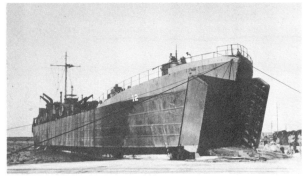

▼LST 12 at Barletta, July 1944. (T. Hill collection)

▲ A closer view of Gosport Hard during 'the build-up'. (J. H. E. Haslett collection)

▶LST 165 in convoy in the North Sea during the shuttle service. The convoy is forming into a single column for arrival at Ostend. (W. West)

▶ LST 12 appears to be sailing up a village high street on the island of Vis, October 1944. (T. Hill collection)

▶ Christmas greetings from LST 401, 1944. (C. Hooper)

Christmas! 1944

401

▶ LST 12 responds to rough seas while on passage to Piraeus, Christmas Day 1944. (T. Hill collection)

noted as having carried a total of 273 officers, 1,610 men, 454 vehicles and 35 tons of loose stores during that time.

LST 404 torpedoed in convoy FTM69

As the beaches of southern France were being invaded, LST 404 left the Normandy coast with 138 casualties on board, most of whom were German. Lieutenant-Commander Shaw, RNR, sailed her to rendezvous with convoy FTM69 – two merchant ships with a destroyer escort.

The convoy had been detected by *U 741* which fired a torpedo at about 1630. Its target was LST 404. A direct hit was scored to starboard, blowing out the side between frames 22 and 25. The tank deck and ship's bottom in this area were also blown away from the centre-line. The upper deck turned back and a crack appeared right round on the port side at frame 25.

The engines died and all lights went out. Lieutenant-Commander Shaw ordered all able-bodied men to the tank deck to hoist out stretcher cases through the after hatch, and this was completed in twenty minutes. One trapped man was released fifteen minutes later.

Shaw ordered the anchor to be let go which brought the ship's head up to wind and sea, thereby steadying her and reducing the strain across the damaged section. LST 413 was about four miles distant at this time, so a signal was made to her to come alongside. This she did at 1720, leaving with 404's injured soon after.

The American rescue tug ATR 4 had seen 404's plight and came alongside at about the same time. A line was passed and secured aft, anchor was slipped and 404 proceeded in tow, stern first. She made it to Ryde Sands in the Isle of Wight.

Six of 404's SBAs were killed together with eighteen PoWs. The U-boat was detected shortly afterwards by HMS *Orchis* and sunk within an hour.

LST 420 hits mine off Ostend

Bill Chalk was a 19-year-old Stoker in LST 420: 'I returned to the ship on Sunday 5 November, having had a run ashore with fellow Stoker, Reg Wilson. During the afternoon, we loaded with men and equipment of an RAF Signals and Radar Unit, the first unit of its kind to be sent to occupied Europe.

'From previous experience, the crew knew that many of these men would be apprehensive about being aboard a ship, particularly if it was their first sea voyage. We found that it helped put them at ease if we moved amongst them, chatted, offered them cups of tea and inquired if anyone was from our own home towns.'

In the early hours of 7 November 1944, LSTs 405, 367, 320, 200 and 420 sailed in that order in single column from Southend for Ostend. The wind was westerly, Force 4, but gradually increased during the night. On arrival off Ostend at 1330, the wind was up to Force 7 or 8 with a heavy sea. The convoy Senior Officer, Lieutenant-Commander J. T. Sheffield, RNR, in LST 405, was told that Ostend was closed because of the weather and that he was to make for the Small Downs (between Deal and Margate) for shelter.

LST 200 reported that she was rolling heavily at the time with a violent, lurching roll. Vehicle lashings had to be

► LST 404 is down by the head after being torpedoed. A sister ship is alongside. (J. H. E. Haslett collection)

▼ LST 404 broken in half on Ryde Sands. (J. Bainbridge collection)

tightened on the upper deck and several tanks in the tank space had swung out of position. A leeway of 27° were being allowed for in the strong wind.

Bill Chalk came off watch at 0800, had breakfast and went up on deck for a chat and a breath of fresh air. A little later, he 'turned in' to get some rest before his 1st Dog Watch at 1600. He fell into a deep sleep. At 1520, his sleep was violently interrupted. 'I felt a tremendous thump. The chains holding my bunk to the deckhead parted and I was thrown on to the deck. As I got up, I could feel the ship pitching forward. The crew's quarters were in total darkness. I was alone.

'I made my way up on deck and went aft. We had struck a mine and the ship had broken completely in half at the bridge. Both halves were alight and drifting apart. My friend, Reg, must have been killed instantly as the mine struck directly beneath the engine room.'

LSTs 405, 367 and 320 turned to the aid of LST 420 even though they were rolling violently. By now, the fire on 420 was severe. The storm was blowing hard, the sea was rough and it was very, very cold.

Bill Chalk stood holding the stern handrail wearing just a singlet and a pair of pants. 'I glanced down. One of the Stewards was sitting astride the port propeller guard. He was sobbing – too fearful to let go.

'There was only one other person left on the quarter-deck with me – Lieutenant Hogg. He said to me, "I suppose we'd better go, Stokes." With those words in my ears, I jumped. As I went under, I started kicking my legs. When I broke the surface, I started to swim into the tide to get away. I heard someone call, "Chalkie, I can't swim." I could see no one. I kept swimming and eventually found a Carley float. On it were Able Seaman Harrington, Sub-Lieutenant Monny, RANVR, an airman and one other man.

'They pulled me on to the float and I realized just how cold I was. The two halves of LST 420 were about 100 yards from us, still burning. On the bow section we could see a man clinging to the sloping deck – but there was nothing we could do.'

Lieutenant-Commander C. C. Page, RNR, positioned LST 367 to drift between the two parts of LST 420. Bill Chalk remembers: 'The crew threw heaving lines out to us, but they fell short. Harrington dived off the float, swam to one of the lines and brought it back. We held on tight as the LST crew hauled us in, but the rope parted leaving us to drift again.'

LST 367 then proceeded towards the wreckage of the bow section where half a dozen or so survivors were grouped. Sheffield's LST 405 and LST 320 under Lieutenant-Commander J. H. E. Haslett, RNVR, also searched the area and picked up survivors, most of whom were weak from shock and exposure.

Bill Chalk: 'Suddenly, from out of the gloom, a trawler appeared. It was the *Greenfly* and we were safely picked up. When I stepped ashore at Tilbury the next morning, the first person I saw was Lieutenant Hogg. He said, "I see you made it, Stokes." Indeed, I had.'

LST 420 lost 55 of her crew, the worst loss of life of any British LST during the war. Many RAF personnel also died. On a happier note, the Steward whom Bill had seen on the propeller guard was plucked to safety at first light on 8 November.

Bill thought that LST 420 was a closed chapter in his life. He was wrong. In 1966 he met and married Margaret. In the course of conversation, they found that her father was one of the RAF men who perished with 420 that fateful day. His body had been recovered with 53 others from LST 420 and subsequently buried by the Belgians in Blankenberg.

In 1986, Stanley Marsh of the Allied Graves Committee in Blankenberg, invited Bill and Margaret to the cemetery. There, Margaret was able to lay a wreath on the grave of the much-loved father she had lost 42 years earlier. Bill was able to pay his respects to the shipmates he lost.

In 1988, Bill Chalk became one of the founder members of the LST & Landing Craft Association.

LST 321 hits mine in convoy

An example of the sturdy construction of an LST is shown by LST 321. At 2130 on 29 November 1944, she weighed anchor and proceeded from Southend in convoy TAL50. Single column was formed. Ahead of her was LST 180; astern of her were LSTs 160 and 408. In command temporarily was Lieutenant George Pemberton, RNR. Draft was 6 feet forward, 13 feet aft.

Out in the Channel, the first of four reports was received warning of E-boat activity. Lieutenant Pemberton ordered ballast tank A415W to be pumped out, thus reducing the draft in event of torpedo attack.

Just before 0630 on 30 November, Pemberton heard a noise which resembled the escaping of compressed air. Within seconds, a dull, muffled explosion occurred under the starboard bow. The vessel shuddered and a 30-foot column of water shot into the air. Pemberton reported: 'I stopped both engines, piped "hands to action stations" and troops to "emergency stations". Steering gear, gyro compass, alarm bells and tank space klaxons were out of action.' The starboard main engine block had also been cracked.

Investigation revealed that the tank deck and starboard troop deck were thick with smoke. There was a strong smell of cordite and acid. Casualties were fortunately restricted to shock and superficial cuts only, even though a hole some 25 feet by 30 feet had been blown out.

The ship was manoeuvred by engines until the steering gear was rectified and Pemberton was able to anchor LST 321 off Ostend by 1100, subsequently berthing in the Mud Dock at 1345. Here, the damage was inspected and it was decided to weld strips over the split plates in the tank deck to facilitate passage to England.

LST 321 left Ostend on 1 December and headed for the Thames. No dockyards were available, so she had to sail back across the Channel in her 'temporarily repaired' condition to Antwerp where she was taken in hand on about 12 December. She was the first of many LSTs to be repaired or refitted there.

LST 415 damaged in convoy TAL97

At 2300 on the night of 15 January 1945, LST 319, as Senior Officer of convoy TAL97, led LSTs 323, 159 and 415 out from Southend, bound for Ostend. The sea was smooth and the wind was light. The sky was cloudy but visibility was good.

At approximately 0245 on the morning of 16 January, C in C Nore signalled the LSTs that E-boats were in the vicinity of Tongue Sands Fort. Lieutenant-Commander Gilbey, RNVR, was in command of LST 415 and noted seeing flares and hearing gunfire. He ordered 'action stations'.

Gunfire increased but no flashes were seen. Very faint throbbing sounds were heard. Gilbey was on the upper bridge on the gyro repeater platform but could not establish the direction from which the sound was coming. Look-outs on the wings of the bridge could see nothing.

Gilbey was naturally expecting trouble from his port side. At 0300, however, a torpedo found LST 415, entering and exploding on the starboard side in the region of the main engine room. The explosion shattered the bulkhead between the main and auxiliary engine rooms and both were flooded. The ship remained on an even keel although she started to sink by the stern until her draught aft was 24 feet. The tank space contained 12 feet of water.

Both primary and secondary lighting failed, causing some confusion with the troops. However, the fact that ship's officers and men were already at action stations meant that they were quickly on the scene. Panic was averted, and the troops were soon on the upper deck with the aid of torches. Captain Heap, RAMC, is noted as having gone round the ship in bare feet looking for casualties.

▶ LST 415 on the beach in the River Thames at Grays, Essex. (H. W. Stevens)

LST 159 obtained permission to go to 415's aid and by 0345 was made fast to her port side. Troops and eight minor casualties among the ship's crew were transferred.

LST 159 dropped anchor to prevent her drifting. An order was received from Tongue Sands Fort at 0405 for 159 to tow 415 clear. LST 159's anchor fouled a cable on the sea bed, and heaving up caused great difficulty. However, it finally cleared and an attempt at towing was made. Lieutenant-Commander Gilbey feared that the fracture in her deck was opening, so the towing was abandoned in case 415 broke in half.

By 0815, the tug Saucy had arrived. A 4½ inch wire was rigged from the port bollard aft of the crack across the deck and through the bow fairlead. The ship towed well at 5 knots back towards the Thames Gate. LST 159 stood by until she was certain she could be of no further assistance and made for Tilbury where troops and casualties were promptly disembarked. 159 joined convoy TAL98 and sailed that same night.

Five members of LST 415's crew were killed.

LST 364 struck by torpedo in convoy TAM87

At 0245 on the morning of 22 February 1945 LST 364 left Margate Roads in convoy TAM87. Her commanding officer was Lieutenant-Commander Coventry, RNR. LST 364 was position 30 in port column, speed 8 to 9 knots. Her steering gear broke down but was repaired within ten minutes, enabling her to rejoin the convoy in her original position.

At 0545 she was struck on the starboard side between frames 35 and 41 by what was believed to be a torpedo. A 30-foot hole was blown from the upper deck to below the waterline and the engine room soon flooded. Lighting and power failed because of the overloads.

Fires broke out and petrol tanks of vehicles in the tank deck exploded. The petrol continued to burn on the surface when the vehicles became submerged. The ship settled rapidly by the stern and her bows rose clear of the water.

HM Trawler Turquoise was contacted by Aldis lamp to come alongside. She took off all 220 personnel, the last of whom only just got across as 364 sank at about 0700. Although 24 men had been injured, there was no loss of life.

LST 80 hits two mines

Convoy ATM97 sailed from Terneuzen (Antwerp) at 1400 on 19 March 1945. The single-line convoy comprised 25 merchant ships plus LSTs 366 and 80. Lieutenant-Commander Grandage, DSC, RD, RNR, was in command of LST 366 in position 20 and Lieutenant-Commander Smyth, RNR, had LST 80 astern of her.

At 1838, near NF 12 Buoy, Grandage saw SS Samselbu explode and break in half. She went down with her guns firing to starboard. Other vessels were also firing to starboard, so he ordered 'action stations'. LSTs 366 and 80 made for the ship at 320 revs to pick up survivors, having signalled their intention to the Senior Officer of the escort vessel, HMS Versatile. She was nearby investigating a submarine contact and was dropping depth-charges.

With the exception of two men killed in the explosion, the entire crew of the Samselbu were picked up by the two LSTs and an ML. Those aboard LST 80 were transferred to the ML which subsequently made for Ostend.

At 1900 the two LSTs regained station in the convoy which had been ordered to form two columns. The weather had deteriorated, wind Force 5, and visibility greatly restricted. Just after passing NF 9 Buoy at 2012, Grandage noted a vessel on the starboard beam signalling 'Have been hit, stand by me.' Course was altered and the vessel was recognized as LST 80.

The Master of *Samselbu* was on the bridge of LST 366 and suddenly shouted, 'Hard-a-starboard, full ahead!' He told Grandage that he had seen a torpedo coming for them. Grandage could see nothing, but heeded the warning. Later inquiries showed that two crew members saw the track of a torpedo pass fifteen yards ahead of the ship.

It is thought that LST 80 hit a mine right under her bottom. Many men suffered leg and ankle injuries. Leading Motor Mechanic Poundall and Stoker Dowling who had been on watch in the engine room could not be accounted for. A rescue attempt was impossible due to flooding. The ship appeared to be down by the stern and a large split ran from below the waterline on both sides and across the main deck forward of the main engine room escape hatch.

LST 366 managed to get alongside LST 80 even though she was lying beam on to the strong wind and rolling heavily. 366 took off casualties, and an American tug took off some of LST 80's crew. LST 80 was by then taking water in the tank space. A total of 129 survivors were taken on to 366.

Smyth and Grandage decided that it was worth making a towing attempt. A heavy 5-inch wire was manhandled over to LST 80 under extremely difficult conditions, and towing commenced shortly before midnight. LST 80 could not be steered as her tiller flat was flooded.

Grandage wrote: 'As the anchor was weighed, our bow fell off to port and tremendous difficulty was experienced in trying to get the ship back to the required course. 100 fathoms of our 5-inch stern wire, being used for towing, were paid out and various manoeuvres were tried to bring the ship round to the wind. "Emergency full ahead" on the port engine, and astern on the starboard engine, with the wheel "hard-a-starboard" failed, as did every other

manoeuvre. We were in the meantime drifting further away from the swept channel and towards various wrecks.'

The weather was just too bad and by 0200 the towing bridle had parted. Although LST 80 settled further during the night, prospects for towing still looked good. Rescue tugs had been expected by 0545, but these failed to appear.

Doggedly, Grandage took 366 alongside 80 once again, allowing fourteen officers and ratings from both ships to board her. Smyth insisted on returning to his ship, even though he was suffering from leg and hand injuries.

At about 0830 rescue tug *Antic* arrived and took over the task of towing. Smyth directed the towing arrangements from the forecastle of LST 80, and progress was made at 3–4 knots.

At about 0900 LST 80 hit another mine – this time on the starboard side forward. Almost all the forecastle party were injured. The impact blew Lieutenant-Commander

▲ Several RN LSTs were fitted with railway tracks in the tank space to enable them to carry rolling stock to Cherbourg. Seen here is LST 323. (IWM BU648)

◄ LST 215 converted to LSE(LC)51. (IWM FL7197)

Smyth and Shipwright Collins overboard. It was later reported that a body had been seen floating past the port side, face down.

LST 80 began to list to starboard and sink rapidly. Survivors were taken off by a boat from *Antic*, the main deck then being about 2 feet out of the water. LST 80 finally sank by the head about twenty minutes after the explosion.

FOIC London wrote: 'I am of the opinion that the efforts of LST 366 to salve LST 80 were outstanding.' Admiral of the Fleet, Jack Tovey, CGB, KBE, DSO, wrote: 'The commanding officer of LST 366 showed fine seamanship and I consider his action highly commendable.'

The body of Lieutenant-Commander Smyth drifted ashore on the Dutch island of Vlieland on 6 April. German Military HQ on the island noted that he was buried the next day in grave 79 of the Vlieland District Cemetery.

▶ LST 430 brings troops from Hamburg into Tilbury. (A. Wright collection)

▼ LST 80. Note her 12-pounder gun right over the stern. Many LSTs had the 12-pounder sited on the superstructure aft of the bridge. (IWM ref A23745)

11. Operations in the Final Months of the War

LST(3)s built in UK and Canada

During the last few months of 1943 it became apparent to the war planners that more LSTs would be required if Japan was to be overthrown. Plans were drawn up for the LST(3), originally code-named 'Seasack'. The feasibility of building these vessels at the Tosi yard at Taranto was studied but discarded in favour of British and Canadian yards.

The requirements for the LST(3) were that they should have the same beaching characteristics as the LST(2) but with a higher speed, slightly larger bow doors, and a greater height between decks. A ramp was to be provided from the upper deck to the tank space, replacing the elevator of the LST(2).

The main bottleneck was engines. The only ones available in sufficient quantity were steam reciprocating. These were from a frigate programme which had been cancelled as a consequence of the reduced submarine menace. The ships would be riveted as neither British nor Canadian yards were equipped to produce all-welded vessels.

The first orders were placed in December 1943 even though the detailed plans were not ready until January 1944. Eighty ships were ordered, of which 45 were to be built in the UK and 35 in Canada; a further 36 ships were to be ordered from Canada towards the end of 1944. The war ended before they were all built and the programme was scrapped. Those built in the UK were numbered 3001 up, and those built in Canada 3501 up. They were originally referred to as 'Transport Ferries'.

First of class trials

LST 3019 was used as the British-built LST(3) to undergo 'first of class trials' which took place early in 1945, probably in Scotland. The report of the trials, written by L. H. Maund (RALSCU), noted that 'The ship is a fine stiff job

▼LST 3505 enters Malta. Notice the two derricks (either side of the bridge) and the for'ard gun mounts. She was later named *Ravager*. (L. Everett collection)

▼ The ramp of an LST(3). Japanese PoWs unload supplies. (N. D. Britten)

and the accommodation is better than that of LST(2). She handles well and can sail in a 10½-knot convoy.'

However, six points were noted where the LST(3) was not as good as the LST(2):

1. The stern winch was seriously deficient in power.
2. Ballast pumps insufficiently powerful to allow speedy alterations of trim and draught.
3. The ship drew a foot more water which would increase the water gap.
4. The addition of derricks on the upper deck reduced the vehicle carrying capacity.
5. The view from the bridge over the stem was obstructed by ammunition lockers and screen.
6. The stern fairlead for the 5½ inch anchor wire was quite unsuitable and damaged two stern wires in two ships in half a dozen beachings.

LSTs transferred to RN from USN

From October to December 1944 35 LST(2)s were transferred to the RN from the USN. Two of the vessels were part of a later build of LST in the USA known as the LST 542 Class. These two, LSTs 538 and 1021, were equipped with ramps from the upper deck instead of the usual elevator. Twenty-five ships were transferred at various ports in the UK and the 11th LST Flotilla was formed by the ten LSTs transferred in the Mediterranean. (LSTs 12 and 426 were added to this mainly 6-davit Flotilla.)

Flotillas re-organized

Flotillas were re-organized many times between late 1944 and the end of the war. The detailed changes would occupy a book of their own, but in essence amounted to the following.

▶ LST 366 unloads at what is now known as the Montgomery Dock at Ostend. On the left of the picture is the Vissers Kaai, still there in 1991. A memorial to General Montgomery stands in approximately the position from where this photograph was taken. Of the other two Ostend hards, only the one at Schutsluisplein in the Tijdok is still recognizable in 1991. (R. W. Knights)

▶ One of the ex-USN LSTs transferred to the RN in 1944 in the Clyde – LST 315. Lieutenant Clune, RNR, was in command for a short time. (H. Clune collection)

▲At Ostend on 8 May 1945, LST 303 dresses ship in celebration of the end of the war in Europe – VE-Day. (K. H. Gazzard)

Build-up to Ostend and Antwerp: Under the control of Captain-in-Charge, Tilbury, from about 1 January 1945. Comprised 1st, 3rd, 5th, 7th and 9th Flotillas – approximately 37 ships. Gradually whittled down to thirteen ships by October 1945 when administration was taken over by CLSCU.

Far East: Vessels of 2nd, 4th, 6th and 10th Flotillas were refitted and sailed for India in readiness for Operation 'Zipper'. 12th Flotilla created late in 1945 for duties in SW Pacific area.

LST(3)s: Gradually made up into 50th, 51st and 52nd Flotillas for duties in the Far East.

LST 4 hits mine

LST 4 was one of the ten LSTs transferred to the RN from the USN in the Mediterranean in December 1944. She was on passage from Taranto to Piraeus on Sunday 14 January 1945. Approaching Piraeus at 1400, and just off Aegina Island, she struck a mine almost midships on the port side.

Power failed and she drifted towards rocks. However, she was able to start main engines again by 1425 and reached Piraeus under her own power. A destroyer and trawler stood by throughout.

LST 178 hits two mines

Just one week after LST 4 had been mined, sister vessel LST 178 sailed from Patras loaded with army personnel and vehicles bound for Corfu.

At 0930 on 21 January 1945 her commanding officer felt a heavy thump port forward followed a few seconds later by another explosion aft on the port quarter. This second explosion blew the port rudder off and badly damaged the port propeller. Shell plating was caved in

badly by the blast which also caused several small holes – the largest of these was 2 feet 6 inches by 8 inches. Fortunately, the only casualty sustained was a cut on the right ankle of a cook in the galley.

All compasses and steering gear were put out of action, so an MGB was signalled to lead her back to Patras. LST 178 was able to make 3½ knots. Although ordered to beach the ship, the commanding officer took her into Patras Harbour, fearing that the beaching would break her back.

The ship entered the harbour at 1400. Her two LCV(P)s were lowered in order to push her into the berth, and she was made fast by 1425.

Operation 'Nestegg'

Operation 'Nestegg' was a plan for the re-occupation of the Channel Islands following the signing of the German surrender on 9 May 1945. Among the armada to sail on 11 May were both British and US LSTs.

Sailing for Guernsey were US LSTs 516, 59, 137, 139 and 295 accompanied by British LST 324. US LST 516 went into the Old Harbour at St. Peter Port followed later by US LSTs 295 and 139. LST 324 went to L'Ancresse Bay with US LSTs 59 and 137 before returning to St. Peter Port.

Sailing for Jersey were US LSTs 521, 527 and 542 accompanied by British LST 238. These vessels beached at St. Aubin's Bay to a cheering crowd of islanders.

On 20 May four US LSTs berthed in Braye Harbour, Alderney, leaving LST 324 at anchor. It seems that all the LSTs were on their way back to England by 1700 that day, carrying with them many PoWs.

In September 1945 LST 365 became the first LST to enter St. Helier.

Operation 'Doomsday'

Operation 'Doomsday' was the code-name for the re-occupation of southern Norway. Little is known of this operation other than that a convoy sailed from Leith in Scotland at 1900 on 15 May 1945 in which were the following LSTs and destinations:
LSTs 214 and 239 for Stavanger.
LSTs 315 and 320 for Stavanger and Oslo.
LST 3019 for Stavanger and Kristiansand.
LSTs 65, 161, 162, 165, 180, 200 and 3014 for Oslo.

It is believed that this was the first operational use of LST(3)s – 3014 and 3019.

On 1 June the first of many LST convoys sailed from Hamburg to aid the operation. Destinations of Bergen and Trondheim were added to those above, using LSTs 198, 319, 365, 401 and 430. The farthest north destination was Tromsö, served by LSTs 165, 214 and 239 in early June 1945.

▶ Operation 'Nestegg' – LST
238 in the harbour at St.
Peter Port, Guernsey.
(A. Mellor collection)

▲ From the bridge of LST
365, an Operation
'Doomsday' convoy forms a
single line to enter the River
Elbe, en route to Hamburg.
(R. C. Pickering collection)

▶ LST 365 anchored at
Brunsbüttel, where the Kiel
Canal joins the River Elbe.
(R. C. Pickering collection)

Operation 'Crosskeys'

'Crosskeys' was the code-name for the opening up and
relief of Denmark. A convoy sailed in connection with this
operation from Leith for Copenhagen on 18 May 1945.
Among the vessels were LST 416, carrying stores, and
Tasajera.

John McFadden (Signalman LST 416): 'On the passage
from Leith we sighted several floating mines. We took on
several pilots before arriving off Copenhagen at midnight
on 22 May. We berthed in Copenhagen the next day and
were given a wonderful welcome. The ship was opened to
visitors, and we were showered with invitations to visit
homes and take trips around the city. The captured
German ships *Nürnberg* and *Prinz Eugen* were in dock.

◀ LST 365 is a welcome sight for the people of Stavanger. (R. C. Pickering collection)

◀Officers, crew and dog – LST 401. The plaque lists the operations in which 401 took part. The words at the foot of the plaque read 'Ubique Pongos' ('Soldiers every-where') (C. Hooper collection)

◀LST 403 has been fitted with a flying bridge to assist visibility over LCT 2120. This view is thought to show her leaving the UK for the Far East. (L. Everett collection)

▶ LST 2 passing through the Suez Canal. Note the awnings over the upper deck. (L. Robson)

▼ Operation 'Zipper'. LST 410 carries identification serial number 'C1' as Flotilla Leader. LST 538 alongside carries 'C2'. (H. Blake)

'We sailed for Kristiansand and left there for Leith on 3 June, passing seventeen LSTs on passage. We left Leith on 10 June and went to Stavanger, Bergen and Trondheim before arriving back in Leith on 21 June.'

Tasajera sailed through the Kiel Canal from Brunsbüttel to Kiel, into the Baltic Sea, and discharged at Nakskov in Denmark before returning to the UK in August 1944.

Operation 'Zipper'

From late 1944 LSTs began to be removed from the build-up convoys to Ostend and Antwerp, and refitted. They were to be 'tropicalized' for operation in the Far East, and many were fitted with LCT launchways.

The first ships to leave the UK for Calcutta were LSTs 8, 11, 163, 199 and 403 of the 4th Flotilla. Senior Officer was Commander Clitherow in LST 199. They left Milford Haven at 0900 on 19 December 1944, joining convoy KMS73 by mid-afternoon.

En route it was discovered that LSTs 11 and 163 had 5.25-foot propellers; LSTs 8 and 199 had standard 4.93-foot propellers; and LST 403 had 4.58-foot propellers fitted. As a consequence the flotilla took its speed from LST 403.

The ships spent Christmas Day rolling in Force 4 to 8 winds, but passed Gibraltar safely. On entering Port Said, LST 163 suffered a steering failure and collided with a merchant ship. Leaving Port Said on 4 January 1945, the ships arrived in Cochin on 21 January, and Calcutta on 31 January.

Many more LSTs followed over the next few months until the invasion force was at full strength. About 70 LST(2)s and (3)s were shown as being 'in India' in September 1945.

Operation 'Zipper' is often referred to as 'the invasion that never was'. The atom bomb was dropped on Hiroshima on 6 August and on Nagasaki three days later. Japan surrendered on 15 August. About 50 LSTs beached in the Port Swettenham and Port Dickson area on 9 September, totally unopposed.

Many months of clearing-up operations followed around Singapore and the islands of Borneo, Java and Sumatra. Dutch women and children were taken out to hospital ships and PoWs were transported from the notorious Changi Jail. At least three LSTs (160, 324 and 419) travelled as far as Brisbane, Australia, returning Australian troops to their homeland. LSTs 303 and 324 are believed to have gone to Japan.

Andy Robertson was a 'Jack Dusty' in LST 160: 'We sailed to Borneo, where the sky seemed to lay heavy on your shoulders. The heat was dense. The wind could be heard in the trees but it never reached the ground.

'We were sent to a small port in the north of the island to collect some Japanese men, women and children who had been brought there to start a colony. An appalling sight met our eyes – there were hundreds of them. The filth was something we had never seen before. They had

◀Operation 'Zipper'. LST 8 (C119) off-loads at Port Dickson, 12 September 1945. (D. Robb)

▼Sonny Griggs aboard LST 199. (S. Griggs)

no food; they were utterly demoralized; there were dead and dying; the smell made us sick. They suffered from malaria, typhoid, beri-beri, dysentery and ulcers.

'We sailed for Jesselton, North Borneo. There were several burials at sea en route. It took some time to get everyone off the ship as we had beached some distance from the shore. The next day, the Australian soldiers marched a squad of Japanese soldiers on board to clean up.

'With 400 Aussie troops on board, we sailed into Brisbane with LST 419 on the morning of 16 November 1945. As we steamed up the river, we were cheered from every jetty and headland. We were met by a brass band and lorries took the soldiers off to a hospital camp. We suffered more breakdowns whilst tied up in Brisbane than when we were in the thick of it all – no one seemed to mind, and we were still there in March.'

LST 199 mined
On 5 November 1945, LST 199 struck a mine in Surabaya seriously damaging her engines and shafts. She was considered uneconomical to repair and was used as a temporary refrigeration ship.

LSTs returned to US authorities
With the end of the war against Japan, there was a reducing need for the LSTs. Many of those in the Far East were sailed for Subic Bay in the Philippines and handed back there. Others were loaded with various types of LCP and sailed from the UK back to the USA.

The War Diary for 19 January 1946 records the frigates *Gardiner* and *Berry* together with LSTs 165, 217, 238, 358 and 416 on passage in the North Atlantic, all being returned to the USA.

Alan Birmingham (LST 416): 'After refitting in Antwerp we returned to the UK and the ship was detailed for return to the USA. She was reduced to a skeleton crew to sail across the Atlantic. Bad weather forced the convoy to shelter in the Azores for 48 hours. Three days out from the Azores, the bad weather returned. Forty-foot waves battered the ships, heavy seas and wind reduced progress to less than one mile in 24 hours. It was a nightmare voyage and we suffered an 11-foot split in the bilges. However, we made it to Norfolk Navy Yard, where we had ammunitioned the ship in 1943, and paid off in February 1946.'

▶ LST 1021 ready to load at
Kyaukpyu, on the Arakan
Coast of Burma, between
Akyab and Ramree, in
November 1945. (A. Smith)

▼ LST 380 transporting
Dutch women and children
from Java to Singapore.
(W. Sutcliffe collection)

▶ In command of LST 304 en route for Hong Kong is Lieutenant-Commander J. F. G. Fotheringham. He joined 304 in November 1942 and left her in Singapore late in 1945. (IWM ref SE4962)

▼ The first two LSTs of the 12th Flotilla into Brisbane, Australia – LSTs 160 and 419. (A. Robertson collection)

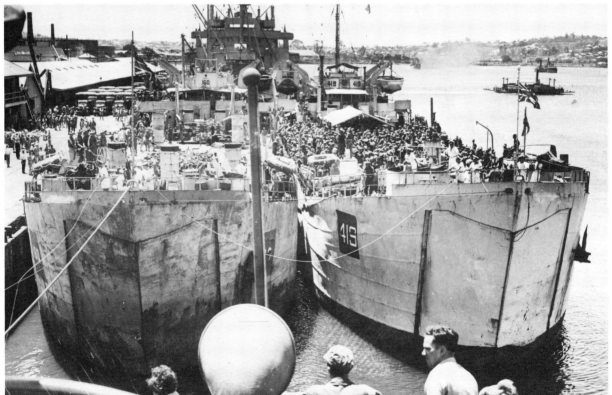

12. The LST After the War

The Atlantic Steam Navigation Company

Frank Bustard had worked for the White Star Line from the age of 16, and by 1934 he was the Passenger Traffic Manager. When the Cunard Line merged with the White Star Line in that year, Bustard decided that he didn't want to work for the new company. He left and formed the Atlantic Steam Navigation Company Limited two years later.

Called up for the Army Reserve during the Second World War, he was present at the LST(2) trials near Liverpool in 1943. He immediately saw their commercial potential. After the war, his entrepreneurial skills helped him secure the charter of three LST(3)s for a period of three years. The vessels were LSTs 3512, 3519 and 3534. They were subsequently named *Empire Celtic*, *Empire Baltic* and *Empire Cedric*.

The first commercial 'ro-ro' voyage began on 11 September 1946, when *Empire Baltic* sailed from Tilbury to Rotterdam with 64 vehicles for the Dutch government. The vessels were used to ferry thousands of Army vehicles between Tilbury and Hamburg up to 1955, and Antwerp thereafter. *Empire Doric* (ex-LST 3041) joined the fleet in 1948.

On 21 May 1948 the company started their Preston–Larne 'drive on/drive off' service for commercial vehicles and trailers, the inaugural run being undertaken by *Empire Cedric*. *Empire Doric* also worked on the service.

The *Baltic* and *Doric* were chartered by the British government to augment RN LST(3)s for the evacuation of the British Army from Egypt in 1952. They were on a 6-month charter from January of that year and operated in

◄ Ex-LST(3) 3043 – renamed *Messina* in 1947 and carrying the pennant number L3043. Seen here leaving Malta, she has causeways secured to her sides and is towing a Rhino ferry. (J. D. Fyffe collection)

▲ Royal Navy LST 3516 *Striker* in the background with Atlantic Steam Navigation Company vessel *Empire Baltic* at Tobruk in February 1952. (M. Bustard collection)

◀ *Empire Gaelic* arrives at Douglas, Isle of Man, with a cargo of buses from Preston, *c.* 1955. (M. Bustard collection)

◀ *Empire Nordic* in Atlantic Steam Navigation livery with trailers on her upper deck. (J. Clarkson)

the Mediterranean (Tripoli, Malta, Benghazi, Tobruk, Port Said and Famagusta). They returned to the UK in July 1952.

In 1956 ASN vessels were again called upon. Operation 'Musketeer' was put into action following the Egyptian government's decision to nationalize the Suez Canal Company.

For more detailed reading on the ASN, see the bibliography.

The Royal Fleet Auxiliary LSLs

The RFA Landing Ship Logistics are the modern military version of the roll-on/roll-off passenger and cargo ferry. With a displacement of 5,674 tons, these five civilian manned ships were seen as the ultimate development of the LST. With a range of 8,000 nautical miles at 15 knots, they were designed to transport in the region of 300 troops together with tanks, vehicles and heavy equipment. Fitted with bow doors and a stern ramp, they are capable of operating directly on to a beach.

RFA *Sir Bedivere* was part of the amphibious warfare force during the Falklands operation in 1982. In San Carlos water she was hit by a bomb which failed to explode. At Fitzroy, her sister ship, *Sir Galahad*, suffered so severe damage that she was later sunk as a war grave. *Sir Tristram*, after being abandoned during the same attack, was later

lifted home and extensively rebuilt. On her return to the UK, *Sir Bedivere* brought home the remains of 64 servicemen killed in action. Her commanding officer was decorated for distinguished service.

Epilogue

And so ends this history of the Royal Navy's LSTs. The words of two LST crewmen sum up.

John Holden (LST 418): 'These great, 328-foot long vessels had surprised everyone who served in them. When crews first saw them in America in late 1942 and early 1943, they doubted their ability to sail across the Atlantic, never mind cover the thousands of miles that they did with maximum loads, sometimes in mountainous seas and, in the Med, almost continuous action. The engineering department did a first class job throughout the difficult and often scary conditions.'

Andy Robertson (LST 160): 'The LSTs were a breed of their own. We swore at them in bad weather, yet we protected them, with violence if need be, if we heard them being made fun of by someone off a "big ship". We hated them – yet we loved them. They were happy ships.'

A reminder of the poem . . .

'. . . *So at last I believe they almost agree,*
She's a useful old tub . . . that LST.'

▶ The founder members of the LST & Landing Craft Association. From left to right, back row: Arthur Bailey, George Townsend, Ted Hewitt, Les Marren, Cliff Bellamy. Front row: Henry Baker, Alan Mellor, Jim Travers, Bill Chalk. (W. Chalk collection)

▶ The Royal Fleet Auxiliary, *Sir Bedivere*, L3004, is a Landing Ship Logistic (LSL). Helicopters can be operated day and night from her two helicopter platforms. (Thomas A. Adams collection)

▶ Pongos and LSTs – the efforts of both will never be forgotten. (IWM ref NA4256)

13. Technical Details, LST(2)

Extracted from various naval records and builders' records.

While every care has been taken in compiling this data, it should be noted that the various publications consulted did contain slightly differing information.

LST Technical Instructions

Description: Landing Ships Tank (previously known as ATLs) are designed primarily to disembark on beaches where no unloading facilities exist, and can be used to transport tanks and their crews on long ocean passages. They can also transport and disembark a variety of vehicles or a Landing Craft Tank (unloaded) can be transported and launched sideways, or liquid and solid cargoes can be carried.

In the event of a withdrawal, ships can evacuate tanks and MT, stores, animals or large bodies of troops.

These large capacity, shallow draught vessels with unique loading arrangements may be considered as general purpose carriers of high operational value.

They have no protection except around the guns, the wheelhouse and conning station, and are not designed to take part in any initial assault on defended beaches.

The ship may be described as consisting of a tank garage under a parking place and over ballast compartments flanked by storerooms, the garage and parking place communicating by means of a lift.

The metacentric height of such a vessel unloaded is extremely high (30 feet) resulting in heavy rolling with a short period. This can be reduced by loading weight as high and as far outboard as possible. The light draught reduces the ship's manoeuvrability at slow speeds. This can be improved by increasing the draught forward by filling the ballast compartment.

Loading: Since the number of permutations of combinations of different types of vehicles, tanks and guns which can be put in an LST is almost infinite, it is impossible to give exact capacity figures. Where the load has consisted entirely of small vehicles, up to 120 have been carried.

With larger assorted vehicles and no tanks, a good planning figure would be about 70.

Tanks can only be carried in the tank deck. Vehicles and guns can be carried in the tank deck or on the upper deck, subject to the limitation that unless loaded and unloaded by crane, nothing can be put on the upper deck that weighs more than 10 tons (lifting capacity of truck elevator) or which measures more than 23 feet 6 inches × 13 feet 6 inches (dimensions of truck elevator hatch).

There is space in the tank deck for 18 Churchill or 20 Sherman tanks, stowed two abreast, but the number which can actually be carried is in practice limited by operational requirements. LST(2) are designed to beach carrying a 500-ton load, 72 tons of fuel, 50 tons of water and with a full complement of troops on a beach gradient of 1 in 50, drawing 3 feet 1 inch forward and 9 feet 6 inches aft. To load the tank deck to its full capacity with tanks brings the weight of tanks up to 700–720 tons. If vehicles are also carried on the upper deck, the load might come to about 850 tons. This may be acceptable if the ship is to unload on to a pontoon causeway, Rhino ferry, hard or jetty; or to beach on a really steep beach, say 1 in 30 or better. It is not acceptable if the ship is to beach on a flatter beach and the load must be reduced proportionately to the gradient of the beach.

Weight of load in relation to beach gradient must therefore always be considered if a substantial number of tanks are carried. If, however, only vehicles are carried, it is unlikely that the weight of load will come up to the designed beaching load of 500 tons, and the number of vehicles which can be carried is therefore limited only by the space available and the size of vehicles.

Dimensions:

Length (oa)	327ft 9in
Beam	50ft 1½in
Height above mdd of mast	76ft 0in
Height above mdd of conning position	31ft 6in
Height above mdd of wheelhouse	24ft 0in
Height above mdd of upper deck	16ft 6in

Displacement: *Light*: 1,435 tons. Draught: 2ft 6in

forward; 6ft 1in aft (no fuel, fresh water, ballast, tanks or MT). *Beaching:* 2,100 tons. Draught: 3ft 1in forward; 9ft 6in aft (70 tons fuel, 40 tons fresh water, no ballast, 500 tons of tanks. Slope of keel 1 in 50). *Ocean:* 3,800 tons. Draught: 7ft 1in forward; 13ft 6in aft (all ballast full, full fuel and fresh water, no tanks or MT).

Speed: Approx. 10–11½ knots. Sea-going economical 8¾ knots.

Endurance: 19,000 nautical miles at 10 knots (loaded), 21,000 nautical miles at 10 knots (light), 23,000 nautical miles at 8¾ knots (loaded).

Propellers: Twin screw diameter 7ft 0in. Pitch 4.935ft or 4.583ft. Four blades each. Rotation: Port, outboard; Starboard, outboard.

Machinery: *Main engines:* Two General Motors Type 12–567 V12 diesel. 900hp each.

Generators: Three 100kW, 120–240 volts DC. Average consumption 12gph. Refrigerating plant fitted.

Auxiliary boiler: One oil-fired, Cleaver Brookes Co. for steam heating.

Ballast pumps: Two 30hp, 1,500gal/min. Gardner-Denver centrifugal, driven by Century 30hp 230volt DC motors.

Fire and Bilge pumps: Two 30hp 250gal/min. Goulds Pumps Inc. centrifugal.

Elevator winch: 20hp motor sited on deck, 2 × 18-inch gipsies, 2 × 24-inch diameter lift. Drums by Warsaw Elec. Co. NY. Will take a 10-ton load. Four portable guide posts require to be fitted in hold before lift can be used. Dimensions: 23ft 6in fore and aft, 13ft 6in athwartships. Speed: Lift raised in 56 seconds. Lift lowered in 52 seconds (approx. 2½ minutes per vehicle complete operation).

Boat winch: 25hp GEC motor. Welin Davit & Boat Corp. winch NJ, type BWB with horizontal rope drums.

Ramp motor: GEC 10hp mechanism by Western Gear Works, Seattle. Maximum angle of depression of ramp 26°, ramp resting on beach will take 50-ton load. Length of ramp, 23ft 3½in. Ramp operated by 10hp electric motor driving a cross shaft over which 2 × ¾in chains pass. These chains are attached to the ramp and after passing over the shaft are led to a cable locker and secured. Hand brake is also fitted for lowering. Ramp is pulled home on to its seating by bottle screws. When ramp is fully lowered and supported by ship's structure, the outboard end projects 2 feet below the line of keel. Ramp chains are designed to handle weight of ramp only.

Bow door: GEC 3hp mechanism by Western Gear Works, Seattle. Driving a rack and pinion gear. Doors are pulled together by ratchet device. Minimum height of entrance 13ft 7in. Minimum width 13ft 3in.

▶ The General Motors 12-567 diesel engine with Falk clutch and reduction gears. (Falk Corporation)

Air compressors: Two vertical, 2–stage, aircooled, 10 cu.ft/min. 150psi.

Capstan engine: 20hp motor driven, and steam winch for anchor handling.

Steering gear: Steering motor Cracker-Wheeler 10hp, mechanism by Baldwin Locomotion Works, Philadelphia. Twin rudders telemotor control. Hand steering from steering gear compartment.

Cargo hatch: A cargo hatch is fitted with hatch covers and tarpaulin is fitted at the after end of the deck. This has no lift but is plumbed by two 30cwt derricks in the case of ships which have carried out Alteration & Amendment No. 74. Dimensions: 29ft 6in fore and aft, 12ft 6in athwartships.

Tank deck: 231 feet long (level portion only) × 29 feet 6 inch wide × 12ft 0 inch high. Maximum height is 13 feet. Limiting height for vehicles entering tank deck is 11ft 3in. For vehicles entering elevator, 10ft 6in. Ventilation of tank deck is by natural supply through upper deck gratings and exhaust by fans through tall portable cylinders on upper deck.

Fuel: For ship's machinery. Diesel oil. 607 tons stowage capacity. An additional 890 tons can be carried in ballast tanks. Where beaching operations are involved, fuel carried must be reduced to the minimum required for the operation. 10 tons per day's steaming at 10 knots should be allowed and about 2 tons per day to run generators, etc., in harbour. 300 gallons of petrol can be stored on deck for Landing Craft.

Water capacity: Domestic, 446 tons. Note: operational requirements may necessitate very considerable reduction in amount of water carried so that ship may be in lightest possible trim for beaching on a flat beach.

Complement: 7 officers and 53 men.

Capacity for 12 officers and 165 men in addition to ship's complement. Considerably larger numbers can be carried on short passages, or in the tropics where sleeping on the upper deck can be accepted. Note: the galley is adequate to provide hot meals for 250 men in addition to ship's company.

Armament: Six 20mm Oerlikons. One 12-pounder sited aft. Four PAC. (Some vessels fitted with twin Oerlikons).

Anchors/Cables: One 5,000lb Port forward with 120 fathoms 1¼-inch chain cable. One 3,000lb Danforth aft with 150 fathoms 1⅝-inch diameter steel wire rope. Each anchor has its own capstan. Spare mooring wire, 45 fathoms, 3½-inch.

Casualties: In stretcher racks (where fitted), 144. In troop's quarters 135.

For short passages, 200 plus can be carried on the tank deck in stretchers.

Life–rafts: Ten × 25 persons each.

Radio and navigational equipment: 2 × TCE transmitters, RAO/RBL receiver, RBH bridge, DAE (D/F) TW12 emergency broadcast receiver. RG2 transmitter, RG receiver. QH2 – two per squadron. H/F, D/F – one per six ships. Radar: Type 271P, LSTs 199 and 324; Type 271Q, LSTs 13, 33, 180, 217 and 322; Type 79B, LST 365. Hailing equipment Types 431, 432. Sperry MkXIV gyro compass with 108v stand-by battery, repeaters at conning platform, wheelhouse and after steering position. Two × USN(1) magnetic.

Smoke apparatus: The following are fitted with Besler fog-making machine Model 317: LSTs 9, 13 (now FDT 13), 62, 65, 80, 163, 164, 180, 215, 216 (now FDT 216), 217 (now FDT 217), 322, 423 and 430. The following carry smoke floats: LSTs 80, 215, 238, 239, 302, 304, 320, 323, 361, 364, 365, 367, 402, 428. (Author's note: it seems likely that this is not a complete list.)

Food stowage: Meat, 90 days. Dry provisions, 90 days. Green vegetables, 14 days. Potatoes, 21 days. Refrigerating capacity, 21 tons (841.7ft³).

Notes on ship handling: Data obtained on LST 320

Turning data

At speed 9 knots:	15 degrees rudder	30 degrees rudder
Tactical diameter:	550 yards	375 yards
Time to turn 180°:	3 minutes 56 seconds	2 minutes 57 seconds
Alter course 90°:	Advance 450 yards;	Advance 360 yards;
	transfer 320 yards;	transfer 190 yards;
	2 minutes 7 seconds	1 minute 36 seconds

Notes on stopping

(a) Coming to single anchor from 9 knots: stop at 4 cables.

(b) When stopping from 9 knots, ship had not completely lost way after advancing 6½ cables in 7 minutes, against a stream of about 1 knot.

(c) When stopping from 9 knots and going Full Astern immediately, ship lost way after advancing 2½ cables in 3 minutes.

Speed – Revolutions

220 revolutions is equal to 9 knots. Working about this datum, approx. 30 revs go to 1 knot. Maximum continuous revolutions should not exceed 250 per minute at a displacement of 4,100 (American) tons. For short periods or in an emergency, revolutions can be increased to 275 under above conditions.

One-third speed can be taken as:	110 revolutions
Two-thirds speed can be taken as:	190 revolutions
Standard speed can be taken as:	250 revolutions

14. Individual Ships

Bachaquero Launched 7 May 1937; commissioned in RN 10 July 1941
Built by Furness Shipbuilding and North Eastern Marine Engineering Co. Took part in invasions of Madagascar, North Africa, Normandy. The first ever tank landing ship. Paid off 6 Aug 1945.

Misoa Launched 22 June 1937; commissioned in RN 11 July 1941
Built by Furness Shipbuilding and North Eastern Marine Engineering Co. Took part in invasions of North Africa, Pantelleria, Sicily, Taranto, Normandy. Used as a Coastal Forces Depot Ship during the invasion of Normandy. Paid off, date uncertain.

Tasajera Launched 3 Mar 1938; commissioned in RN Approx Dec 1941
Built by Furness Shipbuilding and North Eastern Marine Engineering Co. Took part in invasions of North Africa, Normandy. Assisted in relief of Denmark. Damaged 19 July 1944 when she dragged into a 'Gooseberry' breakwater off Normandy. Paid off, date uncertain.

Boxer Launched 12 Dec 1942; commissioned in RN 10 April 1943
Built by Harland & Wolff, Belfast. Took part in invasions of Sicily, Salerno, Anzio. Later converted to serve as a Fighter Direction Ship. Paid off, date uncertain.

Bruiser Launched 24 Oct 1942; commissioned in RN 12 Mar 1943
Built by Harland & Wolff, Belfast. Took part in invasions of Sicily, Salerno, Anzio, southern France. Operated in the Adriatic. Later became a training ship. Paid off, date uncertain.

Thruster Launched 24 Sept 1942; commissioned in RN 28 Jan 1943
Built by Harland & Wolff, Belfast. Took part in invasions of Sicily, Salerno, Anzio, southern France. Operated in the Adriatic. Paid off, date uncertain.

LST 2 Launched 19 Sept 1942; commissioned 29 Nov 1944
Built by Dravo Corporation, Pittsburg, Pa. Served as US

▶ HMS *Boxer* after conversion to Fighter Direction Ship. (F. Thomas collection)

▲ LST 2 loads up at   Operation 'Zipper'.
Southampton in 1945 for   (L. Robson)

LST 2 until commissioned in the RN. On trials in Scotland during Dec 1944. Took part in invasions of North Africa, Sicily, Salerno, southern France(?), and Normandy. At Tyne Dec 1944–Aug 1945 for preparation for Far East. Sailed from Southampton 17 Aug 1945 to Port Said and then Bombay, arriving 21 Sept 1945. Railway lines installed (metre guage?). Various trips between Madras, Singapore and Trincomalee. Ship de-stored at Changi Mar 1946. Arrived Subic Bay, Philippines, 1 Apr 1946, and returned to USA, 13 Apr 1946.

LST 3 Launched 19 Sept 1942; commissioned in RN 24 Dec 1944.
Built by Dravo Corporation, Pittsburg, Pa. Served as US LST 3 until commissioned in the RN. Took part in the invasions of Sicily and southern France. Transferred to the RN from the USN at Bizerta. Known to have visited Messina, Taranto, Brindisi, Bari, Venice, Trieste, Naples, Piraeus, Malta and Gibraltar. Was at Taranto from 28 Sept 1945 for repairs. Sailed back to USA by RN crew Apr 1946, and returned to the USN 12 May 1946.

LST 4 Launched 9 Oct 1942; commissioned in RN 24 Dec 1944.
Built by Dravo Corporation, Pittsburg, Pa. Served as US LST 4 until commissioned in the RN. Took part in the invasions of Sicily, Salerno, Anzio and southern France. Struck a mine 14 Jan 1945 while on passage between Taranto and Piraeus. Was able to make Piraeus. Stayed there until about June when she went to Alexandria. In Malta for repairs 10–24 Oct 1945. Sailed back to USA by RN crew early 1946. Port screw lost en route, and was towed to Norfolk, Virginia, by another LST.

LST 5 Launched 3 Oct 1942; commissioned 18 Nov 1944.
Built by Dravo Corporation, Pittsburg, Pa. Served as US LST 5 until commissioned in the RN. Took part in the invasions of Sicily, Salerno and Normandy. At Belfast for machinery refit 22 Jan–11 Apr 1945. Sailed for Far East during the summer of 1945. Paid off 19 Feb 1946. It is thought that she may have been subsequently scuttled in the Bay of Bengal.

LST 8 Launched 29 Oct 1942; commissioned in RN 23 Mar 1943.
Built by Dravo Corporation, Pittsburg, Pa. Sailed from New York for the Mediterranean in convoy UGS8A, 14 May 1943. Took part in the invasions of Sicily, Reggio, Salerno, Anzio, Normandy and Malaya. At Barry for docking 4–6 May 1944. At Liverpool for refit in September 1944. Paid off Subic Bay, Philippines, 4 May 1946.

LST 9 Launched 14 Nov 1942; commissioned in RN 20 Mar 1943.
Built by Dravo Corporation, Pittsburg, Pa. Sailed from New York for the Mediterranean in convoy UGS8A, 14 May 1943. Took part in invasions of Sicily, Reggio, Vibo Valentia, Anzio, Normandy, Malaya. Performed a regular ferry service across the Messina Straits. Noted as having made 57 crossings. At Leith for refit 11 Apr–3 June 1944. Sailed from Leith in time for D-Day. Operated on the shuttle service to Normandy. Repairs carried out at various times at Thames, Portsmouth and Southampton from June 1944 to February 1945. Collided with a jetty at Tilbury Dock 25 Jan 1945. At Antwerp for minor defects in April 1945, and was refitted there from May to June. Paid off at Subic Bay, Philippines, 4 May 1946.

LST 11 Launched 18 Nov 1942; commissioned in RN 23 Mar 1943.
Built by Dravo Corporation, Pittsburg, Pa. Sailed from New York for the Mediterranean in convoy UGS8A, 14 May 1943. Took part in invasions of Anzio, Normandy and Malaya. (It is uncertain whether she took part in the other Mediterranean landings.) At Cardiff in May 1944 for defects. Visited Thames and Portsmouth for repairs during June and August 1944. At Cardiff for refit 12 Sept–23 Oct 1944. Paid off at Subic Bay, Philippines, 13 April 1946.

LST 12 Launched 7 Dec 1942; commissioned in RN 26 Mar 1943
Built by Dravo Corporation, Pittsburg, Pa. Trials carried out in Mississippi River. Sailed via Norfolk Navy Yard, Virginia, to New York. Sailed from New York in convoy UGS8A, 14 May 1943 for the Mediterranean via Bermuda,

but broke down en route. Took part in invasions of Sicily, Reggio, Salerno, southern France. The only British LST(2) to take part in the invasion of southern France in August 1944. Struck a mine 13 Nov 1943 but made Ferryville under her own power. Operated between Italy, Yugoslavia and Greece from Sept 1944 to Jan 1945. At Antwerp for refit from August to October 1945. Paid off at New York, 5 Jan 1946.

LST 13 (FDT 13) Launched 5 Jan 1943; commissioned in RN 3 Apr 1943.
Built by Dravo Corporation, Pittsburg, Pa. Sailed from Halifax, Nova Scotia, in convoy SC131 carrying general cargo, 18 May 1943. Returned to Halifax with defects and sailed with convoy SC132 26 May 1943 arriving Liverpool 11 June 1943. Went to the Clyde area. Stayed there until November 1943 when she sailed for Southampton. Back in the Clyde by 31 December and taken in hand at Messrs John Brown for conversion to Fighter Direction Tender. Took part in invasion of Normandy. (*See* also LSTs 216 and 217.)

LSTs 33, 35, 36, 37. Launched N/A; commisioned in RN N/A
Built by Dravo Corporation, Pittsburg, Pa. All four at Anzio. 33, 35, 36 at southern France, Adriatic. Transferred from the USN to the Hellenic Navy 18 Aug 1943. Operated partly under direction of Captain LST. All four sailed from New Orleans via New York, Boston and Halifax (convoy SC144) for Scotland, arriving 26 Oct 1943. Then proceeded to London's West India Docks to unload lumber carried from Newark, then back to

Scotland. They sailed for the Mediterranean on 7 Dec 1943 less LST 35 which required generator repairs. She followed on 4 Jan 1944. LST 37 ran aground on passage from Catania to Bizerta on 6 Jan 1944 and was subsequently declared a loss.

LST 62 Launched 23 Nov 1942; commissioned in RN 4 Mar 1943.
Built by Jeffersonville Boat & Machine Co., Indiana. Took part in invasions of Reggio, Anzio, Normandy. Converted for carriage of rolling stock. Paid off at New York 10 June 1946.

LST 63 Launched 19 Dec 1942; commissioned in RN 29 Mar 1943
Built by Jeffersonville Boat & Machine Co., Indiana. Sailed in convoy SC131 from Halifax, Nova Scotia, on 18 May 1943 carrying general cargo. Arrived Liverpool 31 May 1943 (with LSTs 64, 164, 198 and 200). Sailed from Clyde 25 June 1943 as part of convoy KMS19 for the invasion of Sicily. Took part in invasions of Sicily, Salerno, Anzio, Normandy. Paid off at New York 17 Dec 1945. Appears in Imperial War Museum film AYY 509 at Sousse. Imperial War Museum photograph A19146 depicts her south of Naples with a barrage balloon.

LST 64 Launched 8 Jan 1943; commissioned in RN 2 Apr 1943.
Built by Jeffersonville Boat & Machine Co., Indiana. Sailed from Halifax, Nova Scotia, on 18 May 1943 in convoy SC131 carrying general cargo (with LSTs 63, 164, 198 and 200). Arrived Liverpool 31 May 1943. Sailed from Clyde

▶Ex-LST 13 serving as FDT 13 during Operation 'Neptune'. (J. Lindop)

25 June 1943 as part of KMS19 for the invasion of Sicily. Took part in invasion of Sicily (possibly also Salerno). Stranded at Naples in rough weather 26 Feb 1944. Towed to Ferryville – considerably damaged and laid aside. Paid off into Care & Maintenance 7 July 1944 and handed back to US authorities at Palermo 15 Oct 1945.

LST 65 Launched 7 Dec 1942; commissioned in RN 18 Mar 1943.
Built by Jeffersonville Boat & Machine Co., Indiana. Sailed from New York in convoy UGS8A, 14 May 1943. Took part in invasions of Sicily, Vibo Valentia, Anzio and Normandy. Badly damaged during Operation 'Ferdy'. Converted for carriage of rolling stock. Assisted in relief of Norway. Reduced to Care & Maintenance 18 July 1945. Believed loaded with LCT 2243 at Portsmouth for return to USA. Paid off and transferred to US custody at New York 5 Jan 1946. Photographs at Imperial War Museum: one in Foxhill Collection; NA4378 (with LST 302); NA6422–24 at Vibo Valentia.

LST 76 Launched 14 Apr 1943; commissioned in RN 24 Dec 1944
Built by Jeffersonville Boat & Machine Co., Indiana. Served as US LST 76 until commissioned in the RN. Took part in the invasion of southern France. Noted at Taranto for docking 2 Feb–10 Mar 1945. Repairs at Rosyth and on the Clyde during 1945. Devonport for repairs 19–25 Feb 1946. Transferred to USN at Norfolk, Virginia, USA, 23 Apr 1946.

LST 77 Launched 21 Apr 1943; commissioned in RN 24 Dec 1944.
Built by Jeffersonville Boat & Machine Co., Indiana. Served as US LST 77 before commissioning in the RN. Took part in the invasion of southern France. Operated mainly in the Adriatic as part of 11th LST Flotilla, carrying troops, partisans and civilians. Known to have visited Piraeus, Trieste, Patras, Prevezia(?), Ancona, Taranto. Dry-docked in Malta October 1945. Prepared for return to USA in Malta February–March 1946. Returned to US custody 12 May 1946.

LST 79 Launched 8 May 1943; commissioned in RN 17 July 1943
Built by Jeffersonville Boat & Machine Co., Indiana. Believed sailed from USA in convoy UGS15, 16 Aug 1943. Sunk by aerial torpedo in Ajaccio Harbour, 30 Sept 1943.

LST 80 Launched 18 May 1943; commissioned in RN 19 July 1943
Built by Jeffersonville Boat & Machine Co., Indiana. Believed sailed from New York in convoy UGS15, 16 Aug 1943. Operated in the Mediterranean before returning to UK. At Falmouth Feb–Mar 1944. Took part in invasion of Normandy. Operated in the shuttle service between London, Ostend and Antwerp. Struck two mines while in convoy ATM97 and sank 20 Mar 1945. Photograph at Imperial War Museum: A23745. Also appears in IWM film ADM1254 (D-Day).

◀ **LST 76 at Taranto in 1944.** The figure '76' and the words 'The Gateway to Glory' are painted above her bow doors. (F. J. Gray)

LST 81 (LSE 1). Launched 28 May 1943; commissioned in RN 30 July 1943
Built at Jeffersonville Boat & Machine Co., Indiana. Converted to LSE 1. Exact date unknown, but does not appear to have done any work as an LST. Believed returned to USA and paid off 21 May 1946.

LST 82 (LSE 2). Launched 9 June 1943; commissioned in RN 2 Aug 1943
Built at Jeffersonville Boat & Machine Co., Indiana. Converted to LSE 2 at Norfolk, Virginia, USA, 2 Sept 1943. Left Norfolk for Oran December 1943 in convoy carrying US troops. Sailed to Algiers and Bougie, then Malta. Left Malta February 1944, arrived Portland Mar 1944. Anchored off Normandy approx. D+5, repairing small vessels until end of July. Back to Portsmouth then Larne, Northern Ireland. Took part in the invasion of southern France and visited Toulon and Marseilles. Visited Ajaccio, Naples, Taranto, Palermo, Malta, Aden, Cochin, Bombay, Madras. Transported Doctors and Nurses from Colombo to Sumatra. Went to Batavia, Java, then Singapore at Christmas 1945. Ship returned to USA and paid off 21 May 1946.

LST 157 Launched 31 Oct 1942; commissioned in RN 30 Nov 1944
Built by Missouri Valley Bridge & Iron Co., Evansville, Indiana. Served as US LST 157 before commissioning in the RN. Took part in the invasions of Sicily, Salerno, Normandy and Malaya. Believed taken in hand for preparation for service in the Far East at Penarth Pontoon Co., Penarth, early 1945. Transferred to the USN at Subic Bay, Philippines, 13 Apr 1946.

LST 159 Launched 21 Nov 1942; commissioned in RN 4 Mar 1943
Built by Missouri Valley Bridge & Iron Co., Evansville, Indiana. Sailed from New York in convoy UGS9, 28 May 1943. Took part in invasions of Sicily, Anzio and Normandy. Selected for conversion to LSE(LC) 54, but conversion was cancelled. Transferred to USN at Norfolk, Virginia, USA, 23 Apr 1946.

LST 160 Launched 30 Nov 1942; commissioned in RN 10 Mar 1943.
Built by Missouri Valley Bridge & Iron Co., Evansville, Indiana. Sailed from New York in convoy UGS8A, 14 May 1943. Took part in invasions of Reggio, Normandy, Malaya. (Involvement in Sicily, Salerno and Anzio is uncertain.) Operated in shuttle service between Tilbury, Ostend and Antwerp. Prepared for Far East at Antwerp Mar–Apr 1945. Repatriated Australian troops in Brisbane. Returned to USN at Subic Bay, Philippines, 4 May 1946. Photograph at Imperial War Museum: NA6280.

LST 161 Launched 7 Dec 1942; commissioned in RN 16 Mar 1943.
Built by Missouri Valley Bridge & Iron Co., Evansville, Indiana. Sailed from New York in convoy UGS8A, 14 May 1943. Took part in invasions of Anzio and Normandy. Also relief of Norway. (Other operations uncertain.) Converted for carriage of rolling stock. Was in the Clyde area for refit for Far Eastern service July 1945, but was subsequently not required. Transferred to US custody at New York, 5 Jan 1946.

LST 162 Launched 3 Feb 1943; commissioned in RN 25 Mar 1943.
Built by Missouri Valley Bridge & Iron Co., Evansville, Indiana. Sailed from New York in convoy UGS8A 14 May 1943. Took part in invasions of Sicily, Salerno, Reggio, Anzio and Normandy. Also relief of Norway. Operated in the shuttle service between Tilbury, Ostend and Antwerp. Transferred to US authorities at Greenock, 1 Feb 1946. Photograph Portsmouth Publishing Co. ref 2996.

LST 163 Launched 4 Feb 1943; commissioned in RN 1 Apr 1943.
Built by Missouri Valley Bridge & Iron Co., Evansville, Indiana. Sailed for Liverpool from Halifax, Nova Scotia, in convoy SC131 on 18 May 1943. Took part in invasions of Sicily, Salerno, Anzio, Normandy, Malaya. Paid off probably in Singapore, 15 Feb 1946.

LST 164 Launched 5 Feb 1943; commissioned in RN 5 Apr 1943.
Built by Missouri Valley Bridge & Iron Co., Evansville, Indiana. Sailed for Liverpool from Halifax, Nova Scotia, in convoy SC131, 18 May 1943. Took part in invasions of Sicily, Salerno, Anzio, Normandy, Malaya. Paid off 8 Feb 1946.

LST 165 Launched 2 Feb 1943; commissioned in RN 7 Apr 1943.
Built by Missouri Valley Bridge & Iron Co., Evansville, Indiana. Sailed from New York in convoy UGS8A 14 May 1943. Took part in relief of Norway (others uncertain). Returned to US authorities at New York, 20 Mar 1946.

LST 173 Launched 24 Apr 1943; commissioned in RN 24 Dec 1944.
Built by Missouri Valley Bridge & Iron Co., Evansville, Indiana. Served as US LST 173 before commissioning in the RN at Bizerta. Took part in the invasion of southern

France. Operated in the Adriatic. Went to Norway in Operation 'Doomsday'. Transferred to USN at Norfolk, Virginia, USA, 23 Apr 1946.

LST 178 Launched 23 May 1943; commissioned in RN 24 Dec 1944.
Built by Missouri Valley Bridge & Iron Co., Evansville, Indiana. Served as US LST 178 until commissioned in the RN. Took part in the invasion of southern France. Operated in the Adriatic until she struck mines on 21 Jan 1945. Paid off into Care & Maintenance 28 May 1945.

LST 180 Launched 3 June 1943; commissioned in RN 9 July 1943.
Built by Missouri Valley Bridge & Iron Co., Evansville, Indiana. Part of 9th Flotilla which sailed for the invasion of the Andaman Islands, which was cancelled. Took part in invasion of Normandy. Prepared for Far East at Liverpool June–Sept 1945, but not required. Believed loaded with LCT 2227 for return to USA. Paid off New York 17 Dec 1945.

LST 198 Launched 17 Jan 1943; commissioned in RN 6 Mar 1943.
Built by Chicago Bridge & Iron Co., Seneca, Illinois. Sailed for Liverpool from Halifax, Nova Scotia, in convoy SC131 18 May 1943. Took part in the invasions of Sicily, Salerno, Anzio and Normandy. Operated in the shuttle service. Bow doors badly damaged in two collisions in Feb–Mar 1945. Paid off New York, 23 Jan 1946.

LST 199 Launched 7 Feb 1943; commissioned in RN 20 Mar 1943.
Built by Chicago Bridge & Iron Co., Seneca, Illinois. Sailed from New York in convoy UGS8A 14 May 1943. Took part in the invasions of Sicily, Salerno, Reggio, Anzio, Normandy and Malaya. Mined off Surabaya 5 Nov 1945. Paid off 29 Mar 1946. Photographs at Imperial War Museum: ref HU49713; NA6216.

LST 200 Launched 20 Feb 1943; commissioned in RN 29 Mar 1943.
Built by Chicago Bridge & Iron Co., Seneca, Illinois. Sailed from Halifax, Nova Scotia, for Liverpool in convoy SC131 18 May 1943. Took part in the invasions of Sicily, Salerno, Anzio and Normandy. Operated in the shuttle service. Paid off and transferred to US custody New York 27 Feb 1946. Photograph at Imperial War Museum: ref FLM1727 (poor quality). Films at Imperial War Museum: ref AYY509 PMA1 Sousse; ADM563. Part log (11 May–13 Sept 1943) at Public Record Office: ref ADM 53/117830–833.

LST 214 Launched 22 June 1943; commissioned in RN 13 July 1943.
Built by Chicago Bridge & Iron Co., Seneca, Illinois. Sailed from Norfolk, Virginia, USA, 16 Aug 1943. Part of 9th Flotilla bound for the invasion of the Andaman Islands, which was subsequently cancelled. Took part in invasions of Anzio and Normandy. Also relief of Norway. Struck by shell at Anzio, 29 Jan 1944. Operated in the shuttle service. Paid off and transferred to US custody at Norfolk, Virginia, 26 Jan 1946. Photograph at US Naval Institute.

LST 215 (LSE(LC)51) Launched 26 June 1943; commissioned in RN 20 July 1943.
Built by Chicago Bridge & Iron Co., Seneca, Illinois. Sailed from Norfolk, Virginia, USA, 16 Aug 1943, as part of 9th Flotilla bound for the invasion of the Andaman Islands, which was subsequently cancelled. Took part in invasion of Normandy. Operated in the shuttle service. Collided with blockship in Ostend 24 Oct 1944. Converted to Landing Ship Emergency Repair (Landing Craft) 51 at Amos & Smith, Hull Nov 1944–June 1945. Paid off 27 July 1946.

LST 216 (FDT 216) Launched 4 July 1943; commissioned in RN 4 Aug 1943.
Built by Chicago Bridge & Iron Co., Seneca, Illinois. Sailed from Halifax, Nova Scotia, for Liverpool in convoy SC143, 28 Sept 1943. Converted to Fighter Direction Tender by Messrs. John Brown, Clyde. Commissioned as FDT 216 13 Feb 1944. Took part in invasion of Normandy. Sunk by aircraft torpedo off Normandy 7 July 1944. Photograph at Imperial War Museum: ref A21922.

LST 217 (FDT 217) Launched 13 July 1943; commissioned in RN 7 Aug 1943.
Built by Chicago Bridge & Iron Co., Seneca, Illinois. Sailed from Halifax, Nova Scotia, for Liverpool in convoy SC143, 28 Sept 1943. Converted to Fighter Direction Tender by Messrs. John Brown, Clyde. Commissioned as FDT 217 13 Feb 1944. Took part in invasion of Normandy. Paid off 16 Apr 1946.

LST 237 Launched 8 June 1943; commissioned in RN 12 July 1943.
Built by Missouri Valley Bridge & Iron Co., Evansville, Indiana. Sailed from Norfolk, Virginia, USA, 16 Aug 1943 as part of 9th Flotilla bound for the invasion of the Andaman Islands, which was subsequently cancelled. Took part in invasions of Anzio, Normandy and Malaya. Operated in the shuttle service. Paid off and returned to US custody, Subic Bay, Philippines, 16 Mar 1946.

LST 238 Launched 13 June 1943; commissioned in RN 16 July 1943.

Built by Missouri Valley Bridge & Iron Co., Evansville, Indiana. Sailed from Norfolk, Virginia, USA, 16 Aug 1943 as part of 9th Flotilla bound for the invasion of the Andaman Islands, which was subsequently cancelled. Collision with corvette off Gibraltar, seriously damaged bow doors. Took part in invasion of Normandy and relief of Channel Islands. Operated in the shuttle service. Paid off and transferred to US custody Norfolk, Virginia, USA, 12 Feb 1946.

LST 239 Launched 18 June 1943; commissioned in RN 19 July 1943.

Built by Missouri Valley Bridge & Iron Co., Evansville, Indiana. Sailed from Norfolk, Virginia, USA, 16 Aug 1943 as part of 9th Flotilla bound for the invasion of the Andaman Islands, which was subsequently cancelled. Took part in the invasion of Normandy. Also in relief of Norway. Operated in the shuttle service. Transferred to US authorities at Norfolk, Virginia, USA, 4 Feb 1946. Photograph held by Associated British Ports, Cardiff. Bow doors view showing Churchill tank disembarking at East Dock, Cardiff, 25 Feb 1944.

LST 280 Launched 26 Sept 1943; commissioned in RN 26 Oct 1944.

Built by American Bridge Co., Ambridge, Pa. Served as US LST 280 until commissioned in RN. Took part in invasion of Normandy. Believed torpedoed by German E-boat. Repaired in Thames 8 July 1944–18 Jan 1945. Loaded with LCT 2124 for Far East. Visited Gibraltar, Malta, Port Said, Port Tewfick, Massawa, Aden, Bombay, Cochin, Trincomalee, Vizagapatam, Madras, Malaya, Rangoon, Siam and Singapore. Took part in the invasion of Malaya. Paid off Subic Bay, Philippines, 13 April 1946.

LST 289 Launched 21 Nov 1943; commissioned in RN 30 Nov 1944.

Built by American Bridge Co., Ambridge, Pa. Served as US LST 289 until commissioned in RN. De-equipped and mudberthed Sandacre Bay, 30 July 1946. Re-delivered to US authorities 10 Dec 1946. (No other details available.)

LST 301 Launched 15 Sept 1942; commissioned in RN 6 Nov 1942.

Built by Boston Navy Yard. First LST(2) in commission with RN. Sailed from Halifax, Nova Scotia, in convoy SC113, 16 Dec 1942. Arrived UK 1 Jan 1943. First RN LST(2) to reach UK. Took part in invasions of Sicily, Salerno, Reggio, Anzio and Normandy. Operated in the shuttle service. Various repairs at Cowes, Portsmouth, Thames and Devonport. Paid off New York, 20 Mar 1946. Photograph held by National Maritime Museum. Also Imperial War Museum, Foxhill Collection.

LST 302 Launched 15 Sept 1942; commissioned in RN 14 Nov 1942.

Built by Boston Navy Yard. Sailed from New York as part of 1st Flotilla on 27 Jan 1943 but had to return. Sailed again 23 Feb 1943 for Mediterranean via Bermuda. Took part in invasions of Sicily, Salerno (probably), Anzio and Normandy. Various repairs after Normandy invasion at Leith, Southampton, Thames, Dundee and Clyde. Believed loaded with LCT 2013 at Clyde for return to USA. Paid off New York, 5 or 16 Jan 1946. Photograph at Imperial War Museum ref NA4378.

▶ LST 301 with Vehicle Landing Ramp during trials in 1943. (Royal Marines Amphibious Trials and Training Unit)

▶ LSTs 302 and 303 at Nisida, Italy. (Also in this view are US LST 349 and LST 402.) (Mr Jackson)

▼Officers of LST 303 – Hong Kong 1945. Back row, left to right: Bob Godwin, Dickie Starling (EO), Ken Gazzard. Front row: Jimmy Cooper (No. 1), Freddy O'Neill (CO), Dennis Melville. (K. H. Gazzard)

LST 303 Launched 21 Sept 1942; commissioned in RN 14 Nov 1942.

Built by Boston Navy Yard. Sailed from New York 27 Jan 1943 as part of 1st Flotilla for Mediterranean via Bermuda. Took part in invasions of Sicily, Salerno, Anzio and Normandy. Operated in the shuttle service. Various repairs in Thames and Antwerp. Allocated to 12th Flotilla. Took part in invasion of Malaya and sailed to Australia and Japan. Paid off Subic Bay, Philippines, 4 May 1946. Appears in Imperial War Museum Film AMY485/01/01. IWM photographs ref BU7045-54 (Hamburg 31.5.45) and NA3956/7 (North Africa).

LST 304 Launched 21 Sept 1942; commissioned in RN 30 Nov 1942.

Built by Boston Navy Yard. Sailed from New York on 27 Jan 1943 as part of 1st Flotilla for Mediterranean via Bermuda. Took part in invasions of Sicily, Salerno, Anzio and Normandy. Operated in the shuttle service. Collision with blockship at Ostend, Oct 1944, badly holed. Sailed to take part in invasion of Malaya but orders changed. Sailed from Trincomalee as part of a special force for Hong Kong (believed to be Operation 'Tiderace'). Paid off, possibly Singapore, 19 Feb 1946. Photographs at Imperial War Museum: SE4944–4973 (Hong Kong).

LST 305 Launched 10 Oct 1942; commissioned in RN 7 Dec 1942.

Built by Boston Navy Yard. Sailed from Halifax, Nova Scotia, in convoy SC122/HX229 in company with LST 365. Sailed from Scotland in convoy KMS18A. Took part in invasions of Sicily, Salerno and Anzio. Hit by torpedo from U 230, 20 Feb 1944, sank early next day.

LST 311 Launched 30 Dec 1942; commissioned 18 or 20 Nov 1944.

Built by New York Navy Yard. Served as US LST 311 until commissioned in the RN. Took part in the invasions of Sicily, Salerno and Normandy. Took part in invasion of Malaya. Fitted for carriage of rolling stock. Collided with LST 3036 Singapore 25 Mar 1946. Paid off Subic Bay, Philippines, 13 Apr 1946.

LST 315 Launched 28 Jan 1943; commissioned in RN 30 Nov 1944.

Built by New York Navy Yard. Served as US LST 315 until commissioned in the RN. Took part in the invasions of Sicily, Salerno and Normandy. Assisted in relief of southern Norway. Took part in invasion of Malaya. Paid off Subic Bay, Philippines, 16 Mar 1946.

LST 319 Launched 5 Nov 1942; commissioned in RN 15 Dec 1942.
Built by Philadelphia Navy Yard. Sailed from Halifax, Nova Scotia, for Liverpool 31 Mar 1943, in convoy SC125 in company with LSTs 366 and 406. Sailed from Scotland in convoy KMS18A. Took part in invasions of Sicily, Salerno, Anzio and Normandy. Collided with pier Ostend early October 1944. Assisted relief of Norway. Believed loaded with LCT 2228 at Liverpool for return to USA. Paid off New York 17 Dec 1945.

LST 320 Launched 5 Nov 1942; commissioned 28 Dec 1942.
Built by Philadelphia Navy Yard. Captain LST, Burges Watson's ship. Sailed from New York as part of 1st Flotilla 27 Jan 1943, but broke down. Returned to New York and sailed again 23 Feb 1943 for the Mediterranean via Bermuda. Took part in invasions of Sicily, Salerno, Anzio and Normandy. Operated in the shuttle service. Assisted in relief of Norway. Paid off Norfolk, Virginia, 23 Apr 1946.

LST 321 Launched 5 Nov 1942; commissioned in RN 31 Dec 1942.
Built by Philadelphia Navy Yard. Sailed from Halifax, Nova Scotia, for Liverpool in convoy SC126 8 Apr 1943. Sailed from Scotland in convoy KMS18A. Took part in invasions of Sicily, Salerno, Anzio and Normandy. Operated in the shuttle service. Hit mine 29 Nov 1944. Repaired at Antwerp. Took part in invasion of Malaya. Paid off Subic Bay, Philippines, 13 or 16 Apr 1946. Appears in Imperial War Museum film 565.

LST 322 Launched 5 Nov 1942; commissioned in RN 9 Jan 1943.
Built by Philadelphia Navy Yard. Sailed from New York for the Mediterranean in convoy UGS8, 28 Apr 1943. Broke a crankshaft en route, repaired in Bermuda. Took part in invasions of Sicily, Salerno, Anzio and Normandy. Fitted with rails for carriage of rolling stock. Operated in the shuttle service. Paid off into Care & Maintenance 29 Jan 1945. Returned to US authorities at Bremerhaven, 2 Aug 1946. Appears in Imperial War Museum film 563. Also IWM photograph ref NA3941.

LST 323 Launched 5 Nov 1942; commissioned in RN 18 Jan 1943.
Built by Philadelphia Navy Yard. Sailed from New York for the Mediterranean in convoy UGS6A, 19 Mar 1943. Took

part in invasions of Sicily, Reggio, Salerno, Anzio and Normandy. Fitted with rails for carriage of rolling stock. Operated in the shuttle service. Paid off probably at Plymouth, 26 Jan 1946. Photographs at Imperial War Museum ref BU648/9/50/1–6.

LST 324 Launched 5 Nov 1942; commissioned in RN 23 Jan 1943.
Built by Philadelphia Navy Yard. Sailed from New York in company with LSTs 412 and 421 13 Mar 1943. Took oil refinery equipment to Curaçao, then logs from Georgetown to Freetown, Sierra Leone. Took part in invasions of Sicily, Salerno, Anzio and Normandy. Operated in the shuttle service. Assisted in liberation of the Channel Islands. Took part in invasion of Malaya. Paid off Subic Bay, Philippines, 4 May 1946. Photographs at Imperial War Museum: A17840–6; H38976–84 (with LST 361).

LST 326 Launched 11 Feb 1943; commissioned in RN 30 Nov or 9 Dec 1944.
Built by Philadelphia Navy Yard. Served as US LST 326 until commissioned in the RN. Took part in invasions of Sicily, Anzio and Normandy. Believed to have taken part in invasion of Malaya. Paid off Subic Bay, Philippines, 16 Mar 1946.

LST 331 Launched 11 Feb 1943; commissioned in RN 20 Nov 1944.
Built by Philadelphia Navy Yard. Served as US LST 331 until commissioned in the RN. Took part in invasions of Sicily, Salerno and Normandy. Transferred to RN at Southampton and sailed to Clyde for refit late 1944. Took part in invasion of Malaya as SO of 6th Flotilla. Paid off Subic Bay, Philippines, 16 Mar 1946.

LST 336 Launched 15 Oct 1942; commissioned in RN 18 or 29 Nov 1944.
Built by Norfolk Navy Yard. Served as US LST 336 until commissioned in the RN. Took part in invasions of Sicily, Salerno and Normandy. Transferred to RN at Rosneath. Sailed for invasion of Malaya but broke down en route. At Port Said for repairs 5 June–27 Sept 1945. Returned to Rosneath about November 1945. Paid off Norfolk, Virginia, 7 Mar 1946.

LST 337 Launched 8 Nov 1942; commissioned 18 Nov or 2 Dec 1944.
Built by Norfolk Navy Yard. Served as US LST 337 until commissioned in the RN. Took part in invasions of Sicily, Salerno and Normandy. Transferred to RN at Rosneath. Took part in invasion of Malaya. Paid off Subic Bay, Philippines, 16 Mar 1946.

LST 346 Launched 15 Dec 1942; commissioned 18 or 20 Nov 1944.
Built by Norfolk Navy Yard. Served as US LST 346 until commissioned in the RN. Took part in invasions of Sicily, Salerno and Normandy. Refit at Leith. Took part in invasion of Malaya. Paid off Subic Bay, Philippines, 4 May 1946.

LST 347 Launched 7 Feb 1943; commissioned 6 or 19 Dec 1944.
Built by Norfolk Navy Yard. Served as US LST 347 until commissioned in the RN. Took part in invasions of Sicily, Salerno and Normandy. Transferred to RN at Rosneath. Refit at Cardiff. Operated in the Far East: Singapore, Port Swettenham, Java. Ship handed to French Navy in Singapore 28 Jan 1946.

LST 351 Launched 7 Feb 1943; commissioned 10 Dec 1944.
Built by Norfolk Navy Yard. Served as US LST 351 until commissioned in the RN. Took part in invasions of Sicily, Salerno, Anzio and Normandy. Does not appear to have done any LST work while in RN commission. Mudberthed Sandacre Bay, Saltash, 30 July 1946. Re-delivered to US authorities 10 Dec 1946.

LST 352 Launched 7 Feb 1943; commissioned in RN 24 Dec 1944.
Built by Norfolk Navy Yard. Served as US LST 352 until commissioned in the RN. Took part in invasions of Sicily, Salerno, Anzio, Elba and southern France. Refit at Rotterdam. Paid off at Bremerhaven, 2 Aug 1946. Part log at Public Record Office: ADM 53/121666–121673.

LST 358 Launched 15 Dec 1942; commissioned in RN 24 Dec 1944 approx.
Built at Charleston Navy Yard. Served as US LST 358 until commissioned in the RN. Took part in the invasions of Sicily, Salerno, Anzio and southern France. Does not appear to have done any LST work while in RN commission. Paid off Norfolk, Virginia, 27 Feb 1946. Appears in film at Imperial War Museum: AYY665 (Anzio area). Also photograph at IWM ref NA22299 (Visit by Sir Anthony Eden).

LST 360 (LSE(LC)52) Launched 11 Jan 1943; commissioned 18 or 29 Nov 1944.
Built by Charleston Navy Yard. Served as US LST 360 until commissioned in the RN. Took part in the invasions of Sicily, Anzio and Normandy. Fitted for carriage of rolling stock. Believed transferred to RN at Rosneath. Converted to LSE(LC) 52 at Wallsend Slipway 18 Dec 1944–30 June 1945. Paid off, location unknown, 10 June 1946. Appears in Imperial War Museum film AYY665 at Anzio.

LST 361 Launched 10 Oct 1942; commissioned in RN 16 Nov 1942.
Built by Bethlehem Steel Co., Quincy, Mass. Sailed from New York as part of 1st Flotilla, 27 Jan 1943, but had to turn back. Sailed again 23 Feb 1943 for the Mediterranean via Bermuda. Took part in invasions of Sicily, Salerno, Anzio and Normandy. Operated in the shuttle service. Paid off, location unknown but probably in the USA, 7 Mar 1946.

LST 362 Launched 10 Oct 1942; commissioned in RN 21 or 23 Nov 1942.
Built by Bethlehem Steel Co., Quincy, Mass. Sailed from

◄ LST 352 (R. Willis)

New York as part of 1st Flotilla, 27 Jan 1943, for the Mediterranean via Bermuda. Took part in invasions of Sicily, Salerno and Anzio. Torpedoed and sunk by *U 744* while returning from the Mediterranean to the UK in convoy MKS40 in Biscay area, 2 Mar 1944. Photographs at Imperial War Museum ref NA3962/4.

LST 363 Launched 26 Oct 1942; commissioned in RN 30 Nov 1942.
Built by Bethlehem Steel Co., Quincy, Mass. Sailed from New York as part of 1st Flotilla, 27 Jan 1943, for the Mediterranean via Bermuda. Took part in invasions of Sicily, Salerno, Anzio and Normandy. Operated in the shuttle service. Various repairs at Portsmouth, Thames and Antwerp. Paid off Norfolk, Virginia, 26 Jan 1946. Photographs at Imperial War Museum ref BU7045–54.

LST 364 Launched 26 Oct 1942; commissioned in RN 7 Dec 1942.
Built by Bethlehem Steel Co., Quincy, Mass. Sailed from New York approx. 19 Mar 1943 as straggler to convoy UGS6A. Took part in invasions of Sicily, Salerno, Anzio and Normandy. Operated in the shuttle service. Sunk by torpedo 22 Feb 1945. Photographs at Imperial War Museum ref H38511/12/14.

▼ Oerlikon gun cleaning aboard LST 366. (R. W. Knight's collection)

LST 365 Launched 11 Nov 1942; commissioned in RN 14 Nov 1942.
Built by Bethlehem Steel Co., Quincy, Mass. Sailed from Halifax, Nova Scotia, in convoy SC122/HX229 in company with LST 305. Equipped at Palmers, Jarrow, to serve as Fighter Direction Ship. Sailed from Scotland in convoy KMS18A. Took part in invasions of Sicily, Salerno, Anzio and Normandy. Operated in the shuttle service. Assisted in relief of Norway. Made one trip to Channel Islands, Sept 1945. Suffered considerable damage in storm on passage to Greenock in December 1945. Mudberthed at head of Loch Striven and paid off 29 July 1946. Believed sold to Fresh Frozen Foods, Ayr.

LST 366 Launched 11 Nov 1942; commissioned in RN 21 Dec 1942.
Built by Bethlehem Steel Co., Quincy, Mass. Sailed from Halifax, Nova Scotia, in convoy SC125, 31 Mar 1943. Sailed from Scotland in convoy KMS18A. Took part in invasions of Sicily, Reggio, Salerno, Anzio and Normandy. Operated in the shuttle service. Paid off at Norfolk, Virginia, 26 Jan 1946. Photograph at US Naval Institute.

LST 367 Launched 24 Nov 1942; commissioned in RN 29 Dec 1942.
Built by Bethlehem Steel Co., Quincy, Mass. Sailed from New York for the Mediterranean in convoy UGS6A, 19 Mar 1943. Took part in invasions of Sicily, Salerno, Anzio and Normandy. Operated in shuttle service. Buckled bow doors in collision Nov 1944. Believed loaded with LCT 2285 for return to USA. Paid off New York, 17 Dec 1945. Photographs at Imperial War Museum ref NA3993; NA4264/5

LST 368 Launched 24 Nov 1942; commissioned in RN 4 Jan 1943.
Built by Bethlehem Steel Co., Quincy, Mass. Sailed from New York for the Mediterranean in convoy UGS6A, 19 Mar 1943. Took part in invasions of Sicily, Salerno, Anzio and Normandy. Operated in shuttle service. Sailed to India 1945, took part in invasion of Malaya. Paid off Subic Bay, Philippines, 16 Mar 1946.

LST 369 Launched 24 Nov 1942; commissioned in RN 29 Nov 1944.
Built by Bethlehem Steel Co., Quincy, Mass. Served as US LST 369 until commissioned in the RN. Took part in invasions of Sicily, Salerno and Normandy. Transferred to RN at Rosneath. Sailed to India 1945. No further details known. Paid off, location unknown, 15 Feb 1946.

LST 371 Launched 12 Dec 1942; commissioned in RN 18 Nov 1944.
Built by Bethlehem Steel Co., Quincy, Mass. Served as US LST 371 until commissioned in the RN. Took part in invasions of Sicily, Salerno and Normandy. Transferred to RN at Portland. Took part in invasion of Malaya. Paid off Subic Bay, Philippines, 16 Mar 1946.

LST 373 Launched 19 Jan 1943; commissioned in RN 30 Nov or 9 Dec 1944.
Built by Bethlehem Steel Co., Quincy, Mass. Served as US LST 373 until commissioned in the RN. Took part in invasions of Sicily, Salerno and Normandy. Took part in invasion of Malaya. Paid off Subic Bay, Philippines, 16 Mar 1946.

LST 380 Launched 10 Feb 1943; commissioned in RN 18 Nov 1944.
Built by Bethlehem Steel Co., Quincy, Mass. Served as US LST 380 until commissioned in the RN. Took part in invasions of Sicily, Salerno and Normandy. Fitted for carriage of rolling stock. Believed refitted for Far East at Manchester Dry Dock Co., Nov 1944. Took part in invasion of Malaya. Paid off Subic Bay, Philippines, 13 Apr 1946.

LST 381 Launched 10 Feb 1943; commissioned in RN 6 or 19 Dec 1944.
Built by Bethlehem Steel Co., Quincy, Mass. Served as US LST 381 until commissioned in the RN. Took part in invasions of Sicily, Anzio and Normandy. Believed transferred at Rosneath then sailed to Falmouth. Paid off into Care & Maintenance 15 Jan 1945. Re-commissioned 11 Feb 1946. Paid off New York, 10 June 1946.

LST 382 Launched 3 Feb 1943; commissioned in RN 18 Nov 1944.
Built by Bethlehem Steel Co., Quincy, Mass. Served as US LST 382 until commissioned in the RN. Took part in invasions of Sicily, Salerno and Normandy. Fitted for carriage of rolling stock. Believed transferred to RN at Rosneath. Took part in invasion of Malaya as SO of 10th Flotilla. Transferred to French Navy 28 Jan 1946, location unknown.

LST 383 Launched 28 Sept 1942; commissioned in RN 18 or 20 Nov 1944.
Built by Newport News Shipbuilding & Drydock Co. Served as US LST 383 until commissioned in the RN. Took part in invasions of Sicily, Salerno, Anzio and Normandy. Fitted for carriage of rolling stock. Believed transferred to

RN at Southampton. Took part in invasion of Malaya. Paid off Subic Bay, Philippines, 4 May 1946.

LST 385 Launched 28 Sept 1942; commissioned in RN 29 Nov 1944.
Built by Newport News Shipbuilding & Drydock Co. Served as US LST 385 until commissioned in the RN. Took part in invasions of Sicily, Salerno, Anzio and Normandy. Took part in invasion of Malaya. Paid off Subic Bay, Philippines, 16 Mar 1946.

LST 386 Launched 28 Sept 1942; commissioned 30 Nov or 9 Dec 1944.
Built by Newport News Shipbuilding & Drydock Co. Served as US LST 386 until commissioned in the RN. Took part in invasions of Sicily, Salerno, Anzio and Normandy. Used as pontoon instructional ship in Gareloch from about Mar 1945. Mudberthed at head of Loch Striven and paid off 29 July 1946. Believed sold to Fresh Frozen Foods, Ayr.

LST 394 Launched 11 Nov 1942; commissioned in RN 24 Dec 1944.
Built by Newport News Shipbuilding & Drydock Co. Served as US LST 394 until commissioned in the RN. Took part in invasions of Sicily and southern France. Repaired at Malta Nov 1945. Prepared for re-delivery to USA at Malta Feb–Mar 1946. Returned to US authorities 12 May 1946, location unknown.

LST 401 Launched 16 Oct 1942; commissioned in RN 1 Dec 1942.
Built at Bethlehem Fairfield Co., Baltimore, Md. Yard No.2173. Sailed from New York as part of 1st Flotilla 27 Jan 1943, but had to turn back. Sailed again for the Mediterranean via Bermuda 23 Feb 1943. Took part in invasions of Sicily, Salerno and Anzio. Was under repair at Wallsend Slipway at time of invasion of Normandy. Made several trips Southampton to Cherbourg with rolling stock up to 31 Dec 1944. Operated in the shuttle service. Assisted in relief of Norway. Paid off at Norfolk, Virginia, 7 Mar 1946.

LST 402 (LSE(LC)53) Launched 9 Oct 1942; commissioned in RN 9 Dec 1942.
Built at Bethlehem Fairfield Co., Baltimore, Md. Yard No. 2174. Sailed from New York as part of 1st Flotilla for the Mediterranean via Bermuda, 27 Jan 1943. Took part in the invasions of Sicily, Salerno, Anzio and Normandy. Taken in hand for conversion to LSE at Wallsend Slipway 5 Mar 1945. Went to Far East summer 1945. Paid off 24 Sept 1946, location unknown.

LST 403 Launched 24 Oct 1942; commissioned in RN 9 Dec 1942.
Built at Bethlehem Fairfield Co., Baltimore, Md. Yard No. 2175. Sailed from New York as part of 1st Flotilla 27 Jan 1943, but had to turn back. Sailed again for the Mediterranean via Bermuda 23 Feb 1943. Took part in invasions of Sicily, Reggio, Salerno, Anzio and Normandy. Refit at Hull Oct–Nov 1944. Took part in invasion of Malaya as SO of 4th Flotilla. Paid off Subic Bay, Philippines, 13 Apr 1946. Photograph at Imperial War Museum (with LST 427 in Foxhill Collection).

LST 404 Launched 28 Oct 1942; commissioned in RN 15 Dec 1942.
Built at Bethlehem Fairfield Co., Baltimore, Md. Yard No. 2176. Sailed from Norfolk, Virginia in convoy UGL2 for Mediterranean via Bermuda, 9 Apr 1943. Took part in invasions of Sicily, Reggio, Salerno, Anzio and Normandy.

Torpedoed by *U 741* in English Channel, 15 Aug 1944. Beached on Isle of Wight. Paid off 8 June 1945.

LST 405 Launched 31 Oct 1942; commissioned in RN 28 Dec 1942.
Built at Bethlehem Fairfield Co., Baltimore, Md. Yard No. 2177. Sailed from Norfolk, Virginia, for the Mediterranean via Bermuda in convoy UGL2, 9 Apr 1943. Took part in invasions of Sicily, Reggio, Salerno, Anzio and Normandy. Operated in the shuttle service. Refit at Antwerp Apr–June 1945. Took part in invasion of Malaya. Collision with troopship Colombo Harbour, 25 Oct 1945. Possibly sunk, location unknown, in agreement with US authorities as a total loss, March 1946. Photograph at Imperial War Museum ref NA6287 (with LST 62).

LST 406 Launched 28 Oct 1942; commissioned in RN 26 Dec 1942.
Built at Bethlehem Fairfield Co., Baltimore, Md. Yard No.

▶ The guns of LST 401. (Both W. Collison)

2178. Sailed from Halifax, Nova Scotia, in convoy SC125 31 Mar 1943. Sailed from Scotland in convoy KMS18A. Took part in invasions of Sicily, Salerno, Anzio and Normandy. Operated in the shuttle service. Refit on Clyde Aug–Dec 1944 for Far East. Believed sailed to Colombo. Paid off Subic Bay, Philippines, 13 Apr 1946. Photographs at Imperial War Museum ref B5128/9/39/53.

LST 407 Launched 5 Nov 1942; commissioned in RN 31 Dec 1942.
Built at Bethlehem Fairfield Co., Baltimore, Md. Yard No. 2179. Sailed from New York for Mediterranean via Bermuda in convoy UGS6A, 19 Mar 1943. Took part in invasions of Sicily, Salerno and Anzio. Blown aground in storm off Nisida 26 Feb 1944. Damaged beyond repair. Stripped of engines, etc. Paid off 24 Apr 1944. Believed sold to a local scrap firm.

LST 408 Launched 31 Oct 1942; commissioned in RN 23 Dec 1942.
Built at Bethlehem Fairfield Co., Baltimore, Md. Yard No. 2180. Sailed from Norfolk, Virginia, for Mediterranean via Bermuda in convoy UGL2, 9 Apr 1943. Took part in invasions of Sicily, Salerno, Anzio and Normandy. Fitted for carriage of rolling stock. Operated in the shuttle service. Took part in invasion of Malaya. Visited Brisbane, Australia. Paid off Subic Bay, Philippines, 4 May 1946.

LST 409 Launched 15 Nov 1942; commissioned in RN 6 Jan 1943.
Built at Bethlehem Fairfield Co., Baltimore, Md. Yard No. 2181. Sailed from New York for Mediterranean via Bermuda in convoy UGS6A, 19 Mar 1943. Took part in invasions of Sicily, Reggio, Salerno, Anzio and Normandy. Fitted for carriage of rolling stock. Operated in the shuttle service Southampton to Cherbourg. At Falmouth February 1945, paid off into Care & Maintenance. Handed over to US authorities at Bremerhaven, 2 Aug 1946. Photograph at Imperial War Museum ref NA6232.

LST 410 Launched 15 Nov 1942; commissioned in RN 14 Jan 1943.
Built at Bethlehem Fairfield Co., Baltimore, Md. Yard No. 2182. Sailed from New York in convoy UGS7A but broke down and had to return. Sailed again for the Mediterranean in convoy UGS8, 28 Apr 1943. Took part in invasions of Sicily, Salerno, Anzio and Normandy. Converted to Flotilla Leader at Liverpool Sept 1944–Jan 1945. Took part in invasion of Malaya as SO of 2nd Flotilla. Paid off Subic Bay, Philippines, 16 Mar 1946. Photograph at Imperial War Museum ref A24040.

LST 411 Launched 9 Nov 1942; commissioned in RN 8 Jan 1943.
Built at Bethlehem Fairfield Co., Baltimore, Md. Yard No. 2183. Sailed from New York for Bermuda in convoy UGS6A, 19 Mar 1943. Broke down and remained at Bermuda before re-sailing in convoy UGL2, late Apr 1943. Took part in invasions of Sicily and Salerno. Hit mine off La Maddalena 31 Dec 1943, broke in two. Paid off 31 Dec 1943.

LST 412 Launched 16 Nov 1942; commissioned in RN 27 Jan 1943.
Built at Bethlehem Fairfield Co., Baltimore, Md. Yard No. 2184. Sailed from New York 13 Mar 1943 in company with LSTs 324 and 421. Took oil refinery equipment to Curaçao, then logs from Georgetown to Freetown, Sierra Leone. Took part in invasions of Salerno, Anzio and Normandy. Operated in the shuttle service. Paid off New York, 23 Jan 1946. Photographs at Imperial War Museum ref A17840–6 (with LST 324, some good, some not so good).

LST 413 Launched 10 Nov 1942; commissioned in RN 6 Jan 1943.
Built at Bethlehem Fairfield Co., Baltimore, Md. Yard No. 2185. Sailed from New York for the Mediterranean via Bermuda in convoy UGS6A, 19 Mar 1943. Took part in invasions of Sicily, Reggio, Salerno, Anzio and Normandy. Operated in the shuttle service. Took part in invasion of Malaya. Paid off Subic Bay, Philippines, 13 Apr 1946.

LST 414 Launched 21 Nov 1942; commissioned in RN 20 Jan 1943.
Built at Bethlehem Fairfield Co., Baltimore, Md. Yard No. 2186. Sailed from Norfolk, Virgina, for the Mediterranean via Bermuda in convoy UGL2, 9 Apr 1943. Took part in invasion of Sicily. Hit amidships by torpedo from torpedo-bomber, 15 Aug 1943. Beached north of Bizerta. Vessel cannibalized.

LST 415 Launched 21 Nov 1942; commissioned in RN 19 Jan 1943.
Built at Bethlehem Fairfield Co., Baltimore, Md. Yard No. 2187. Sailed from New York for the Mediterranean via Bermuda, 6 Apr 1943, convoy unknown. Took part in invasions of Sicily, Reggio, Salerno, Anzio and Normandy. Operated in the shuttle service. Hit by torpedo in English Channel, believed from E-boat, 16 Jan 1945. Beached in the Thames near Grays, Essex. Reduced to Care & Maintenance 17 Feb 1945. Written off approx. 18 Sept 1945. Cut up 1947.

LST 416 Launched 30 Nov 1942; commissioned in RN 5 Feb 1943.
Built at Bethlehem Fairfield Co., Baltimore, Md. Yard No. 2188. Sailed from New York for the Mediterranean via Bermuda, 6 Apr 1943, convoy unknown. Took part in invasions of Sicily, Reggio, Salerno, Anzio and Normandy. Operated in the shuttle service. First LST into Ostend, 4 Oct 1944. Assisted in relief of Norway. Paid off Norfolk, Virginia, 12 Feb 1946.

LST 417 Launched 24 Nov 1942; commissioned in RN 1 Feb 1943.
Built at Bethlehem Fairfield Co., Baltimore, Md. Yard No. 2189. Sailed from New York for the Mediterranean in convoy UGS8, 28 Apr 1943. Took part in invasions of Sicily and Reggio. Severely damaged by torpedo-bomb, 7 Sept 1943. Towed to Ferryville, then to Taranto. Believed to have had new stern fabricated. Believed sailed back to USA and handed over to US authorities at Norfolk, Virginia, 31 May 1946.

LST 418 Launched 30 Nov 1942; commissioned in RN 1 Feb 1943.
Built at Bethlehem Fairfield Co., Baltimore, Md. Yard No. 2190. Sailed from Halifax, Nova Scotia, in convoy SC127, 16 Apr 1943. Sailed from Scotland in convoy KMS19. Took part in invasions of Sicily, Salerno and Anzio. Hit by torpedo-bomb, 21 Oct 1943. Repaired at Oran and back at sea by 26 Nov 1943. Sunk by torpedoes from *U 230* off Anzio, 16 Feb 1944.

LST 419 Launched 30 Nov 1942; commissioned in RN 9 Feb 1943.
Built at Bethlehem Fairfield Co., Baltimore, Md. Yard No. 2191. Sailed from New York for the Mediterranean in convoy UGS8, 28 Apr 1943, but had to return. Sailed again in convoy UGS8A, 14 May 1943. Operational activities in the Mediterranean uncertain, but took part in invasion of Normandy. Operated in the shuttle service. Sailed for the Far East as part of 12th Flotilla. Paid off at Subic Bay, Philippines, 4 May 1946.

LST 420 Launched 5 Dec 1942; commissioned in RN 16 Feb 1943.
Built at Bethlehem Fairfield Co., Baltimore, Md. Yard No. 2192. Sailed from New York for the Mediterranean in convoy UGS8, 28 Apr 1943. Took part in invasions of Sicily, Salerno, Anzio and Normandy. Operated in the shuttle service. Sunk by mine off Ostend, 7 Nov 1944.

LST 421 Launched 5 Dec 1942; commissioned in RN 27 Jan 1943.
Built at Bethlehem Fairfield Co., Baltimore, Md. Yard No.

▲Football team of LST 416.
(G. Raitt)

2193. Sailed from New York 13 Mar 1943 in company with LSTs 324 and 412. Took oil refinery equipment to Curaçao, then logs from Georgetown, British Guiana, to Freetown, Sierra Leone. Took part in invasions of Sicily, Salerno, Anzio and Normandy. Operated in the shuttle service. Refitted for Far East at Sunderland 14 Sept–14 Nov 1944. Took part in invasion of Malaya. Paid off 8 Feb 1946, location unknown. Photographs at Imperial War Museum. In file V113, side view; A25035 and A25037 show crew members; IWM 7976/7 large model of LST bearing number LST 421.

LST 422 Launched 10 Dec 1942; commissioned in RN 5 Feb 1943.
Built at Bethlehem Fairfield Co., Baltimore, Md. Yard No. 2194. Sailed from New York for the Mediterranean in convoy UGS8, 28 Apr 1943. Took part in the invasions of (possibly) Sicily, Reggio, Salerno and Anzio. Hit mine off Anzio and sank 26 Jan 1944.

LST 423 Launched 14 Jan 1943; commissioned in RN 25 Feb 1943.
Built at Bethlehem Fairfield Co., Baltimore, Md. Yard No. 2195. Sailed from New York for the Mediterranean in convoy UGS8, 28 Apr 1943. Took part in invasions of Sicily, Anzio and Normandy. Fitted for carrying rolling stock. Started taking railway wagons to Cherbourg 18 Aug 1944. Paid off New York, 10 June 1946.

LST 424 Launched 12 Dec 1942; commissioned in RN 1 Feb 1943.
Built at Bethlehem Fairfield Co., Baltimore, Md. Yard No. 2196. Sailed from Halifax, Nova Scotia, in convoy SC127, 16 Apr 1943. Carried general cargo for the Clyde. Sailed from the Clyde in convoy KMS18A. Took part in the invasion of Sicily. Struck a mine off Sousse, 30 July 1943.

Laid up at Ferryville. Repairs discontinued. Handed back to US authorities at Palermo, 7 Jan 1946.

LST 425 (LSE(LC)50) Launched 12 Dec 1942; commissioned in RN 11 Feb 1943.
Built at Bethlehem Fairfield Co., Baltimore, Md. Yard No. 2197. Sailed from New York for the Mediterranean in convoy UGS8, 28 Apr 1943, but believed returned to New York. Took part in invasions of Sicily, Salerno, Reggio, Anzio and Normandy. Operated in the shuttle service (at least 21 trips). Taken in hand at Liverpool for conversion to LSE(LC)50, 15 Sept 1944. Completed about 16 July 1945. Paid off New York, 30 Aug 1946.

LST 426 Launched 11 Dec 1942; commissioned in RN 17 Feb 1943.
Built at Bethlehem Fairfield Co., Baltimore, Md. Yard No. 2198. Sailed from New York for the Mediterranean in convoy UGS7A. Involvement in invasions uncertain. Grounded and damaged at Bagnoli, 23 Nov 1943. Taken in hand for repair at Gibraltar. Paid off Norfolk, Virginia, USA, 23 Apr 1946. Photograph at Imperial War Museum ref NA3938. One logbook (5 Dec 1943–6 Jan 1944) at Public Record Office.

LST 427 Launched 19 Dec 1942; commissioned in RN 16 Feb 1943.
Built at Bethlehem Fairfield Co., Baltimore, Md. Yard No. 2199. Sailed from New York for the Mediterranean in convoy UGS8, 28 Apr 1943. Took part in invasions of Sicily, Salerno, Anzio and Normandy. Operated in the shuttle service. Refitted at Falmouth for Far East, Oct 1944 to Jan 1945. Took part in invasion of Malaya. Paid off Subic Bay, Philippines, 13 Apr 1946. Photograph at Malta War Museum, negative number 10397.

LST 428 Launched 22 Dec 1942; commissioned in RN 10 Feb 1943.
Built at Bethlehem Fairfield Co., Baltimore, Md. Yard No. 2200. Sailed from New York for the Mediterranean in convoy UGS7A. Took part in invasions of Sicily, Salerno, Anzio and Normandy. Fitted for carriage of rolling stock. Paid off New York, 10 June 1946.

LST 429 Launched 11 Jan 1943; commissioned in RN 21 Feb 1943.
Built at Bethlehem Fairfield Co., Baltimore, Md. Yard No. 2201. Convoy from USA unknown. Lost by fire in the Mediterranean, 3 July 1943 – the first RN LST to be lost. No other details known.

LST 430 Launched 31 Dec 1942; commissioned in RN 21 Feb 1943.
Built at Bethlehem Fairfield Co., Baltimore, Md. Yard No. 2202. Sailed from New York for the Mediterranean in convoy UGS8, 28 Apr 1943. Took part in invasions of Sicily, Salerno, Anzio and Normandy. Fitted for carrying rolling stock. Operated in the shuttle service. Assisted in relief of Norway. Paid off Norfolk, Virginia, USA, 26 Jan 1946.

LST 538 Launched 5 Jan 1944; commissioned in RN 26 Oct 1944.
Built at Missouri Valley Bridge & Iron Co., Evansville, In. Transferred to the RN from the USN in London, 26 Oct 1944. Took part in the invasion of Malaya. Paid off Subic Bay, Philippines, 16 Mar 1946.

LST 1021 Launched 16 May 1944; commissioned in RN Approx. 24 Dec 1944.
Built by Bethlehem Steel Co., Quincy, Mass. Transferred

◀LST 427 during Operation 'Neptune'. (L. Roberts)

▶LST 430 at Tilbury.
(A. Wright collection)

▶LST 1021 almost dried-out
at Kyaukpyu, Burma,
November 1945. (A. Smith)

▼LST 1021 loading a jeep up
her ramp to the upper deck.
Kyaukpyu, Burma, November
1945. (A. Smith)

to the RN from the USN at Bizerta. Transported British
army units from Taranto to Patras. Visited Salonika, Oran,
Algiers and Malta before returning to Liverpool from
Gibraltar, March–April 1945. Took part in invasion of
Malaya. Paid off Subic Bay, Philippines, 8 Feb 1946.

LST(3)s: Virtually no operational detail has come to light
concerning these vessels. Therefore, only outline detail is
given below.

LST 3001 Launched 15 Jan 1945; completed 29 June
1945.
Built by Vickers-Armstrong, Newcastle. Handed to WO
on charter 31 Oct 1946. Renamed *Frederick Clover* in
1946.

LST 3002 Launched 9 Apr 1945; completed 27 Sept 1945.
Built by Vickers-Armstrong, Newcastle. Transferred to Royal Hellenic Navy and renamed *Aliakmon* 28 Apr 1947. Sold in Greece 1972.

LST 3003 Launched 8 June 1945; completed 30 Nov 1945.
Built by Vickers-Armstrong, Newcastle. Named *Anzio* in 1947.

LST 3004 Launched 30 July 1945.
Built by Vickers-Armstrong, Newcastle. Cancelled and sold to Ministry of Transport, 18 June 1946.

LST 3005
Scrapped incomplete Barrow 1945.

LST 3006 Launched 3 Sept 1944; completed 29 Mar 1945.
Built by Harland & Wolff, Belfast. Renamed *Tromsö* in 1947. Renamed *Empire Gannet* in 1956.

LST 3007 Launched 16 Sept 1944; completed 15 May 1945.
Built by Harland & Wolff, Belfast. Transferred to Royal Hellenic Navy and renamed *Axios* 26 Apr 1947. Sold in Italy 24 July 1962.

LST 3008 Launched 31 Oct 1944; completed 4 May 1945.
Built by Harland & Wolff, Belfast. Transferred to Royal Australian Navy. Photograph at Imperial War Museum: A29822; FL7161–3.

LST 3009 Launched 30 Dec 1944; completed 11 May 1945.
Harland & Wolff, Belfast. Handed over to WO and renamed *Reginald Kerr* in 1946. Served as Royal Army Service Corps vessel.

LST 3010 Launched 30 Sept 1944; completed 5 Apr 1945.
Built by Harland & Wolff, Belfast. Renamed *Attacker*. Chartered by Atlantic Steam Navigation Company, Nov 1954. Renamed *Empire Cymric*. Took part in Operation 'Musketeer'. Sold to Shipbuilding Industries, Faslane, 1 Oct 1963. Photographs at Imperial War Museum: A28921; FL7199–7200.

LST 3011 Launched 12 Feb 1945; completed 14 Aug 1945.
Built by Harland & Wolff, Belfast. Renamed *Avenger*. Sold to Royal Indian Navy 1 Mar 1949 and renamed *Magar*.

LST 3012 Launched 12 Mar 1945; completed 25 Sept 1945.
Built by Harland & Wolff, Belfast. Renamed *Ben Nevis* (LST(Q)1). Sold 1965.

LST 3013 Launched 24 Apr 1945; completed 24 Nov 1945.
Built by Harland & Wolff, Belfast. Renamed *Ben Lomond* (LST(Q)2).

LST 3014 Launched 11 Nov 1944; completed 29 Mar 1945.
Built by Barclay Curle, Glasgow. Took part in Operation 'Doomsday', relief of Norway. Sold to Royal Australian Navy. Commissioned in RAN 8 July 1946.

LST 3015 Launched 16 Mar 1945; completed 21 Sept 1945.
Built by Barclay Curle, Glasgow. Renamed *Battler*, then *Empire Puffin*.

LST 3016 Launched 14 Dec 1944.
Built by Hawthorn Leslie, Hebburn-on-Tyne. Renamed *Dieppe*.

◀LST 3010 enters harbour at Malta. (M. Cresswell collection)

LST 3017 Launched 28 Nov 1944; completed 9 June 1945.
Built by Hawthorn Leslie, Hebburn-on-Tyne. Recommissioned in Royal Australian Navy 4 July 1946. Renamed *Tarakan* 7 Dec 1948.

LST 3018 12 June 1945.
Built by Hawthorn Leslie, Hebburn-on-Tyne. Cancelled.

LST 3019 Launched 4 Sept 1944; completed 30 Dec 1944.
Built by Swan Hunter, Newcastle. Took part in Operation 'Doomsday', relief of Norway. Renamed *Vaagso* in 1949. Sold to a Portsmouth company in 1959. Photographs at Imperial War Museum: FL7201–4

LST 3020 Launched 31 Oct 1944; completed 6 Apr 1945.
Built by Swan Hunter, Newcastle. Transferred to Royal Hellenic Navy on loan. Renamed *Alfios*, 7 May 1947. Sold in Italy 1962. Photographs at Imperial War Museum: FL7150–4.

LST 3021 Launched 23 Oct 1944; completed 20 Apr 1945.
Built by Lithgows, Port Glasgow. Paid off and transferred to WO 29 Aug 1946. Renamed *Charles Macleod*. Served as Royal Army Service Corps vessel.

LST 3022 Launched 26 Jan 1945; completed 8 Oct 1945.
Built by Lithgows, Port Glasgow. Transferred to Royal Australian Navy 8 July 1946. Sold in Australia 1949.

LST 3023 Launched 13 June 1945.
Built by Lithgows, Port Glasgow. Cancelled.

LST 3024 Launched 5 Oct 1944; completed 15 Mar 1945.
Built by Smiths Dock Co. Ltd., Middlesbrough. Handed over to Royal Army Service Corps 31 Oct 1946 and renamed *Maxwell Brander*.

LST 3025 Launched 14 Jan 1945; completed 27 June 1945.
Built by Smiths Dock Co. Ltd., Middlesbrough. Renamed *Bruiser*. Sold to a Singapore company 1954.

LST 3026 Launched 30 Oct 1944.
Built by Blyth Shipbuilding. Renamed *Charger*. Taken over by Atlantic Steam Navigation Company 8 Dec 1955 and renamed *Empire Nordic*. Took part in Operation 'Musketeer'.

▲Bow view of LST 3025. (S. H. Hall)

◀Ex-LST 3026. *Empire Nordic* in service with the Atlantic Steam Navigation Company. (J. Clarkson)

LST 3027 Launched 26 Jan 1945.
Built by Blyth Shipbuilding. Renamed *Lofoten* in 1947.
Became an accommodation ship.

LST 3028 Launched 16 Nov 1944; completed 19 May 1945.
Built by A. Stephen & Sons, Glasgow. Renamed *Snowden Smith* and served as Royal Army Service Corps vessel.
Photographs at Imperial War Museum: FL7148/9.

LST 3029 Launched 12 Jan 1945; completed 29 Aug 1945.
Built by A. Stephen & Sons, Glasgow. Renamed *Chaser*.
Sold in Italy 1961. Photographs at Imperial War Museum: FL7145-7.

LST 3030 Launched 12 June 1945.
Built by Hall Russell & Co. Ltd., Aberdeen. Cancelled.

LST 3031 Launched 14 Dec 1944; completed 11 July 1945.
Built by Chas. Connell & Co. Ltd., Glasgow. Renamed *Sultan*.

LST 3032 Launched 27 Apr 1945.
Built by Chas. Connell & Co. Ltd., Glasgow. Cancelled.

LST 3033 Launched 11 Feb 1945; completed 19 July 1945.
Built by Wm. Pickersgill & Son, Sunderland. Renamed *Empire Shearwater*. Photographs at Imperial War Museum: A30624; A30840; FL7205-7.

LST 3034 Launched 25 Aug 1945.
Built by Wm. Pickersgill & Son, Sunderland. Cancelled.

LST 3035 Launched 24 Oct 1944; completed 10 Mar 1945.
Built by Wm. Denny & Bros Ltd., Dumbarton. Transferred to Royal Australian Navy 18 July 1946. Renamed *Lae* 7 Dec 1948. Sold in Sydney 1955. Photographs at Imperial War Museum: FL7208-10.

LST 3036 Launched 20 Nov 1944; completed 5 May 1945.
Built by Ailsa Shipbuilding, Ayrshire. Renamed *Puncher*.
Sold to Belgian company 29 May 1961.

LST 3037 Launched 30 Jan 1945; completed 31 May 1945.
Built by Fairfield, Glasgow. Served as Royal Army Service Corps vessel and renamed *Evan Gibb* 10 Sept 1946.

LST 3038 Launched 14 Mar 1945; completed 27 July 1945.
Built by Fairfield, Glasgow. Renamed *Fighter*, then *Empire Grebe*.

LST 3039 Launched 27 June 1945.
Built by Fairfield, Glasgow. Cancelled.

LST 3040 Launched 22 Sept 1945.
Built by Harland & Wolff, Belfast. Cancelled.

LST 3041 Launched 31 Oct 1944; completed 6 June 1945.
Built by Harland & Wolff, Glasgow. Chartered to F. Bustard & Son for five years. Renamed *Empire Doric*. Took part in Operation 'Musketeer'. Sold to a Portsmouth company 12 Jan 1960.

LST 3042 Launched 31 Jan 1945; completed 16 Nov 1945.
Built by Harland & Wolff, Glasgow. Renamed *Hunter* then *Empire Curlew*.

LST 3043 Launched 27 Apr 1945.
Built by Scotts. Renamed *Messina*. Took part in Operation 'Grapple', British nuclear tests, Malden Island, South Pacific, 1957 (see also LST 3044). Photographs at Imperial War Museum: FL7211–3.

LST 3044 Launched 29 July 1945; completed 4 Apr 1946.
Built by Vickers-Armstrong, Barrow-in-Furness. Renamed *Narvik*. Took part in Operation 'Hurricane', British nuclear tests, Monte Bello Islands, Western Australia, 1952 and 1956 (see LST 3522 and 3532). Also took part in Operation 'Grapple' (see LST 3043).

LST 3045
Cancelled.

LST 3501 Launched 24 Aug 1944; completed 19 May 1945.
Built by Canadian Vickers, Montreal. Transferred to Royal Australian Navy, 1 July 1946. Renamed *Labuan*, 7 Dec 1948. Sold to a Sydney company and handed over 14 Nov 1955.

LST 3502 Launched 31 Aug 1944; completed 16 May 1945.
Built by Canadian Vickers, Montreal. Transferred to Royal

Hellenic Navy at Rosneath on 12 May 1947 and renamed *Strymon*. Sold in Italy 3 July 1962.

LST 3503 Launched 12 Oct 1944; completed 5 May 1945.
Built by Canadian Vickers, Montreal. Transferred to Royal Hellenic Navy at Rosneath on 12 May 1947 and renamed *Acheloos*. Sold in Italy 16 Nov 1971.

LST 3504 Launched 30 Nov 1944; completed 25 May 1945.
Built by Canadian Vickers, Montreal. Renamed *Pursuer*, then *Empire Tern*.

LST 3505 Launched 23 Nov 1944; completed 20 June 1945.
Built by Canadian Vickers, Montreal. Renamed *Ravager*. Sold in Italy 19 June 1961.

LST 3506 Launched 2 Dec 1944; completed 25 July 1945.
Built by Canadian Vickers, Montreal. Transferred to Royal Hellenic Navy at Rosneath on 18 Apr 1947 and renamed *Pinios*. Sold for breaking up in the UK 28 Feb 1972.

LST 3507 Launched 21 Oct 1944; completed 15 May 1944.
Built by Davie Shipbuilding, Canada. Chartered to F. Bustard & Sons. Renamed *Empire Gaelic*. Took part in Operation 'Musketeer'.

LST 3508 Launched 30 Oct 1944; completed 7 June 1945.
Built by Davie Shipbuilding, Canada. Renamed *Searcher*. Broken up at Milford Haven 1949.

LST 3509 Launched 23 Nov 1944; completed 22 June 1945.
Built by Davie Shipbuilding, Canada. Served as Royal Army Service Corps vessel and renamed *Humfrey Gale*.

LST 3510 Launched 28 Nov 1944; completed 17 July 1945.
Built by Davie Shipbuilding, Canada. Renamed *Slinger*, then *Empire Kittiwake*.

LST 3511 Launched 29 Nov 1944; completed 14 Sept 1945.
Built by Davie Shipbuilding, Canada. Renamed *Reggio*. Sold 1960. Photograph at Imperial War Museum: 'Reggio'. FL5486–93.

LST 3512 Launched 25 Apr 1945; completed 7 Aug 1945.
Built by Davie Shipbuilding, Canada. Chartered by F. Bustard & Sons. Renamed *Empire Celtic*. Took part in Operation 'Musketeer'. Sold in Italy 10 Aug 1962.

LST 3513 Launched 26 Apr 1945; completed 31 Aug 1945.
Built by Davie Shipbuilding, Canada. Renamed *Salerno*. Sold 20 June 1961.

LST 3514 Launched 3 Oct 1944; completed 3 Apr 1945.
Built by Yarrows Ltd, Canada. Transferred to Royal Indian Navy. Renamed *Smiter*. Returned to Royal Navy. Wrecked off Portuguese coast, 25 Apr 1949, and disposed of locally having become a total constructive loss.

LST 3515
Built by Yarrows Ltd, Canada. Renamed *Stalker*.

LST 3516 Launched 15 Feb 1945; completed 10 July 1945.
Built by Yarrows Ltd, Canada. Renamed *Striker*.

LST 3517 Launched 28 Apr 1945; completed 8 Sept 1945.
Built by Yarrows Ltd, Canada. Renamed *St. Nazaire* then *Empire Skua*.

LST 3518 Launched 6 Apr 1945; completed 9 Aug 1945.
Built by Canadian Vickers, Montreal. Renamed *Suvla*. Possibly used for trials with models of vertical take-off aircraft 1948. Sold 9 Aug 1960. A two-page Report of Proceedings of a voyage made by this vessel to Bergen in 1946 is held at Public Record Office, Kew, ref ADM 1/19593.

LST 3519 Launched 20 Apr 1945; completed 21 Sept 1945.
Built by Canadian Vickers, Montreal. Taken over by Frank Bustard & Sons 21 Aug 1946 and renamed *Empire Baltic*. Took part in Operation 'Musketeer'. Sold in Italy, 3 July 1962.

LST 3520 Launched 2 May 1945; completed 25 Oct 1945.
Built by Canadian Vickers, Montreal. Renamed *Thruster*, then *Empire Petrel*.

LST 3521 Launched 27 July 1945.
Built by Canadian Vickers, Montreal. Believed scuttled 1946.

LST 3522 Launched 9 June 1945; completed 30 Sept 1945.
Built by Davie Shipbuilding, Canada. Renamed *Tracker*. Took part in Operation 'Hurricane', British nuclear tests, Western Australia, 1952 (*see also* LSTs 3044 and 3532). Sold to a London company 8 Dec 1970.

LST 3523 Launched 9 July 1945.
Built by Davie Shipbuilding, Canada. Renamed *Trouncer* in 1947, then *Empire Gull*.

LST 3524 Launched 25 July 1945; completed 6 Nov 1945.
Built by Davie Shipbuilding, Canada. Renamed *Trumpeter*, then *Empire Fulmar*.

LST 3525 Launched 29 Aug 1945; completed 13 Nov 1945.
Built by Davie Shipbuilding, Canada. Renamed *Walcheren*, then *Empire Guillemot*.

LSTs 3526 to 3531 Cancelled

LST 3532 Launched 19 May 1945; completed 3 Nov 1945.
Built by Marine Industries, Canada. Renamed *Zeebrugge*. Took part in Operation 'Hurricane', British Nuclear tests, Western Australia, 1952 (*see also* LSTs 3044 and 3522).

LST 3533
Cancelled.

LST 3534 Launched 23 June 1945; completed 25 Oct 1945.
Built by Yarrows Ltd, Canada. Chartered by F. Bustard & Sons 13 Sept 1946. Renamed *Empire Cedric*. Took part in Operation 'Musketeer'. Sold to a Belgian company 12 Aug 1960.

LSTs 3535 to 3537 Cancelled

LSTs and Commanding Officers for Operation 'Neptune'

Assault Group S1 (for SWORD Beach).

1st Flotilla	Acting Commander A. B. Alison, RNR
LST 9[2]	Temporary Acting Lieutenant-Commander W. G. Lock, RNR
LST 302[1]	Temporary Acting Lieutenant-Commander W. A. Burn, RNR
LST 303[1]	Temporary Acting Lieutenant-Commander F. Lawson-Baker, RNR
LST 304[1]	Acting Lieutenant-Commander J. F. G. Fotheringham, RNR
LST 320[1]	Acting Lieutenant-Commander D. Buckley, RNR
LST 324[3]	Acting Lieutenant-Commander A. J. Bell, RNR
LST 361[1]	Acting Commander A. B. Alison, RNR
LST 363[1]	Acting Lieutenant-Commander J. B. McReynolds, RNR
3rd Flotilla	Acting Commander D. S. Hore-Lacy, RN
LST 322[2]	Acting Commander D. S. Hore-Lacy, RN
LST 367[1]	Temporary Acting Lieutenant-Commander C. C. Page, RNR
LST 408[2]	Temporary Acting Lieutenant-Commander R. Cook, RNR
LST 419[2]	Temporary Acting Lieutenant-Commander H. A. Stanfield, RNR
LST 420[1]	Lieutenant-Commander J. F. Twite, RNR
LST 423[2]	Lieutenant-Commander R. M. Naylor, RNR
LST 427[1]	Temporary Acting Lieutenant-Commander W. G. E. Rawlingson, RNVR
LST 428[2]	Temporary Acting Lieutenant-Commander J. T. Hamlyn, RNR
5th Flotilla	Acting Commander G. F. Parker, RD, RNR
LST 162	Acting Lieutenant-Commander R. E. J. Fox, RNR
LST 163[1]	Temporary Acting Lieutenant-Commander F. E. Trout, RNR
LST 164[1]	Temporary Acting Lieutenant-Commander W. W. Hardy, RNR
LST 364[1]	Acting Commander G. F. Parker, RNR
LST 365[1]	Temporary Lieutenant W. N. Pickering, RNR
LST 412	Acting Lieutenant-Commander P. R. Brown, RNR
LST 415	Temporary Lieutenant-Commander H. C. Gaffney, RNR
LST 430[2]	Lieutenant P. V. M. Davey, DSC, RNVR

Assault Group J3 (for JUNO Beach).

2nd Flotilla	Acting Commander C. M. V. Dalrymple-Hay, RN
LST 323[2]	Temporary Acting Lieutenant-Commander N. Stewart, RNR
LST 368	Temporary Acting Lieutenant-Commander J. Livingstone, RNR
LST 404[1]	Acting Lieutenant-Commander H. B. Shaw, RNR (ret.)
LST 405[1]	Acting Lieutenant-Commander J. T. Sheffield, RNR

LST 409[2] Lieutenant-Commander G. M. Dixon, RANVR

LST 410 Temporary Lieutenant-Commander J. K. Jones, RNR

LST 413[1] Temporary Acting Lieutenant-Commander R. J. W. Crowdy, RNVR

LST 425[1] Acting Commander C. M. V. Dalrymple-Hay, RN

4th Flotilla Acting Commander C. B. S. Clitherow, RN

LST 8 Temporary Acting Lieutenant-Commander R. R. Taylor, RNR

LST 11 Temporary Acting Lieutenant-Commander C. A. Payne, RNR

LST 62[2] Temporary Lieutenant-Commander S. Rayer, OBE, DSC, RNR

LST 65[2] Acting Lieutenant-Commander L. J. Smith, RNR

LST 159 Temporary Acting Lieutenant-Commander F. H. Evans, RNR

LST 160 Temporary Acting Lieutenant-Commander J. I. Murray, DSC, RNR

LST 199 Acting Commander C. B. S. Clitherow, RN

LST 416[2] Lieutenant-Commander H. E. Braine, RNR

9th Flotilla Acting Commander G. H. F. Owles, DSO, DSC, RN

LST 80[1] Temporary Acting Lieutenant-Commander T. H. Lowe, RNR

LST 180[1] Unknown

LST 215 Acting Commander G. H. F. Owles, DSO, DSC, RN

LST 238[1] Temporary Lieutenant-Commander J. M. Cunningham, RNR

LST 239[1] Temporary Commander G. A. Moore, RNR

LST 402[2] Lieutenant Commander H. E. Sprigge, RD, RNR

LST 421 Temporary Acting Lieutenant-Commander J. V. Machin, RNR

Fighter Direction Tenders

FDT 13 Lieutenant-Commander R. A. Crozier, RD, RNR

FDT 216 Lieutenant-Commander G. D. Kelly, RD, RNR

FDT 217 Acting Lieutenant-Commander F. A. Smyth, RNR

Assault Group L1

7th Flotilla Acting Commander J. G. Sutton, RN

LST 214 Temporary Acting Lieutenant-Commander R. H. E. Hand, RNR

LST 237 Acting Lieutenant-Commander W. D. Smith, RNR

LST 301 Acting Lieutenant-Commander R. F. Hoyle, RNR (ret.)

LST 319 Acting Commander J. G. Sutton, RN

LST 321 Acting Lieutenant-Commander C. H. Metcalfe, RNR

LST 366 Lieutenant-Commander G. R. Grandage, DSC, RD, RNR

LST 406 Acting Lieutenant-Commander H. J. Chaloner, RNR

8th Flotilla Acting Commander G. B. R. Rudyerd-Helpman, RN

LST 63 Acting Lieutenant-Commander V. Elsom, RNR

LST 165 Temporary Lieutenant-Commander D. M. McFarlane, RNR

LST 198 Acting Commander G. B. R. Rudyerd-Helpman, RN

LST 200 Temporary Acting Lieutenant-Commander J. Barnie, RNR

LST 403 Temporary Acting Lieutenant-Commander W. R. G. Garling, RNR

Assault Group L3

Bachaquero Lieutenant-Commander P. G. Britten, RNR

Misoa Lieutenant-Commander J. W. Grace, DSC, RD, RNR

Tasajera Lieutenant-Commander C. M. Ramus, RNR

Totals: 59 LST(2)s
3 *Maracaibo* class
3 Fighter Direction Tenders.

Notes: LST 161 was at Plymouth still under repair.
LST 401[2] was at Newcastle still under repair.
[1]Fitted with stretcher racks.
[2]Fitted with stretcher racks and railway tracks.
[3]Fitted with railway tracks.

Convoy details of LSTs returning to UK

MKS 38 (left Bizerta 28 Jan 1944, arrived UK 13 Feb 1944)

		Force
80	Falmouth, then Portsmouth approx. mid-March	J
180	Plymouth, then Portsmouth approx. mid-March	J
215	Southampton, then Portsmouth approx. mid-March	J
238	Portsmouth	J

MKS 39 (arrived UK 24 Feb 1944)

163	Clyde, then Invergordon, then Portsmouth mid-April	S
164	Clyde, then Portsmouth mid-April	S
239	Cardiff, then Portsmouth mid-April	J
302	Rosyth, then Portsmouth late April(?)	S
303	London, then Portsmouth early May	S
304	London, then Portsmouth mid-April	S
320	Newcastle, then Portsmouth late April	S
323	Belfast, then Portsmouth for refit early April	J
361	Rosyth, then Leith, then Portsmouth early May	S
363	Hartlepool, then Portsmouth late April	S
364	Chatham (convert to Flotilla Leader), then Portsmouth late April	S
365	Devonport, then Humber, then Portsmouth late March	S
367	Liverpool, then Portsmouth early April	S
404	Devonport, then Portsmouth mid-April	J
405	Portsmouth	J
420	Liverpool, then Clyde(?) late March, then Portsmouth early May	S
425	Devonport, then Portsmouth approx. mid-April	J

MKS 40 (arrived UK 5–7 March 1944)

324	Falmouth, then Portsmouth early May	S
362	Sunk by *U744* in Biscay area, 2 March 1944.	
413	Falmouth, then London, then Portsmouth early May	J
427	Portsmouth	S

MKS 43 (arrived UK 4 April 1944)

9	Rosyth. Arrived Southend 6 June from Leith	S
62	Clyde, then Portsmouth late May(?)	J
65	London, then Portsmouth late May	J
322	Liverpool, then Portsmouth mid-May	S
401	Newcastle. (At Newcastle for D-Day, arr. Portsmouth, 18 June 1944).	J
402	Liverpool, then Portsmouth mid-May	J
408	Devonport, then Portsmouth mid-May	S
409	Cardiff, then Portsmouth mid-May	J
416	Clyde, then Portsmouth late May	J
419	Falmouth, then Portsmouth early May	S

423	Hartlepool, then Portsmouth mid-May	S
428	Humber, then Dover (train trials), then Portsmouth late May	S
430	Chatham, then Portsmouth late May	S

MKS 45 (arrived UK approx. 22 April 1944).

8*	Swansea, then Portsmouth early May	J
11*	Swansea, then Portsmouth late May	J
63	Swansea, then Thames, then Harwich in May	L
159*	Swansea, then Portsmouth early May	J
160*	Swansea, then Portsmouth early May	J
161	Plymouth	L
162*	Swansea, then Portsmouth early May	S
165	Swansea, then Harwich early May	L
198	Swansea, then Harwich early May	L
199*	Swansea, then Portsmouth early May	J
200	Swansea, then Harwich early May	L
214*	Swansea, then Harwich early May	L
237*	Swansea, then Harwich early May	L
301*	Swansea, then Harwich early May	L
319*	Swansea, then Harwich early May	L
321*	Swansea, then Harwich early May	L
366*	Swansea, then Harwich early May	L
368	Swansea (docked Barry 26 April 1944), then Portsmouth late May	J
403	Swansea, then Harwich early May	L
406*	Swansea, then Harwich early May	L
410	Swansea, then Portsmouth early May	J
412*	Swansea, then Portsmouth early May	S
421*	Swansea, then Cardiff, then Portsmouth late May	J

*From Casablanca 11 April 1944 to join MKS 45. The 22 LSTs proceeding to Swansea had embarked: 235 British troops; 2,655 French troops; 847 Italian Pioneer Corps; 5 British naval ratings; 1 British war correspondent; 346 tanks; 701 vehicles; 7 bags of ships' mail.

MKS 46 (arrived UK approx. 3 May 1944).

415	To Portsmouth (Cowes). From Casablanca.	S

The above total 62 LSTs. LST 362 was sunk en route. Therefore, only 61 LSTs got back to the UK. Seven other LSTs were left in the Mediterranean:

12	Taranto	Long-term repairs
64	Ferryville	Long-term repairs
407	Naples	Damaged by grounding in bad weather
414	Bizerta	Cannibalized
417	Ferryville	Cannibalized
424	Ferryville	Cannibalized. Temporary depot ship
426	Gibraltar	Long-term repairs

Acknowledgements

The compilation of this book has brought me into contact with many people, all over the world. Every effort has been made to trace owners of copyright material. For any errors or omissions, I sincerely apologize in advance.

I would especially like to thank Bill and Margaret Chalk, Norman Barrass, John McFadden and Jim Patterson for their support and encouragement on every step of the way.

Many grateful thanks also to Tom Adams and Arnold Hague for painstakingly checking my manuscript and making helpful suggestions for its improvement; to Alan Francis and David Ashby of MoD Naval Historical Branch for all their help; to Paul Kemp and the staff of the Imperial War Museum; the Public Record Office; the National Maritime Museum, the LST & Landing Craft Association; the LST Club; the US LST Association; Associated British Ports; T. Ball (Falk Corporation, USA); H. E. Buttelmann (Gibbs & Cox Inc, USA); Major J. D. C. Mayhew, RM (retd), Royal Marines Amphibious Trials and Training Unit; Dr E. H. Putley, Mr and Mrs P. Whinney and, last but not least, my wife, Anne, for putting up with it all.

However, there is always one shining star. My task has been made so much easier by the immense amount of help I have received from Les Roberts. Les has typewritten in excess of 40,000 words to me concerning his days in LST 366. He has been my mentor and guide through this story of the LSTs — my only regret is that space precludes the use of more of his memories. To Les Roberts — sincere and grateful thanks.

My thanks also to the following who have contributed in various ways: K. Atkinson; N. Aspinall; A. F. Allin; D. W. Allen; I. P. Allen; T. F. J. Adcock; N. D. Britten; J. H. Britton; S. Batty; C. G. Banks; R. Briggs; E. W. Brindley; D. Baker; H. A. Baker; G. Barefoot; E. W. Baxter; R. J. Brend, MBE; A. Bailey; F. A. Beer; D. A. Bone; A. J. Banger; the late J. H. Bayley and Mrs Bayley; W. Brooks; D. W. Bunker; H. Boyle; J. Burns; J. Bainbridge; J. Bell; W. M. Benzie; J. L. Baillie; A. R. Birmingham; E. Bottomley; H. Blake; S. Bicknell; M. F. Brown; D. Barnard; M. Bustard; N. Barnes; A. Clark; D. F. Clark; W. Clark; E. Cheeseman; C. E. Cook; G. R. Cashmore; B. Cairns; R. Crawford; M. A. Crouch; S. J. Cotton; L. Coughlan; Mr and Mrs J. W. Cook; B. J. Chambers; M. Cresswell; D. Carter; H. S. Clune; W. Charles; M. Costeloe; W. Collison; Charlie Chester (BBC Radio, Sunday Soapbox); R. Dosch; R. Desaever; W. C. Dunkinson; A. E. Davis; T. A. Davis; A. Dyason; R. Dunkeld; R. M. Darnell; R. Derrick; A. J. Dawkins; C. B. Dunsford; R. T. B. Davies; Mrs D. Dawson; A. G. Donlan; G. W. Drummond; G. Evans; J. G. Evans; G. A. Edmond; L. W. Edwards; S. Edwards; R. Eaton; L. R. Everett; M. Element; J. Fenney; R. J. Fisher; K. R. Fern; J. F. G. Fotheringham; J. Frame; J. French; G. E. Friberg; W. Fieldhouse; W. Fry; S. Forrest; G. E. Fox; B. Friend; D. Finlayson; J. D. Fyffe; K. J. Gower; F. J. Gray; A. Gardner; J. Green; D. S. Goodbrand; W. J. Gatley; S. Goldberg; J. Glover; S. Griggs; K. H. Gazzard; T. Grieves; R. Gaskell; S. Gleeson; F. Godfrey; J. T. Graham; J. R. Goodwin; A. E. Griffiths; Monsieur D. Georges; J. Gibson; G. Henderson; A. Hatton; R. Hardwick; S. Hardwick; F. H. J. Hall; F. Hall; M. Hall; S. H. Hall; J. B. Heenan; P. Heywood; E. C. Hughes; I. W. Hughes; T. C. Hill; K. Heap; J. H. E. Haslett; R. B. W. Haslett; G. F. Hopkins; E. Humphreys; B. Hunt; F. E. Hart; J. Hutchinson; P. W. Howells; B. Howlett; I. G. Howlett; J. Harris; S. C. Hook, DSM; E. Hardy; W. Horsley; J. R. Holden; C. Hooper; W. Harrington; R. J. Hurry; Mrs N. Hawkins; E. Ingham; F. Irish; D. Jennings; C. Jenkins; R. Jones; W. Johnson; Mr Jackson; L. A. Kelly; R. Kelly; R. B. King; R. W. Knights; W. F. Larham, DSM; W. T. Lammas; J. Lindop; J. Lowe; A. Lawrence; P. A. Lacey; C. Lincoln; S. R. Lane; W. Lane; P. R. Lock; W. Leonard; T. E. Lowe-Troke; E. C. B. Lee; F. Lee; J. R. Lee; E. Mount; W. J. Marshall; L. Morton; B. McDermott; S. Mitchell; C. Madden; W. H. Minards; W. McCauley; T. McFarlane; A. E. Mellor; L. S. Markham; J. McMahon; J. B. McCowen; F. W. May; R. R. Morris; W. McKeever; J. W. Maddern; N. Magson; L. Marren; D. V. Meek; G. Melford; C. Maxwell; the late A. W. McMullan, DSC and Mrs McMullan; the staff of the Directorate of Naval Recruiting; Monsieur J. Noel (D-Day Museum, Arromanches, France); C. Newman; T. Nesbitt; W. J. Norris; R. T. Nunn; W. H. Owen; S. J. Oakes; G. H.

Osborne; Portsmouth Printing & Publishing Co.; R. Patten; G. Parker; A. H. Pembroke; Rear-Admiral J. Paloumbis (Greek Navy); R. E. Parfitt; J. Peplow; C. V. Powell; E. J. Pidcock; R. C. Pickering; T. Pickering; F. Pennington; J. M. Pryce; Royal Institute of Naval Architects; R. Reunbrouck; J. Reiter; L. Robson; D. K. Russell; R. Robertson Taylor; A. Robertson; J. Rollings; J. F. Rutter; J. Reekie; G. W. Raitt; B. Richards; H. Reid; D. R. Robinson; J. D. Robb; A. B. Stakemire; W. Shimwell; P. Spear; G. Spain; E. Stubbs; A. R. Sweetman; J. Sandilands; R. W. Short; H. P. Stokes; W. Spencer; B. Sygrove; E. Swinhoe; H. W. Stevens; F. Standen; A. Smith; F. Smith; V. Suett; R. Sinclair; C. C. Sear; J. Smart; A. E. Thimblebee; F. Thomas; H. R. Taylor; J. Travers; A. Tate; J. Tate; K. Tough (Channel Islands Occupation Society); J. J. Tait; R. W. Tindle; M. Toner; United States Naval Institute; United States National Archives; D. M. Wood; E. Whewell; R. Wootton; D. G. Wilson; E. W. Webber; A. W. West; K. T. Williams; J. R. Wiggins; W. Wells; R. Willis; C. J. Wickens; J. D. Woods; J. Willoughby; E. A. Waller; J. Watson; D. J. Wilkinson; A. Wright; A. F. Wright; W. Whiting; J. White; D. Windens; H. Wroe

◀ HMS *Boxer* in Dockyard Creek, Malta. (A. B. Stakemire collection)

◀ LST 162 after her refit in Belfast, 1945, ready for the Far East. (R. Kelly collection)

◀ LST 367 gingerly makes the double right angle turn into the devastated harbour at Ostend. (K. J. King collection)

Bibliography, Useful Addresses and Abbreviations

Allied Landing Craft of World War Two. Published by Arms & Armour Press. ISBN 085368 6874

Barger, M. *Large Slow Target* vol. 2, USA, 1989. Mainly concerns the US LSTs and contains biographical contributions from members of the US LST Association. Information on this book can be obtained from Taylor Publishing Company, Box 597, Dallas, Texas, 75235, USA.

Brindley, W. *The Ninety and Nine.* Methuen. ISBN 0 417 02960 8. Account of fictional US LST operating between Naples and Anzio, 1944.

Burn, L. *Down Ramps.* Carrol & Nicholson, 1947.

Churchill, Winston S. *The Second World War.* (six volumes), Penguin.

Cowsill, M. *By Road Across the Sea, the History of the Atlantic Steam Navigation Company Ltd.* Ferry Publications, 1990. ISBN 1 871947 07 3.

Clark, A. *A Cornfield Shipyard.* USA, 1991. Details the history of the Evansville Shipyard and the 167 LSTs built there. Information on this book can be obtained from A. Clark, PO Box 5, Haubstadt, Indiana 47639-0005, USA.

Dictionary of American Naval Fighting Ships, vol. VII (Appendix), Historical Center, Department of the Navy,

▶ A Landing Craft Recovery Unit emerges from LST 320 on to the Rhino ferry. The forecastle was always a favourite 'observation platform'. (C. Powell collection)

Washington, USA, 1981.

Hoyt, E. P. *The Battle before Normandy*. Concerns Exercise 'Tiger'. Robert Hale. ISBN 0 7090 3266 8.

Lenton, H. T. and Golledge, J. J. *Warships of World War Two*. Ian Allan Ltd.

Lewis N. *Channel Firing*. Concerns Exercise 'Tiger'. ISBN 0 670 82398 8.

Lund, P. and Ludlam, H. *The War of the Landing Craft*. W. Foulsham & Co. Ltd., 1976. ISBN 0 572 00935 6.

Robb J. D. *Only survivors tell tales*. Vantage Press, USA. ISBN 0 533 08903 4. Available in UK from Clay Maxwell, LST Club, 45 New Road, Water Orton, Birmingham, B46 1QP.

Small, K. *The Forgotten Dead*. Bloomsbury. Concerns Exercise 'Tiger'. ISBN 074 750 30 95.

Selected Papers on British Warship Design in World War II. From the Transactions of the Royal Institution of Naval Architects. Conway. ISBN 0 85177 284 6.

Articles

MeFaul, Jim. 'Ferries to Suez – 1956', in *Ships Monthly*, Dec 1981. Concerning Operation 'Musketeer'.

Taylor, C. M. 'The LST – Kingpin of the Invasion Fleet', in *Marine Engineering and Shipbuilding* (USA), Feb 1945.

'LST (2) – Backbone of the Amphibious Navy', in *Army and Navy Modelworld*, July 1984.

Regular Newsletters are published in Britain by two groups. For membership details, please send stamped addressed envelope to: LST & Landing Craft Association, c/o Bill Chalk, 15 Cobham Way, Merley, Wimborne, Dorset, BH21 1SJ; LST Club, c/o Clay Maxwell, 45 New Road, Water Orton, Birmingham, B46 1QP.

The US LST Association publishes a bi-monthly newspaper, *Scuttlebutt*. Details of membership from US LST Association, PO Box 167438, Oregon, Ohio 43616-7438, USA.

Items at Public Record Office, Ruskin Avenue, Kew, London:

Operation 'Husky': ADM 199/943; 199/2517.
Operation 'Avalanche': ADM 199/860; ADM 199/949.
Operation 'Shingle': ADM 116/4946; ADM 116/5459; ADM 199/873.

Items at MoD Naval Historical Branch, 3–5 Great Scotland Yard, London, SW1A 2HW do not have reference numbers. The Battle Summary Reports (BSRs) contain information on most operations. By appointment only.

Copies of Imperial War Museum photographs can be purchased on application to the Department of Photographs, Imperial War Museum, Lambeth Road, London, SE1 6HZ. The archive is open to the public during the week and visitors are welcome, but it is advisable to make an appointment.

Abbreviations

DUKW	Amphibious vehicle
BYMS	Minesweeper
LSE(LC)	Landing Ship Emergency Repair (Landing Craft)
LSI	Landing Ship, Infantry
LCF	Landing Craft, Flak
LCG	Landing Craft, Gun
LCH	Landing Craft, Headquarters
LCI	Landing Craft, Infantry
LCS	Landing Craft, Support
LCT	Landing Craft, Tank
LCT(R)	Landing Craft, Tank (Rocket)
LCA	Landing Craft, Assault
LCM	Landing Craft, Mechanized
LCP(R)	Landing Craft, Personnel (Ramped)
HDML	Harbour Defence Motor Launch